THE JOURNEY
NARRATIVE
IN AMERICAN
LITERATURE

THE JOURNEY NARRATIVE IN AMERICAN LITERATURE

PATTERNS AND DEPARTURES

Janis P. Stout

Greenwood Press
Westport, Connecticut
London, England

PS169
T74
S7
1983

Library of Congress Cataloging in Publication Data

Stout, Janis P.
  The journey narrative in American literature.

  Bibliography: p.
  Includes index.
  1. American literature—History and criticism.
2. Travel in literature. 3. Narration (Rhetoric)
I. Title.
PS169.T74S7   1983   810'.9'355   82-24256
ISBN 0-313-23235-0 (lib. bdg.)

Library of Congress Catalog Card Number: 82-24256
ISBN: 0-313-23235-0

First published in 1983

Greenwood Press
A division of Congressional Information Service, Inc.
88 Post Road West
Westport, Connecticut 06881

Printed in the United States of America

10 9 8 7 6 5 4 3 2 1

Acknowledgments

Portions of the text have been published previously in somewhat different form. Permission to reprint is gratefully acknowledged.

Janis P. Stout, "The Possibility of Affirmation in *Heart of Darkness* and *Henderson the Rain King*." *Philological Quarterly*, 57 (1978), 115-31.

———, "Journeying as a Metaphor for Cultural Loss in the Novels of Larry McMurtry." *Western American Literature*, 11 (1976), 37-50.

———, "Stevens' 'Comedian' as Journey Narrative." *Concerning Poetry*, 14 (1981), 31-48.

———, "Biblical Allusion in *Henderson the Rain King*." *South Central Bulletin*, 40 (1980), 165-67.

Permission to reprint quoted material was granted as follows:

Excerpts from poems by Wallace Stevens, from *The Collected Poems of Wallace Stevens*. Copyright © 1954 by Wallace Stevens. Reprinted by permission of Random House, Inc.

Excerpt from "The Kid," by Conrad Aiken, and from the author's note on William Blackstone, from *Collected Poems*, Second Edition. Copyright © 1970 by Conrad Aiken. Reprinted by permission of Oxford University Press.

Excerpts from poems by Hart Crane, from *The Complete Poems and Selected Letters and Prose of Hart Crane*, edited by Brom Weber. Copyright © 1933, © 1958, 1966 by Liveright Publishing Corporation. Reprinted by permission of Liveright Publishing Corporation and Laurence Pollinger Ltd.

Excerpts from *The Great American Novel*, by Philip Roth. Copyright © 1973 by Philip Roth. Reprinted by permission of Philip Roth and Holt, Rinehart & Winston.

Excerpt from "Lines Written Near San Francisco," copyright © 1963 by Louis Simpson. Reprinted from *At the End of the Open Road* by permission of Wesleyan University Press.

Excerpts from *Clarel*, by Herman Melville, edited by Walter Bezanson. Copyright © 1960 by Hendricks House, Inc. Reprinted by permission of Hendricks House.

Contents

Preface

The journey is so pervasive a thematic concern and so recurrent a symbolic action in American fiction that its importance would scarcely seem to need demonstration. Nevertheless, the obvious need not remain unexamined. It may be in need of careful examination so that what seems obvious can be either validated or disproven and what is less obvious can be seen more clearly. The journey theme in American letters has not received that careful examination. One purpose of the present study will be to show that American literature is indeed characterized by journeys, even obsessed with journeys, possibly to an even greater degree than has been supposed. Another will be to show that the theme of the journey is more complex, more multidimensional, than it might seem to be.

A study of this kind is in a sense a survey of a given field, a survey that also involves an inventory of the stones in that field. However, full comprehensiveness in examining a literary tradition with the wide scope and to some extent the amorphousness of this one is scarcely feasible and perhaps not even desirable. The stones begin to look much alike after the basic shapes have been identified and a few of the more interesting, more eccentric specimens are examined closely.

My method will be to identify a few basic patterns of journey narrative that recur very often, mentioning or briefly examining works that illustrate each pattern, and then to consider at greater length a small number of major works that may be called departures from the patterns that have been established. These departures are all works in which the journey is particularly important in ways that are not obvious and have not often been considered.

The definition of a literary form is always a complex and difficult matter unless discussion is limited to such broad and one-dimensional terms as the prose/poetry distinction or the mechanics of structures such as the sonnet, the quatrain, or the couplet. More complex problems of form involve content and the relation between content and structure. For example, a minor genre that flourished in England in the seventeenth century, the country house poem, is defined chiefly by its content, the celebration of a country estate, but that content also involves a set of recurrent attitudes and tropes, and the whole is presented in a verse form of some stateliness. Similarly, the epic can be defined as a lengthy narrative poem (form) treating matters of a certain scope and magnitude (content) in an elevated manner (style) and utilizing certain characteristic tropes or incidents (style? content? form?). Of course, all literary scholars know that form and content are or ought to be inseparable. And indeed complex structures are concepts that demonstrate that inseparability. The price of an adequate complexity in defining such a structure, however, is often the loss of neatness or logical consistency. Categories that ring true in their mapping of the literary territory as it is actually experienced may not be mutually exclusive, simply because they are not set up according to a single set of criteria but several overlapping sets, drawing on both form and content.

So it is with the patterns of journey narrative that I have identified in chapters two through six. The definitions derive more from content than from form in that they are based on such matters as direction of journey, motivation for journeying, and reference to actual historic precedents. At the same time, each pattern displays recurrent elements of form such as characteristic incidents, images, and tone. Because the categories I define are derived by reference to several criteria, they do not have that inevitability, that logical consistency and mutual exclusiveness, which one might wish. Nevertheless, they appear as they do because these are the patterns that are encountered regularly in American journey narratives.

The patterns described here do not often occur singly, producing narratives strictly of escape or strictly of quest, but in combination. For instance, though the escape is clearly a form in itself, once a character has escaped, he may engage in an exploration, a colonization, or a state of aimless wandering. A given journey may be conceived as an escape if emphasis is placed on its negation of the existing order from which a character departs or a quest for freedom if emphasis is placed on the condition he or she hopes to find by leaving. A journey to Europe may be a retreat from the overwhelming raw energy of America or a quest for enlightenment. A single work of narrative, then, may bear the marks of more than one journey pattern, either in combination or in series, and in the present study a single work may be mentioned in more than one context. The Western, that most American of fictions, also appears in several contexts because it is actually a composite form, utilizing more than one type of journey.

The chapters on recurrent forms are arranged in a rough chronological order according to their greatest ascendancy in American letters. The exploration, the escape, and the journey of home founding were important patterns very early; the limitless journey of wandering without clear direction or destination tends to occur most insistently in the twentieth century. But the chronology is not clear-cut or absolute, and each pattern is traced as it appears in works of various periods. In these chapters, I have used as illustrations both works often recognized as journey narratives and works that are less familiar, including selections from popular culture, in order to define a pattern and to indicate the breadth and variety of its occurrence.

The chapters given to analysis of specific texts, seven through eleven, are not expansions of the illustrations used in chapters two through six, the chapters of definition; they are considerations of narratives of great complexity combining various patterns of journey. These works demonstrate that the patterns of journey narrative, relatively separable and well defined in theory, are in fact, as they are experienced in real narratives of some complexity, not separable but interwoven. The more complex the work, the more intricately interwoven its narrative patterns, so that the patterns defined in the early chapters become contributing motifs in the richness of the works considered in the later chapters. For these chapters I have not chosen the obvious and classic texts—*Moby-Dick*, for instance, or *Huckleberry Finn*. These have been considered so often precisely in terms of their journeys that they have seemed to me more useful as illustrations for purposes of definition than as subjects of extended analysis. Instead, I have chosen works that have accumulated smaller bodies of criticism or criticism which has not been focussed on their journey motifs.

A word about chapter nine, "Poets' Journeys: Hart Crane and Wallace Stevens." It is important to illustrate the inclusiveness of the American concern with journeys by pursuing it into this somewhat different region. Furthermore, it is in poetry that we can see most clearly the fragmentation of the journey that is characteristic of twentieth-century literature. Because the linguistic structures of poetry are so complex and the patterns of journey narrative enter more obliquely, the pace of this chapter is considerably different, more obviously painstaking, than that of the others.

In the last chapter, *"The Great American Novel* and the Great American Novel,"* commentary on a specific work leads us again, as in the opening chapter, toward the asking and tentative answering of larger questions. These larger questions generally involve the relationship of the fictional journey narrative to the American historic experience and the relationship of the American fictional journey to older and more nearly universal forms of literary journeys. I hope, by this point in the study, to have developed a greater understanding of ways in which the peculiarities of the historic context have affected American writers' responses to the literary traditions within which they work and to the particular visions that they have entertained as they have developed their own fictions. Nevertheless, in spite of that hope, it is well to point out in advance that some questions are too large, too complex, or perhaps too amorphous to permit answers and to concede that I have not provided answers, only notes toward answers. The journey narrative in American literature exists at the center of tensions not only between content and form but between history and aesthetic traditions and between the peculiarities of being American and the embracing generalities of larger human history and a larger literary context. It is more nearly possible to give an account of these tensions than to resolve them, and I hope to have done that. In the process, my concern is primarily with literary history and literary form. But literature does not exist in a vacuum; it does not exist even in the context of its own traditions alone. The very fact that we designate studies as referring to *American* literature demonstrates the existence of a social, historic context. Similarly, the literary concern of this study, operating within an extraliterary social context, reflects back on that context. What we discover here will primarily be of relevance to American literature in general, as well as to specific texts, but it will also be of relevance to American culture. Given the nature of the topic, the two cannot be separated.

Hearty thanks go to certain people who have been especially helpful to me during my work on this study: to J. P. Blumenfeld, Walter Isle, Monroe Spears, and Terrence Doody, who read portions of the manuscript and gave me suggestions from which I have benefited; to Barbara Huval, who took time out from her own graduate studies to verify the references; to Joyce Pyndus and Donna Montez, who typed and retyped; to my family, who have been heroically tolerant of the litter of papers and pens with which I have been surrounded for quite some time.

THE JOURNEY
NARRATIVE
IN AMERICAN
LITERATURE

1
The Journey and American Aspirations

> Like the young partridge, the American is scarcely hatched, ere he sets out, with the shell still clinging to his downy wing, in search of a new region
> James Kirke Paulding, *Westward Ho!* (1832)

> I am afoot with my vision. . .
> Walt Whitman, "Song of Myself"

From its beginnings, the American literary tradition has been characterized to a remarkable and peculiar degree, by narratives and images of journeys. It has been a literature of movement, of motion, its great icons the track through the forest and the superhighway. Works as diverse in nature and period as Cooper's sea novels, Melville's *Moby-Dick*, Twain's *The Adventures of Huckleberry Finn*, Hemingway's expatriate fiction, and Jack Kerouac's *On the Road* are linked by their concern with narrative sequences of travel or voyaging. These are the obvious examples, which have been examined repeatedly in terms of their handling of quest or escape or picaresque motifs. A great many other works—novels, usually, but poems as well—that utilize journey structures in less conspicuous or less controlling ways, as well as works which are themselves, for whatever reason, less often discussed than the ones I have named, also form a part of this tradition, as do yet other works that invoke the image of the journey as a touchstone of value even though they are not cast in narrative structures of journeying.

That this should be so is in great part a reflection of our national history. Space has pressed on us, and spatial movement has been the characteristic expression of our sense of life. The migration to the home country, which commonly forms a part of a people's mythology or prehistory, was for us an observable and much observed fact. If the early ocean crossings of the Puritans and the Pilgrims have been elevated to national myth, as they indeed have, they were first an actual experience with their own recorded accounts and commentaries.[1] Those first westerly voyages to America's eastern shores were, in addition, the prototype for what Walter Allen calls a "principle of recurrence" in American experience.[2] Journeys, both mass and individual, have been the most powerful shaping structure of that experience.

What prompted the early explorers and settlers to launch out on voyages to a New World has been a question much discussed by historians. Whatever the cause or causes—land hunger, commercial development, thirst for glory, religious vision—the fact remains that American history begins with voyages, of exploration or escape or migration. The pattern, once set, continued. From the first, despite Puritan mandates against dispersion, hardy loners, whether positively lured by goals such as land or adventure or freedom or negatively driven to the "safety valve" of the frontier, pushed west. Invariably, the first solitary frontiersmen drew after themselves the homeseeking, society-building waves of westering pioneers that created anew the circumstances for new lone departures. Nor were motives ever distinguishable simply as single or collective. The journey west can be generalized as a move from the known to the unknown or from restriction to freedom, but it meant different things to different groups. As Paul Horgan writes in his novel *The Common Heart* (part of his trilogy *Mountain Standard Time*), "To the successive waves of travelers in the West, the land presented a new meaning each time, for each was looking for something different from what his predecessors had sought."[3]

Westerly movement—of exploration, fortune-hunting, retreat from civilization, or migration—has been an historic pattern not merely for decades but for centuries.[4] For all the doubts, reservations, and qualifications that have been appended like footnotes to Frederick Jackson Turner's great and certainly overstated thesis, the importance of the western spaces and westerly movement can scarcely be exaggerated. And all the while, during the cross-continent westerly migrations, new groups kept making their journeys from the Old World to the New to continue the process begun in the sixteenth century and add their weight to the westward push. The push toward California, the essence of the American Dream, was dramatically continued in the 1930s by the nomads of the depression and indeed continues today in a well-documented flight from the aging cities of the East Coast to the sunny Southwest. Economic motives for journeying continue to apply, as much to the mobile middle class as to migrant workers in agriculture.

Besides the westerly journeys, there has been a continuing counter move toward the East.[5] Such a pattern of eastward journeying is apparent in the turning back of discouraged pioneers; in the European travels first of young intellectuals such as Longfellow and George Ticknor and, later in the nineteenth century, of the genteel social elite; and in our own century in the wartime journeys to Europe and the escapes of the disenchanted Lost Generation and their latter-day counterparts—an ironic reversal of the original hopeful flight from Old World decadence to the New Eden.

And now, journeys to the moon.

The ways in which American literature reflects its historic context can be more fully explored only in the cumulative examination of narrative patterns and individual works. However, some indication of the ways in which history has shaped American writers' predilection for the journey can be made here. First, the historic journeys of exploration and migration have constituted the actual material of a great many writings, either in factual accounts or in historical fiction. Our journey-centered history also set the patterns in which the journey would continue to appear in our fiction, particularly the escape and the home founding. Even more pervasively, the characteristic journeys of

American history influenced our literature by providing images and a framework of values associated with movement and direction.

In accordance with the patterns of history, our journeys are typically westerly, and westerly movement is typically associated with positive values such as freedom and progress.[6] Such connotations clearly reflect the hopeful expectations of the Puritans and other founders as well as successive waves of pioneers. As Edwin Fussell has demonstrated in his provocative study *Frontier*, the receding western frontier signifies the meeting ground of various contrarieties, including the obvious values of civilization and savagery, and thus becomes a narrow zone of intense ambiguity. Since fictional journeys tend to recall the nation's cross-continent westerly march by an implicit allusiveness, the values and ambiguities of this directional symbolism are appropriated by the journey as symbol. More abstractly, like the westerly march of society, the journey symbolizes Progress, mankind's efforts toward intellectual or moral goals, even the search for meaning itself. At its broadest and most completely divorced from the frontier association, the journey collapses into the allegorical, sunset-directed Journey of Life,[7] a familiar, even hackneyed trope by no means peculiar to American literature.

It is in the Western that these directional values are most clearly evident. In relation to American life and letters in general, as well as the journey narrative in particular, the Western assumes a paradigmatic importance.[8] The Western is not, however, a single form, but a rich amalgam, pertinent to the present study at several points, within which two basic types are clearly discernible. One of these is the fiction of the settler, a form already mentioned in reference to the historical derivation of the home-seeking novel. In Westerns of this type, whether novel or film, the West itself is presented dually as opportunity, the land to be settled and the new life it affords, and as obstacle, the rugged spaces intervening between the pioneer and his goal. The journey toward that goal becomes a one-way quest for an object, the special place to be settled, which may be clearly envisioned but uncertainly mapped. The general tone of this type of Western is melioristic and its values collective or at least familial: if the quest is successful, the site of western opportunity will be transformed as it is made to afford a stable social life. Dramatic heightening arises from the struggles of the hero (whether individual or collective, as for instance an entire wagon train)[9] against the natural hazards encountered in the crossing of the obstacle territory and the struggle to tame a harsh land. Determination and endurance are glorified—for instance, in Emerson Hough's *The Covered Wagon* and A. B. Guthrie's *The Way West*.

In a quite distinct type of Western, the often violent melodrama of the lone cowboy, mountain man, or outlaw, the westerly journey is valued for quite other reasons. The austere heroes of this type of Western define themselves singly in an exhilarating symbiosis with their wide open environment, not in their relationship or even subordination to a family or larger social group. They cherish no hope of establishing a social order, but rather value the West precisely because it has none. Therefore, the westerly journey in this form is not one from inadequate society to opportunity for a better society, but from society to the presocial condition. The journey, travelling, itself is the chief value, not some end goal as in the settler's novel.[10] The West is neither obstacle nor opportunity, but a ground for anarchic freedom. If the orientation of the settler's Western is toward the future, that of the heroic primitive Western is inevitably toward the past. Therefore, its tone is often more elegiac than is that of the settler's Western, even though it may be fiercely ecstatic in episodes of the hero's rugged enjoyment of what the wilderness has freely to give: independent action. Probably the pre-eminent example of this form, as it is the pre-eminent primitive Western in aesthetic quality, is Guthrie's *The Big Sky*, with its powerful, asocial hero, Boone Caudill.[11] Even without the relentless march of settlement, the book plunges into pathetic tragedy because the attempt to remove to the primitive West is doomed to failure by the nature of time and of man himself.

Just as the Western is thus divided in its values, so the most common motif in Western tales is the conflict between the two value systems.[12] Whichever side wins, the result is a sense of loss because the free West of the lone hero can never be recovered, and the hopes of the settler are, if not doomed, at least sobered by harsh realities. Like much else about the Western, this conflict plot, familiar from countless movies and television dramas of the range war between the advocates of the free West (cowmen) and the would-be socializers of the West ("sodbusters" and commercial opportunists), derives from James Fenimore Cooper. In his elegiac novel of Natty Bumppo's extreme old age, *The Prairie*, Cooper finds, almost in spite of himself, a crude, sturdy vitality in Ishmael Bush, leader of a family clan heading west to establish itself agriculturally beyond the laws and customs of society.[13] Nevertheless, Bush's trek is shown to be ill advised, morally polluted, and contrary to the natural order of the region—ecologically unsound, so to speak. In the end, his journey is made to yield to the journey-of-life motif of Natty, the lone Westerner facing the setting sun, with its conservative and harmoniously cyclical connotations. Yet it is clear that with Natty's passing the forces of unnatural change, the forces of the settler, will subsequently win out.

It is largely this sense of disparity between hope and reality that distinguishes the realistic or mature Western from its melodramatic, romanticized cousin.[14] Such an awakening to harsh truth occurs, for instance, in *The Big Sky* when Boone Caudill realizes that the carefree, savage life he had embraced is spoiled, and must inevitably have been spoiled, by his own human failings, which cannot be left behind in the escape from society. Similarly, in Guthrie's *The Way West* the common moral and social failings of the East mar even the best, most rationally planned wagon train. Moving west cannot provide the beatitude that eager pioneers expect, because they only move the old problems along with them into the new territory. By contrast, Emerson Hough's standard wagon train novel, *The Covered Wagon*, derives much of its romantic tone from its refusal to engage in this kind of questioning of the nobility and promise of the westerly journey.

Another illustration of the way in which the realistic Western treats the disparity between expectation and fulfillment is a 1935 novel by Edwin Lanham, *The Wind Blew from the West*. In this tale of a fictional town called Rutherford, based on the actual town of Weatherford, Texas, Lanham's home, a series of characters are shown as they examine a promotional pamphlet about Rutherford, decide to make the westward journey to what they believe is a thriving new city, and find that their hopes have been unrealistic. One of these, a wheat farmer from Arkansas, following what he believes to be a divine sign that he should seek a Promised Land, sees his "New Canaan" farm wiped out by flood and his wife brutally mutilated and killed by Indians he had believed amicable. A good-natured French drummer who tries pig farming on the frontier is also flooded out and in the end defrauds his fellow pioneers and returns to the East in disgrace. The main character in the romantic subplot sees his hopes for a new exemplary community ruined partly by the pressures of competing economic forces and partly by his own rigidly narrow righteousness, a trait he had brought with him to the frontier. In each instance, the flaw is the characters' unrealistic hopes, which were unsuited to the opportunities actually offered by the West to those able to recognize and properly assess them.

It is evident, then, that even in the Western, which is built on the value of westerly motion, there exists a counterstrain of directional ambiguity related to a disparity between infinite hope and limited or marred actuality. In fact, such a counterstrain in directional values extends far beyond the Western. The association of the West (sunset) with death is a major source of directional ambiguity in other literatures as well; tension between the West as primitive vigor and renewal and the West as death is very powerful, for instance, in James Joyce's celebrated story "The Dead." In American literature, such tensions have been more nearly subordinated to the West as freedom and new life, but they have nonetheless been present. In the movie Western, the hero's riding into the sunset may only be his departure from our humdrum realities to the realm of endless heroism, but an elegiac feeling in the scene implies his death. Howard Mumford Jones amply demonstrates the conflicting images of the New World in *O Strange New World*, and the lurking savage who spoiled that Eden was simply moved west as the frontier moved from the Atlantic seaboard to the Pacific. Fussell, as mentioned above, demonstrates the sinister ambiguities of the meeting point of savagery and civilization in *Frontier*, and Charles Sanford notes that the westerly journey "combines elements of progress with impulses of infantile regression."[15] Numerous once-hopeful pioneers were glad to escape back East; the rebound of the westerly impulse has often been disillusionment. The tone of disillusionment is struck with particular frequency in literature of the twentieth century, which finds itself with the American dream, as it was represented geographically at any rate, fully unfolded, known, and after all not entirely satisfying. The disparity between infinite hope and finite possibility becomes intensified as the dreamed aspiration is denied a continental dwelling place. Such a disparity is well summarized in Louis Simpson's poem "Lines Written Near San Francisco," from a volume tellingly entitled *At the End of the Open Road*:

> Every night, at the end of America
> We taste our wine, looking at the Pacific.
> How sad it is, the end of America![16]

Even within the Anglo-American experience, then, which has chiefly constituted mainstream American literature, the connotations of the West and westering have never been unambiguous. In addition, American minority cultures have their own directional values, and an analysis of journey patterns by a scholar having specialized knowledge of Chicano and other minority literatures is much to be desired. The outlines, however, can be indicated.

For Chicano culture, the directions of symbolic value, roughly corresponding to the West/East values of Anglo-European Americans, are North and South. For Afro-Americans, too, the original westerly journey to America could scarcely hold the liberating, hopeful connotations of the founders' tradition, and the return to the home continent is necessarily more fraught with anxiety. Like the Chicano culture, Afro-American culture, through the heritage of the Underground Railway and escape in general, finds the North a locus of freedom and betterment (for instance, in the folk song "Follow the Drinking Gourd"). We should add, however, that in the experience of the black cowboy, the West took on the connotations of freedom and self-aggrandisement that it held for other groups. For the native Indian, deprived of his homeland and forced to migrate to a government reservation, going west could never mean progress but only despair and death.

Still, despite the presence of these various directional ambiguities and tensions, it remains true that the West is primarily a locus of such positive values as release and hope. Growing out of the directional values is a tendency to regard westering or pioneering as an end in itself, quite apart from its goals. Thoreau wrote in his 1862 essay "Walking":

Eastward I go only by force; but westward I go free. . . . I should not lay so much stress on this fact, if I did not believe that something like this is the prevailing tendency of my countrymen. I must walk toward Oregon, and not toward Europe. And that way the nation is moving, and I may say that mankind progress from east to west.[17]

The same association of westerly movement with progress is struck by Melville at the end of the thirty-sixth chapter of *White-Jacket*:

We Americans are the peculiar chosen people—the Israel of our time. . . .We are the pioneers of the world; the advance-guard sent on through the wilderness of untried things, to break a new path in the New World that is ours.[18]

The pioneer enterprise tends to be romantically glorified, and the goal of the journey shifted, as Sanford says, to "endless process itself rather than". . .any easily definable end point.[19] John Steinbeck, in his story "The Leader of the People," strikes this characteristically American note of glorying in the process of the journey when Grandfather recalls the days of the wagon train, when he was leader: "It was westering and westering. Every man wanted something for himself, but the big beast that was all of them wanted only westering." The passage has been criticized as a structural flaw in the story and an example of overinflated rhetorical vagueness.[20] However, I regard the very vagueness of "it" ("It was westering and westering. . .") as being a precisely correct rendering of the diffuse, romanticized value-associations commonly attached to the westerly journey. Again, as in so much literature of America's westward expansion, the

tone is elegiac and regretful: the point of the story is that westering of the sort Grandfather remembers is obsolete; there is
nowhere else for the leader to take his people.

The journey-centeredness of the historic context, then, has
provided matter, forms, and directional associations for the literary imagination. A second context of great importance, however, is the presence of journey narrative in other literatures.
Early American writers were keenly aware of such literary precedents. William Bradford and the Puritan divines explicitly invoked, as precedents and interpretive models, the biblical account
of the journey of the Children of Israel to the Promised Land as
well as, secondarily, the Aeneid. Both, of course, are epic accounts of exalted social undertakings involving great migrations;
it is clear that the early American writers regarded their own
experience in epical terms and considered the massive journey
to be an important element of an authentic epic. The well-known
beginning of Cotton Mather's *Magnalia Christi Americana* (1702)—
"I write the Wonders of the CHRISTIAN RELIGION, flying from
the Depravations of Europe, to the American Strand"—deliberately echoes Virgil's opening:

> I sing of arms and of a man: his fate
> had made him fugitive; he was the first
> to journey from the coasts of Troy as far
> as Italy and the Lavinian shores.[21]

We say that a new consciousness was being expressed, and
indeed the discovery even more than the settlement of America
created a newness of mind for all of Europe, let alone the par-
ticipants and theorists themselves. But as they interpreted their
experience of social creation, they appropriated existing forms.
The patterns of road narrative already familiar in world literature
and mythology—the quest, the migration, the homecoming, the
wandering—were reshaped into distinctive, while yet familiar,
patterns of American narrative. The patterns of journey narrative
that we observe in American literature are not unique, but traditional and distinctively adapted.[22]

The simple journey or road narrative is one of the most ancient
of storytelling forms. Scholes and Kellogg point out in *The Nature*

of Narrative that the traveller's tale or lie is a "persistent oral form in all cultures."[23] Similarly, Northrop Frye comments that the marvellous journey is "the one formula that is never exhausted."[24] The journey is a convenient form for fiction because its parameters are so obvious and at the same time so flexible. Yet only the simplest of traveller's tales are merely literal and commentative. We know by its appearance in virtually all mythologies that the form was unquestionably seen to hold a potential for larger meanings even earlier than recorded literature gives us a means of judging men's assumptions. In the biblical myth of the Garden, for instance, a theological idea or supposed historical occurrence, the deterioration of man from created perfection to a state of sin and a consequent world of sorrow and uncertainty, appears in terms of spatial movement, the expulsion from Eden. Spiritual connotations of place and movement appear variously throughout the Bible in a pattern of symbolically meaningful wilderness and desert experiences, a pattern which was later of great importance to the early Puritan writers in the New World.[25] From classical civilization, the Odyssey, another early text of great continuing influence, also clearly demonstrates the usefulness of journey motifs for conveying nonspatial experiences. Disregarding for the moment the structural aspects of Odysseus' "real" journey, we can see that his descent into the underworld, for instance, involves the giving of spatial terms to a nonspatial concept, the integrative encounter and converse with the past and its secrets. Indeed, the horrific journey, usually to an underworld, is a regular feature of the hero tale or monomyth,[26] and in every case it is a means of representing not only the hero's conquest of his environment but some redemptive experience occurring not in space but in another dimension, inner or spiritual.

The facility of the journey in serving as a metaphor was clearly established, then, long before the birth of American culture and literature. The journey is indeed a perennially recurrent fictional form precisely because it is, as Scholes and Kellogg suggest, a "simple linear form" providing an obvious structure which readily accommodates secondary import.[27]

The effectiveness of the journey as symbolic action largely derives from the facility with which space can become an analogue for time. It is this interchangeability of the two dimensions,

spatial and temporal, that is the basic capacity allowing transformation of simple journey narrative into symbolic action. The
journey can readily be used as a metaphor for the passage of
time or for penetration into different levels of consciousness.
(My words *passage*, *penetration*, and *levels* show how difficult it
is to speak of such matters without using spatial metaphors.)
The reason why this interchangeability exists is probably easier
to grasp than to state, but clearly derives from the ways in which
we perceive flux and duration. That is, it involves the elemental
questions of epistemology, the relation between subject and object, knower and known. In such a relation, as we address the
environment, we assume instinctively that we ourselves are fixed
points with changes occurring around us. If we pause to consider
that our selves as consciousness are also changing phenomena,
then we become bifurcated selves, split into considering subject
and considered object (the past self or whatnot). Such an experience of bifurcation of the self illustrates the way in which
modes of perception of the outer world can be transferred to the
perception of the inner self. It is precisely this capacity for mir-
roring between the inner and outer dimensions that makes possible the "inward voyage," an archetypal form in which
movement through the geographic world becomes an analogue
for the process of introspection.[28]

From the fixed vantage of the perceiving self, temporal
changes—the seasons, day and night, the aging of friends, appearance and disappearance of social changes of all sorts—occur
on a kind of 360 degree movie screen. These changes occurring
through time, duration, are perceptually present to the observer
as a succession of images, much as landscape becomes a succession of images as we move through it in travel. The perceived
experience is much the same whether the knower is moving (in
spatial terms) or "fixed" (in temporal/perceptual terms). Ab-
stractions assume much the same quality: experientially, we confront the images which represent or result from ideas as shifting
phenomena flitting around the fixed vantage point of the self
just as roadside images shift when we travel. Through this interchangeability of space and time and the correspondence of
inner and outer dimensions, the simple journey becomes figurative, a metaphor or symbol.

The major patterns or forms of journey narrative are also very traditional, though they occur in distinctive ways, reshaped and with different emphasis, in American literature. We have mentioned the simple tale or boasting lie of the traveller. A form scarcely less primitive than that is the fantastic voyage or mock journey, in which the narrative of travel itself takes second place to satiric and intellectual purposes.[29] A form closely related to the mock journey is the picaresque, in which the character of the rogue-narrator himself is likely to assume as much interest as the outer, social spectacle he confronts. Clearly, the picaro's movement is not restricted to a geographical dimension; he moves also "through a spectrum of society."[30] In the home-seeking narrative, whether individual or collective (the epic migration), the journey is again not only toward a place but toward a quality of life as well. A sense of destiny hangs over this form, as in the epics of the Children of Israel and the Aeneid. Its tone is likely to be much more eschatological than that of the homecoming or return, which tends to affirm the superiority of traditional values over the possibility of new orders resulting from adventure or wandering. (For example, Odysseus' return to Penelope and reassertion of his authority.) The home-founding journey is more likely to reach toward tragedy and a tone of exultation than the homecoming, with its restoration of the domestic status quo. The homecoming, that is, tends to be a comedic form, unless the home itself is somehow unworthy or destructive to the hero.

The heroic quest, closely overlapping the narrowing or conspicuously psychological "night journey" that appears in all mythologies, is also generally a comedic form unless the hero fails to achieve the object of his quest, but because the quest object may involve extremes of self-denial, painful transformation of the hero himself, and disruption of the social order, it is likely to reach those regions of the literary map where high comedy and high tragedy intermix. The designation quest is itself highly general,[31] obscuring the fact that there is great variety in types of quests. In the medieval Grail quest, narrative elements were ritualized, and by gaining the sacred token, the hero also won spiritual rebirth for himself and regeneration or restoration for his society. In later quests, such abstract values themselves tend to appropriate the place of the actual object of the quest, though in some works, which for this very reason have a strongly mythic flavor, a magical totem of a more or less transparently symbolic nature is retained. The quest may be for spiritual enlightenment, or Truth, for a father or lost son, for an artistic or craftly secret, for social establishment, but in any case it is likely to involve quest for the quester himself, through discovery of selfhood or self-definition. Here it is the unfamiliarity of the road ahead that is the key to the correspondence of outer and inner worlds. The quester moves through an unfamiliar landscape toward a guessed-at but still astounding token; the introspective venturer finds new awarenesses at every turn of thought and may at last reach the hidden treasure of full self-knowledge, an integrated personality.

In all of these forms as they occur in antiquity and in medieval times, fictional geography and spatial movement tend to be used (to borrow the terminology of Scholes and Kellogg once again) in an essentially illustrative rather than representational way. Or to put it in what may be more comfortable terminology, spatial structures tend to be nonmimetic. Thus it is a mistake to try to map the wanderings of Odysseus or to suppose that Homer meant us to do so; it would be equal folly to try to chart the movements of a Rasselas, a Dante, a Quixote, a Galahad. The mileposts and borders simply won't tally. The authors had something else in mind.

The question of illustrative spatial patterns is considered very incisively by Charles Muscatine in his essay "Locus of Action in Medieval Narrative."[32] Muscatine suggests that "the orientation of the action in space. . .can be a mode of organizing the narrative and giving it more than probability; it can give it meaning" (p. 117). Such a function of space (setting and movement) is of course clearest in literature that is not governed by mimetic predilections. Medieval allegory, Muscatine notes, whether in painting or in literature, "characteristically deals with moral rather than with physical space." Dante, for instance, uses a "patterned. . .setting to express immutable moral relationships" (pp. 117-19).

In literature more nearly governed by realistic assumptions, particularly in the novel, such a correspondence between spatial pattern and moral import is more difficult to define, while at the same time "moral relationships" have come to seem not at all "immutable" but highly problematic. Spatial patterns may occur only as a function of probability, to create the texture of felt life. That is, setting and movement may become devices in the establishment of fictive illusion. They may serve to convey comment on social or historic conditions depicted or echoed in a given work. Or the spatial patterns of a work may derive meaning from their appropriation of traditional, persisting literary forms. In this way, for instance, the fact that Leopold Bloom's movements parallel Odysseus' creates a resonance in *Ulysses* that has nothing to do with the accuracy of Joyce's depiction of Dublin. The formal or aesthetic context of resonance conditions and enriches our reading of specific journey narratives, just as the resonating social or historic context does.

American journey fiction draws on both these contexts, the context of its unique history and the context of journey narrative in world literature. The question of how or why American journey narrative differs from its literary predecessors is perhaps not susceptible to a full answer. Critics and literary historians have been pursuing the issue of an American literary character since Revolutionary times with only limited success. In a sense, the full course of this study will be an attempt to provide an answer to the question of distinctive development of the journey narrative. As a preliminary, however, one can say that this distinctiveness is related to the interplay of the two contexts, history and literary tradition. Even as American writers have worked within long established formal traditions, they have reshaped those traditions out of their response to the patterns and values of the journey in American history. Not that there is an operative determinism of history or that every American writer is primarily or directly concerned with history and social theory, but since American history has been so pervasively concerned with journeys and so forcefully enunciated as myth, there is an overwhelming tendency for American writers who utilize journey narratives to perceive them after the patterns of history. American history, one might say, provides a kind of filter through which writers perceive literary traditions.

Part of the distinctiveness of American journey narrative is simply the insistence with which the journey occurs in our literature. It is, as we have seen, an important recurring form in all literatures, but in American literature it is the dominant form in which experience has been interpreted in fiction. Beyond simple recurrence, the traditional patterns of journey narrative occurring in American literature are reshaped by assuming the coloration of insistent though often ambiguous directional values in which the West, with all its associations, is the primary direction of significance. In addition, the traditional patterns absorb an admixture of motifs and motives of escape and—not necessarily in contradiction—a zest for the ongoing motion of the journey itself, quite apart from its putative goals.

Probably the most distinctively American, and at the same time the least traditionally patterned, engagement with the journey form is Whitman's noted and influential poetry of tribute to the open road. It has generally been recognized that Whitman's poetry affirms journeying as an end in itself. By making his a "perpetual journey" he makes it coterminous with life. This association is quite unlike the allegorical journey of life, a concept that emphasizes stages rather than movement itself. It is desirable, Whitman says, to "know the universe itself as a road, as many roads, as roads for travelling souls."[33] His tone has none of the misgivings that gather around the narratives of rootless wandering in our own day. Instead, he rejoices in the endlessness of the road, hence his own continuing state of motion:

> Afoot and light-hearted I take to the open road,
> Healthy, free, the world before me
> The long brown path before me leading wherever I choose.
>
> (p. 108)

He stresses glad beginnings:

> On journeys through the States we start,
> (Ay through the world, urged by these songs,
> Sailing henceforth to every land, to every sea,)
> We willing learners of all, teachers of all, and lovers of all.
>
> (p. 11)

He is confident of fulfillment, though the end of the journey is beyond calculation:

They go! they go! I know that they go, but I know not where they
   go,
But I know that they go toward the best—toward something great.
                                                       (p. 114)

. . .

My rendezvous is appointed, it is certain,
The lord will be there and wait till I come on perfect terms,
The great Comerado, the lover true for whom I pine will be there.
                                                       (p. 63)

Journeying is apparently a precondition for imparting the mystical word of Truth. Indeed, it may itself, as process, *be* the Truth:
when the dramatically projected Whitman, the hero of "Song
of Myself," leads "each man and each woman of you. . .upon
a knoll," with his embracing left arm "hook[ed]. . .round the
waist" as oracle, the truth to which he points is "landscapes of
continents and the public road" (p. 64). He insists that the open,
outdoor world of the road is the necessary setting for communication of the true Word:

I swear I will never again mention love or death inside a house,
And I swear I will never translate myself at all, only to
   him or her who privately stays with me in the open air.
                                                       (p. 65)

   Clearly, the Word Whitman has to give is himself. Yet he finds
himself impossible to know or define except as a kind of sibylline
utterance. He is thrown back on defining himself in terms of
images from the outer world, as he had also defined the other,
the outer world, in terms of its participation in his self. Since
the road is for him the most significant feature of the outer
world—representing as it does endless process, his own enterprise of comradely knowing, and the way to survey or catalog
his world—it becomes the best correlative for the self. In exploring the open road or "Mannahatta" and other parts of America, Whitman reflexively explores himself.[34]

> O public road, I say back I am not afraid to leave you, yet I love
>   you,
> You express me better than I can express myself,
> You shall be more to me than my poem.
>
> (p. 109)

Further, the road is also the medium for comradeship; it provides
the possibility for all walkers to share their participation in endless process. Whitman means to

> . . .merge all in the travel they tend to, and the days and nights
>   they tend to,
> Again to merge them in the start of superior journeys.
>
> (p. 113)

Sharing, for Whitman, resolves itself into the question,

> Will you give me yourself? will you come travel with me?
> Shall we stick by each other as long as we live?
>
> (p. 115)

For Whitman, then, the journey means ongoing life, possibility,
the interaction of subject and object, communion. But finally the
journey is confirmed solely because it is journey.

In later work, retreating somewhat from his expansive affir-
mations of the future and progress, the aging poet calls us to a
voyage to India, the past, and to a "Passage to more than India!"
(p. 294). Without his earlier assurance regarding the goal of the
journey of self and society, he is left with only an insistence that
we go, whatever the direction:

> O my brave soul!
> O farther farther sail!
> O daring joy, but safe! are they not all the seas of God?
> O farther, farther, farther sail!
>
> (p. 294)

In the very late "Sands at Seventy" annex to Leaves of Grass
(1889), though he continues to view life as "an endless march"
with all people "surely going somewhere" (p. 362), he falls back

even further on conventional utterance, voicing the familiar "great beyond" metaphor: "A far-stretching journey awaits him, to return no more" (p. 369). Nevertheless, in the early period of his creativity, Whitman had utilized the conventional imagery of the road narrative in a distinctively zestful way that has seemed to many readers to be peculiarly American.

Whitman's praise of journeying, voicing as it did both the expansive hope and the restlessness that, in less wholehearted manner, have seemed to many the prevailing tone of the American imagination, has held the attention of American writers, who, like Ezra Pound, have had to find themselves sooner or later making their peace with him. Probably his sweeping lines, like the sweeping roads themselves, have been partly responsible for the clarion-like appeal of his celebrations of the road, but certainly a few of the pictures he creates—the comrade with his arm about the waist, his other hand sketching out the prospect of the hazy beyond; the hardy, democratic foot-traveller in strong shoes and slouch clothes, striking out into the countryside unbothered by civilization at his back—have appealed by their approximation of the ideal guises in which America likes to picture itself. He has been limited, however, to an influence of tone and image. Formally he has had little to give. Narratives must have structure; they cannot proceed in disjointed rapturous utterances. Though Whitman is the fountainhead of American praise of journeying, our poets have tended to abandon his all-inclusiveness for more stringent limits of subject and tone as well as poetic form. Other writers, using more clearly defined and traditional forms of the journey narrative, have had a greater influence than Whitman on the formal patterns of American journey narrative. But in his insistence on seeing the journey as the right pattern of life and as an act of liberation and community, Whitman captured and resoundingly interpreted the one best image of American aspiration.

NOTES

1. But even the recording of the primary explorations and migrations was shaped by pre-existing forms and myths, as scholars have

often noted. See especially Howard Mumford Jones, O *Strange New World* (New York: Viking Press, 1964).

2. Walter Allen, *The Urgent West: The American Dream and Modern Man* (New York: E. P. Dutton, 1969), p. 217. In connection with such a principle of recurrence involving accretions of symbolic meaning to the events of history, my colleague Louise K. Barnett comments, "Think of Kennedy's 'new frontier'—space runs out, but the metaphor continues."

3. Paul Horgan, *The Common Heart* (1942); reprinted in *Mountain Standard Time* (New York: Farrar, Straus and Cudahy, 1962), p. 287.

4. John M. Anderson in *The Individual and the New World* (State College, Pa.: Bald Eagle Press, 1955), p. 5, called the journey west "the nineteenth century pattern of culture and thought." But the nineteenth century only produced the most intensive and dramatic version of what has been characteristic all along. Alan Heimert demonstrates westerly aspiration and movement by 1677 in his essay "Puritanism, the Wilderness, and the Frontier," *New England Quarterly*, 26 (1953), 361-82.

5. A provocative consideration of the contrary directional pulls is Ferner Nuhn's *The Wind Blew from the East: A Study in the Orientation of American Culture* (New York: Harper and Brothers, 1942).

6. The directional values are widely recognized. Walter Allen is typical and quite sound in observing that "movement westward. . .remains the great image of the American sense of possibility" (*The Urgent West*, p. 58). Cf. Nicholas J. Karolides, *The Pioneer in the American Novel, 1900-1950* (Norman: University of Oklahoma Press, 1967).

7. For example, Thomas Cole's four-part allegorical series of paintings *The Voyage of Life*, which depict typical stages in human life in four emblematic scenes. For a commentary on Cole's paintings and the traditional iconography of pilgrimage, see Joy S. Kasson, "*The Voyage of Life*: Thomas Cole and Romantic Disillusionment,"*American Quarterly*, 27 (1975), 42-56.

8. The most thoughtful examination of the Western and its relation to American experience is James K. Folsom's *The American Western Novel* (New Haven: College and University Press, 1966). John R. Melton notes that for the western novelist the "travel narrative" is a "given form." "The Novel in the American West," in *Western Writing*, ed. Gerald W. Haslam (Albuquerque: University of New Mexico Press, 1974), p. 80.

9. Cf. Karolides, *The Pioneer in the American Novel*. In wagon-train novels the entire group are "in the center stage" with the hero only "one of them" (p. 30).

10. Cf. a book that can in some ways be seen as a modern parody of the Western, Jack Kerouac's *On the Road*. John Cawelti observes in

The Six Gun Mystique (Bowling Green, Ohio: Bowling Green University Press, 1971) that motion is a regular attribute of the Western hero.

11. Karolides, *The Pioneer in the American Novel*, refers to Boone as "antisocial" (p. 197). I would demur from the destructive implications of the term.

12. Folsom, *The American Western Novel*, sees in Westerns such as Conrad Richter's *The Sea of Grass* and Jack Schaefer's *Shane* an ideological conflict between individualism and cooperation. He generalizes that "whether the coming of civilization is good or ill is the burden of Western Fiction" (pp. 29-31).

13. Similarly, Cooper accorded grudging admiration to Aaron Thousandacres in *The Chainbearer* and Guert Ten Eych in *Satanstoe*. Cooper's ambiguous responses to his own characters are often seen as evidence of conflict within himself. See, for instance, Jesse Bier, "The Bisection of Cooper: *Satanstoe* as Prime Example," *Texas Studies in Literature and Language*, 9 (1968), 511-21. For a more moderate statement, Richard Chase, *The American Novel and Its Tradition* (New York: Doubleday, 1957), p. 46.

14. Cf. David Lavender, "The Petrified West and the Writer," in *Western Writing*, ed. Haslam, p. 151.

15. Charles L. Sanford, *The Quest for Paradise: Europe and the American Moral Imagination* (Urbana: University of Illinois Press, 1961), p. 56.

16. Louis Simpson, *Selected Poems* (New York: Harcourt, Brace, and World, 1965), p. 124.

17. *The Writings of Henry David Thoreau*, 14 vols. (Boston: Houghton Mifflin, 1946), vol. 5, p. 217.

18. *The Works of Herman Melville*, standard edition, 16 vols. (London: Constable, 1922), vol. 6, p. 189.

19. Sanford, *The Quest for Paradise*, p. 17.

20. For example, Donald E. Houghton, " 'Westering' in 'Leader of the People'," *Western American Literature*, 4 (1969), 117-24.

21. *The Aeneid of Virgil*, trans. Allen Mandelbaum (Berkeley: University of California Press, 1979), p. 1. Sacvan Bercovitch notes that Mather refers to the Aeneid "more frequently, more consistently, than to any other work (except for the Bible)" and mentions the "long exegetical tradition that christianized Aeneas in his role as leader, saint, and father of the people." *The Puritan Origins of the American Self* (New Haven: Yale University Press, 1975), p. 66. Especially in his first two chapters, Bercovitch provides searching examination of the typological significance of the Israelites for the early Puritan writers.

22. Joseph Addison Davis defines the "road novel" as a distinctive

American form related to the picaresque and other traditional journey forms but "different from them" largely because of the shaping effect of the American westward journey of history. See his dissertation "Rolling Home: The Open Road as Myth and Symbol in American Literature, 1890-1940," University of Michigan, 1974; abstracted in *Dissertations Abstracts International*, 35 (1975): 4509A.

23. Robert Scholes and Robert Kellogg, *The Nature of Narrative* (New York: Oxford University Press, 1966), pp. 73-77. See also an indication of the history and relationships of various forms of journey narrative, pp. 228-237.

24. Northrop Frye, *Anatomy of Criticism* (Princeton, N.J.: Princeton University Press, 1957), p. 57.

25. George H. Williams, *Wilderness and Paradise in Christian Thought* (New York: Harper and Brothers, 1962), e.g., pp. 4-6, 99-100, 124-30.

26. See Joseph Campbell, *Hero with a Thousand Faces*, Second Edition (Princeton,. N.J.: Princeton University Press, 1968).

27. Scholes and Kellogg, *Nature of Narrative*, p. 73.

28. Joseph Campbell uses the word journey as a metaphor for introspection and discusses the correspondence between outward and inward discovery in *Myths to Live By* (New York: Viking Press, 1972). For example, "We carry their laws [the laws of space and time] within us, and so have already wrapped our minds around the universe. . . .In searching out its wonders, we are learning simultaneously the wonder of ourselves. That moon flight as an outward journey was outward into ourselves" (p. 239). Also, "Our depths are the depths of space" (p. 266).

29. Scholes and Kellogg define the form as a journey told "for an intellectual and satiric purpose rather than a mimetic or fictional one," p. 28. Philip Babcock Gove, whose study *The Imaginary Voyage in Prose Fiction* (London: The Holland Press, 1961) is the standard commentary on the subject, concedes that "no completely satisfactory definition. . .has ever been devised" but sums it up as a journey of large scope which takes "all knowledge to be its province," pp. 3-4, 174.

30. Scholes and Kellogg, *Nature of Narrative*, pp. 73-74.

31. The quest is one of the three "typical plots of. . .heroic romance." The three are the "journey to a distant goal," the "return home," and the quest, "which involves voyage out, achievement, and return." Ibid., p. 228.

32. Charles Muscatine, "Locus of Action in Medieval Narrative," *Romance Philology*, 17 (1953), 115-22.

33. Walt Whitman, *Complete Poetry and Selected Prose*, ed. James E. Miller, Jr. (Boston: Houghton Mifflin, 1969), p. 113. Citations in parentheses are to this edition.

34. Cf. Todd M. Lieber, *Endless Experiments: Essays on the Heroic Experience in American Romanticism* (Columbus: Ohio State University Press, 1973). Lieber argues, for instance, that Whitman's "perpetual journey" is a metaphor for the poet's endless evolution of identity, a process that has "culmination" in each moment but never a "completion" (pp. 75-102). He finds a tendency in American romanticism to "make the heroic journey the drama of the creative self" (p. 243).

I
PATTERNS

2
Venturing Out:
Exploration and Escape

> The soul has moments of Escape—
> When bursting all the doors—
> She dances like a Bomb, abroad. . .
> > —Emily Dickinson

> Rise from the dates and crumbs. And walk away. . .
> > —Hart Crane, "The Wine Menagerie"

In his study of the literature and mythology of the voyaging hero, *The Adventurer*, Paul Zweig states that for the eighteenth and nineteenth centuries the primary image of society, or of what we like to call "the human condition," was that of a vast prison. The literature of these centuries, Zweig argues, betrays an obsessive concern with "images of helplessness and. . .impotence" and, in response to this obsession, a development of a characteristic hero whose adventure is the act of breaking out of restraint, breaking past barriers. He is a hero of "instinctual" and often amoral freedom whose characteristic journey is the journey out, the escape.[1]

Zweig's comments have a particular though unstated relevance to American literature, which first came to maturity, in the traditional belles lettres at any rate, in the nineteenth century. However, if there was, as Zweig suggests, a kind of spirit of the age bending fictional narrative toward the journey of escape, there was also, in the case of American letters, the equally powerful force of history bending the fledgling literature in precisely the same direction.

As we observed in the previous chapter, American history begins with voyages of exploration, escape, and home founding. These three are the primary—in the sense of being the earliest and the most basic—patterns of journey narrative in American literature. All three are, in their own ways, journeys of venturing out; they share an overall structure of movement away from society toward unfamiliar or unsocialized space. The main differences among them are related to the issue of motivating force. The home-founding journey, a highly specialized form that will be considered in a separate chapter, is a strongly goal-directed journey with its own set of characteristic incidents and values. The exploration is also goal-directed, but not in so specifically focussed a way, since the territory "out there" is by definition terra incognita and therefore the goal cannot so confidently be fixed in advance. Still, the explorer or adventurer is firm in his purpose to venture forth and may be clear as to his hopes or expectations of what he will find, though ultimately the discoveries that await him impose their own shape. In the journey of escape, on the other hand, the force is propulsive; the escape is not a journey *toward* but a journey *away from*.

Journeys of exploration were, of course, the source of the earliest writings associated with the American tradition, the accounts of their voyages written by Christopher Columbus, Captain John Smith, and others. The explorer's account persisted as a clearly defined sub-genre of nonfiction through the nineteenth century in the exploration accounts of Lewis and Clark, John C. Fremont, and Nathaniel Pitt Langford (who explored and described the Yellowstone Park), among others. It enticed such literary notables as Washington Irving, Walt Whitman, and Mark Twain. Edgar Allan Poe produced a spurious explorer's account in his abortive *Journal of Julius Rodman*, and even in recent years John Steinbeck resuscitated the form to great popular applause in *Travels with Charlie*. The explorer's account or geographical account is of great rhetorical interest, particularly as close examination reveals ways in which these supposedly factual writings reflect both pre-existent rhetorical formulas and the intellectual presuppositions of their times. It is in the direct geographical account that the spatial orientation of the American tradition is most clearly evident.[2] Nevertheless, the exploration has played only a minor role in what is more narrowly called literature; its terms have been evident in fiction in popular adventure stories and historical romance, but the journey of exploration itself has remained a structure of nonfictional writings chiefly historical in interest. For this reason, it is not of great pertinence here.

The escape, however, is pervasive and of central concern to us. As critics have often remarked, it is the most fully characteristic form adopted by the American imagination and comprises a part of the mythology of the American experience from its origins.[3] Within that mythology, the journeys of the Pilgrims and the founding Puritans, however mixed their purposes were in actuality, are viewed as visionary escapes from religious oppression. It is also firmly established in popular myth that motives of escape rather than expansionist ambitions impelled frontiersmen of the Daniel Boone variety.[4] They were men, the story goes, who loaded up and moved on when they could hear a neighbor's axe, complaining that the country was getting crowded.[5] In actuality the Daniel Boone of popular fame is a figure more of legend than of fact, created as a fabulous being in the conflicting fictionalized accounts that purported merely to set down his biography. History gives us Boone the colonizer and developer, the man of social vision; folk legend, the more powerful of the two as far as widespread impact, gives us Boone the footloose loner, forever turning his back on society.

In fiction, the motif of the escape appears early and persists to the present. Our earliest fictionalized narratives were the Indian captivity narratives of Mary Rowlandson and others, who chronicled their escapes from the savages who embodied a nightmare version of the New World. Our first great fictional hero, Natty Bumppo, is shown at the end of the first novel in which he appears, *The Pioneers*, poised for westerly flight. His example has been followed ever since, generally through resort to the woods or open spaces.[6] When Hester Prynne and Arthur Dimmesdale decide to shed their false social roles in *The Scarlet Letter*, they meet in the woods and plot an escape either to the wild interior of the continent or back to Europe. Ishmael escapes the "damp, drizzly November" in his soul, in the opening chapter of *Moby-Dick*, by going to sea, while New Yorkers less adventurous than Ishmael, and thus less heroic, only wish they could do so; they stand "like silent sentinels" in "ocean reveries." Poe's Arthur Gordon Pym indulges a perverse and doom-seeking restlessness when he goes off to sea, but the strong implication of the early portion of the *Narrative* is that Pym needs to escape the restraints of his more reputable social self. Sherwood Anderson's young men in *Winesburg, Ohio* and F. Scott Fitzgerald's Jay Gatsby in *The Great Gatsby*, two of the standard modern classics, define themselves as exceptional men by their need, whether fulfilled or not, to escape the narrow confines of their midwestern environments. Like Stella-Rondo in Eudora Welty's comic masterpiece "Why I Live at the P.O.," they deserve credit for getting out of town.

As this summary suggests, the escape was at its greatest ascendancy in the classic texts of the nineteenth century. But it is still very much alive. At the end of Norman Mailer's *An American Dream* (1965), for instance, the hero escapes to the wilds of Mexico, continuing the nineteenth century's pattern of resort to unsocialized spaces even though such spaces, in the modern world, have become rarer and farther off, exotic. The list of escape narratives proliferates largely because the escape so often appears in limited segments of works also utilizing other journey patterns. The tone of the escape narrative or escape sequence, however, has generally darkened as the possibility of real escape has diminished and disillusionment with the outcome of earlier escapes has deepened.

Structurally, the typical fiction of escape is a motivational buildup toward the culminating act of breaking out. Therefore, the course and scope of the ensuing journey may embrace great distance or only a symbolic removal to an inward space of liberation. Indeed, the journey that follows the initial act of breaking out is not typically elaborated in the escape narrative; it is not the important part of the story. If a resultant journey is elaborated, it typically appears as a series of new compulsions to repeated acts of escape (in *Huckleberry Finn*, for instance, or Cooper's *The Last of the Mohicans* or Melville's *Typee*) or as a modulation into another form of journey (for example, Ishmael's complex journey in *Moby-Dick*). After the decisive breaking out, the escape often merges into the quest or the narrative of home founding, as the motive impulse of the hero is modified and defined through experience.

American fiction has traditionally presented the escape as a victory, a rite of passage in celebration of personal transcendence. By escaping, the lone hero pronounces judgment on his society, implicitly shaking its dust from his feet in assertion of his freedom from its conventionalism or corruption. Such a judgment is pronounced by Huckleberry Finn, for instance, when he "lit out" from a repressive and devious society. In more recent fiction, it is pronounced both implicitly and explicitly in the very similar escapes of Ralph Ellison's *Invisible Man* and Richard Wright's "The Man Who Lived Underground." But as Zweig notes in *The Adventurer*, the counterpart of the social prison is "the prison of the lonely self"; the escaping hero must break out of both forms of constraint, as Ishmael has to escape not only the tameness of life on land and its falsification of ultimate truth, but the megrims in his soul. Therefore, the hero's journey of escape often has strong overtones of self-destruction. Such overtones, as well as a sense of futility or uncertainty, have become increasingly prevalent, producing the darkening of the tone of escape fiction. In occasional texts the tone of celebration of the lone escaping hero is still heard. Alison Lurie gives a positive rendition of the escape in *Real People* (1969) by bringing her writer/housewife to a clear realization of reality or truth after she escapes her day-to-day obligations. Such an affirmative tone, however, is no longer typical.

Twain gave the advance notice of this aspect of the literary future (and others) in *Huckleberry Finn*. Huck's first departure is an escape that modulates into a quest. But his final departure for the Territory, the free West, is an escape doomed to failure. He is lighting out "ahead of the rest," but as the phrase indicates they, and thus the society Huck wants to escape, will catch up with him. The implications are tragic, and that overtone of tragic frustration is one of the qualities that make Twain's "boy's book" both prophetic and enduring.[7]

The tone of frustration continues in fiction of the modern period, as increasingly the escape tends to modulate into directionless wandering or a sense of futility, a giving up. Modern fiction tends to put up a No Exit sign, and its heroes are likely to find themselves, like Jay Gatsby, gazing at illusory lights with no place to go. In *Gatsby* and many novels of Fitzgerald's contemporaries, as well as later writers, escape tends to lead into a dead-end street, or often literally to death. (Or worse: the frustrated attempt to escape by means of suicide in Edith Wharton's *Ethan Frome*.) In Paul Horgan's little-read novel of abortive westering, *Far from Cibola* (1938), a bum hitchhiking to California in hopes of escaping the miseries of the depression dies along the way. A more familiar example is Thomas Wolfe's *You Can't Go Home Again*, in which George Webber's great urge is to "flee," to "escape"—the very words punctuate his narrative. What Webber wants to escape is a deadening society, as well as himself. But he becomes a mere "wanderer in strange countries" and finds that, after all, he has been "seeking to escape what now he had returned to."[8] He comes to perceive the world as an aggregate of people all "moving through the moments of their lives to death" (p. 43). Wolfe's turgid autobiographical novel typifies the disillusioned tone of escape fiction in the twentieth century. Webber's and his own final wisdom, stated in a section called "A Wind is Rising, and the Rivers Flow," is the message of homelessness stated in the title. But Wolfe adds a vague, unsubstantiated hope that the process all tends toward something.

Much the same tone of futility and entrapment is heard in William Faulkner's great story "The Bear," a work clearly reflecting the pervasive influence of Twain. As Ike McCaslin grows older he must travel farther and farther to reach the escape valve of the raw wilderness until in "Delta Autumn," the story of Ike's old age which ends *Go Down, Moses*, only a small patch of woods remains for the annual rite of hunting. Ike's own moral vision and courage have shrunk correspondingly. In "The Bear," when Ike makes his final trip and finds Boon Hogganbeck beating at his gun with a rock, he goes by logging train, the very instrument of the economic process that is destroying the sacred wilderness and its opportunities of flight from society to essential reality. That flight had been reflected in Ike's moral life by his "escape" from his familial position in society, with its property and consequently its involvement in social and economic evil, to the holy but uncommitted role of the humble carpenter. The tragedy of *Go Down, Moses* is a tragedy for American life: not only the disappearance of her resources and natural beauty, but the impotence and waste of her finest visionary leaders, her Ike McCaslins, who have chosen to escape from social evils rather than engage them and cope with them.

Despite what has been called the "claustrophobia" of twentieth-century fiction,[9] however, some contemporary works continue to utilize the escape motif in positive ways. At this point we shall briefly examine three important novels that offer the possibility of an affirmation by means of the escape despite a generally dark view of society. These three novels also illustrate very clearly the typical structure of escape fiction, in which the act of breaking out is not the beginning but the culminating event.

The most nearly conventional of the three is John Updike's *Rabbit, Run*, which develops as a series of alternations between movements toward and away from home. We first meet Rabbit Angstrom on his way home from work, but the oppressive atmosphere he finds there—the apartment's shabbiness, his wife's drinking, irritability, and disorderliness—quickly drives him to escape. On impulse, he drives out the main highway from town, thinking he wants to drive straight through to the Gulf of Mexico, avoiding the confusions of cities. Though he quickly returns to his hometown, he does not return home; instead, still trying to escape, he moves in with a girl picked up in a bar. She diagnoses his condition at once: "You just wander, don't you?"[10] In a practical sense the girl is all too correct; Rabbit lacks direction, he is unable to persevere in his intentions. But there is another dimension she has missed. Confused as he is, Rabbit is searching for a better way. His plight is that of the "tender-minded" idealist.[11] Responding intensely to fleeting moments of innocence, vulnerability and generosity, as he senses them in even the smallest gestures or sensations, he cannot accept the mixed condition of life in which such moments are immersed in a daily dinginess. He posits an absolute goodness (God) beyond the daily muddle, and his escapes are efforts to reach that goodness beyond. This dimension of Rabbit's character is clearly seen by his friend the Reverend Eccles, but Eccles sees too that Rabbit's inchoate yearnings for the ideal are futile. "Of course, all vagrants think they're on a quest," he says. "At least at first" (p. 127).

The problem of the novel is whether Rabbit's escapes indicate vagrancy or a questing heroism. Updike does not provide an answer, but he does affirm the possibility of the heroic interpretation. After returning home to his wife and son at the birth of a second child, Rabbit finds the same dispiriting shabbiness, both of spirit and of physical surroundings. He tries to escape to his girl friend once again, and when his conscience again pulls him back toward home, he finds that his drunken wife has accidentally drowned the baby. At the end, confused and oppressed by the rival claims of his two "homes"—wife and pregnant girl friend—Rabbit makes his final escape. Updike's elevated, even ecstatic, language places the action squarely within the American tradition of the solitary retreating hero:

His hands lift of their own and he feels the wind on his ears even before, his heels hitting heavily on the pavement at first but with an effortless gathering out of a kind of sweet panic growing lighter and quicker and quieter, he runs. Ah: runs. Runs. (pp. 306-7)

Just as *Rabbit, Run* leaves its wavering hero at the moment of departure, so Joseph Heller's *Catch-22* (1955) and Ken Kesey's *One Flew Over the Cuckoo's Nest* (1962), two of the most celebrated novels of the post-World War II period, leave their heroes at the moment of setting out on journeys of escape. Despite the thoroughgoing unconventionality of both these novels, they are solidly rooted in the American fictional tradition that has given us a sequence of heroes poised for escape from a repressive society.[12] Like Crane's visionary poet in "The Wine Menagerie," these heroes express their superiority to their surroundings by rising and walking away.

The entire course of Heller's *Catch-22* leads up to Yossarian's moment of escape, which is presented in a mere page or two. The novel as a whole, with all the improbable craziness of the military world that it depicts, prepares the reader to see Yossarian's decision to escape to Sweden as the most positive response he could possibly make to the irrational, death-dealing world he has lived in. Yossarian's verbal exchange with one of his officers just before he sets out states very clearly the positive interpretation Heller has developed.

"But you can't just turn your back on all your responsibilities and run away from them," Major Danby insisted. "It's such a negative move. It's escapist."

Yossarian laughed with buoyant scorn and shook his head. "I'm not running *away* from my responsibilities. I'm running *to* them. There's nothing negative about running away to save my life."[13]

His claim is substantiated narratively by the final words of the novel: "The knife came down, missing him by inches, and he took off." The journey of escape for Yossarian, however hazardous and uncertain, is the moral move from a state of irrationality and repression, an inner death corresponding to the physical death dealt by war, to a state of freedom and individual ethical responsibility.

The same sorts of positive connotations are attached to Chief Bromden's escape at the end of *One Flew Over the Cuckoo's Nest*, both dramatically and by means of a very powerful imagery of water and baptism. In a structure very similar to Heller's, Kesey's involved and certainly reifying depiction of the asylum world[14] of *Cuckoo's Nest* prepares for and justifies Chief Bromden's spectacular departure on the last page of the novel:

I put my back toward the screen, then spun and let the momentum carry the panel through the screen and window with a rippling crash. The glass splashed out in the moon, like a bright cold water baptizing the sleeping earth. . . .I put my hand on the sill and vaulted after the panel, into the moonlight.[15]

Chief Bromden's destination is vague: a return visit to his tribal home, then after that perhaps Canada. The novel leaves him at the moment of setting out on that journey. But the point is that

Chief Bromden, like Yossarian and Rabbit, has for the moment managed to escape a crazy, confining world and set out on a journey of freedom.

If the modern world does indeed resemble an asylum or a system of murderous bureaucratic machinery gone mad, as Kesey and Heller imply, then it gives all the more justification for a heroism of escape. The darker tone of escape fiction reflects not only the desperateness of the need for escape, however, but the difficulty of negotiating so irrational a world in order to arrive at the open portal and the unavailability of places to go. For this reason, sequences of escape in modern literature have with increasing insistency become narratives of lostness and wandering. Indeed, in all of the novels mentioned in this chapter the escape impulse is bound up with other, generally more complex shaping motives, often of home founding or of quest, if not of wandering. To call such works merely novels of escape, as they have at times been called by critics emphasizing the importance of the escape motif, is seriously reductive. The escape may indeed be the most characteristic action form of the American imagination, but it more commonly appears in limited sequences of action than in full narratives. It seldom appears unmixed, particularly when a complete journey sequence is elaborated. Instead, it tends to be a pervasive presence in journey fiction of all structural patterns. Its presence will appear in subsequent chapters considering other recurrent forms of American journey narrative.

NOTES

1. Paul Zweig, *The Adventurer* (New York: Basic Books, 1974), pp. 167-84.

2. Ferner Nuhn writes in *The Wind Blew from the East: A Study of the Orientation of American Culture* (New York: Harper and Brothers, 1942), p. 4, "Space has been our time." A useful brief survey of the literature of travel and exploration is found in *Literary History of the United States*, 3d ed. rev. (New York: Macmillan, 1963), chapters 45 ("Western Chronicles and Literary Pioneers," by Henry Nash Smith), 46 ("The West as Seen from the East," by George R. Stewart), and 53 ("Western Record and Romance," by Wallace Stegner).

3. Numerous critical articles have been devoted to the motif of flight

or escape in various works. The escape form has also been examined in a monograph, Sam Bluefarb's *The Escape Motif in the American Novel: Mark Twain to Richard Wright* (Columbus: Ohio State University Press, 1972). Wright Morris asserts in *The Territory Ahead* (New York: Harcourt, Brace, 1957), p. 14, "The best American fiction is escape fiction."

4. To be sure, elements of escape motivation were present, though not in so simple a form as the myth would have it. Historian Louis B. Wright notes that the panic of 1837 "ruined many a citizen, townspeople as well as farmers, and made them so despondent over conditions at home that they were ready to seek a new life on the prairies of Indiana, Illinois, or even farther west in Iowa." *Culture on the Moving Frontier* (1955; rpt. New York: Harper and Row, 1961), p. 124.

5. In *These Happy Golden Years*, by Laura Ingalls Wilder, the last in a series of pioneer stories with which more than one generation of American children have grown up, the youthful romantic hero comments in typical style, "This country is settling up fast. . . . We have driven only forty miles and we must have seen as many as six houses." (New York: Harper and Row, 1943; "Newly illustrated, uniform edition," 1953), p. 169.

6. As Bluefarb notes in *The Escape Motif*, "the forest has sometimes represented the fact and, almost always, the symbol of escape" (p. 8). Thomas Philbrick points out in his study *James Fenimore Cooper and the Development of American Sea Fiction* (Cambridge: Harvard University Press, 1961), pp. 1 and 71, that in the earlier nineteenth century the sea offered the same appeals of liberation and adventure that the western frontier offered after mid-century.

7. Harold P. Simonson points out the tragic implications of the closed frontier and their appearance in *Huckleberry Finn* in his study *The Closed Frontier: Studies in American Literary Tragedy* (New York: Holt, Rinehart, and Winston, 1970), p. 75.

8. Thomas Wolfe, *You Can't Go Home Again* (1938; rpt. Signet, 1966), pp. 10-11.

9. Zweig, *The Adventurer*, p. 171.

10. John Updike, *Rabbit, Run* (New York: Alfred A. Knopf, 1960), p. 109.

11. William James terms the idealist, who yearns for consistency and order in life, "tender-minded," and the realist, able to tolerate inconsistencies and disorder, "tough-minded."

12. The structure of both, in that they give lengthy development to the reasons impelling the hero's decisive act of escape, leading to an untold journey, is strikingly similar to that of an earlier American classic of classroom fame, Harold Frederic's *The Damnation of Theron Ware* (1896).

The position of Kesey's *One Flew Over the Cuckoo's Nest* within American literary tradition has been examined by several critics, including Leslie Fiedler in *The Return of the Vanishing American* (New York: Stein and Day, 1968), and John A. Baroness in "Ken Kesey: The Hero in Modern Dress," *Bulletin of the Rocky Mountain Modern Language Association*, 23 (1969), 27-33.

13. Joseph Heller, *Catch-22* (New York: Simon & Schuster, 1955), p. 461. Many readers of the novel, however, have resisted Yossarian's claim that his departure is an enabling act. For example, Panthea Reid Broughton, in *William Faulkner: The Abstract and the Actual* (Baton Rouge: Louisiana State University Press, 1974), p. 163, comments that Yossarian's defiant departure is "based on the ultimately naive hypothesis that place can redeem, that the good life can be achieved elsewhere."

14. Robert Boyers points out that Kesey's asylum is "in many respects, a microcosm of the society-at-large" but that Kesey "never strains to maintain the parallel at any cost." See Boyers's article "Attitudes toward Sex in American 'High Culture'," *The Annals of the American Academy of Political and Social Sciences*, 376 (1968), 36-52, reprinted in the very useful Viking Critical Library edition of the novel. The asylum world is the twentieth century's own disturbing extension of the nineteenth century's prison world.

15. Ken Kesey, *One Flew Over the Cuckoo's Nest*, ed. John Clark Pratt (New York: The Viking Press, 1973), p. 310.

3
Venturing Out: The Home-Founding Journey

We detachments steady throwing,
Down the edges, through the passes, up the mountains steep,
Conquering, holding, daring, venturing as we go the unknown
ways,
Pioneers! O pioneers!

We primeval forests felling,
We the rivers stemming, vexing we and piercing deep the
mines within,
We the surface broad surveying, we the virgin soil upheaving,
Pioneers! O pioneers!
—Walt Whitman, "Pioneers! O Pioneers!"

Home is a notion that only nations of the homeless
fully appreciate and only the uprooted comprehend.
—Wallace Stegner, *Angle of Repose*

With the journey of exploration and the journey of escape, the home-founding journey is one of the primary forms of American journey narrative, most directly based on history. The narrative of home founding appeared very early, in the writings of William Bradford and the Puritan divines who both chronicled and interpreted their great migration. Numerous works of historical fiction take the actual home-seeking journeys of the westward pioneers as their material: to name only a few, Caroline Kirkland's marginally novelistic account of her life on the frontier *A New Home—Who'll Follow?* (1839), Emerson Hough's *The Covered Wagon* (1922), A. B. Guthrie's *The Way West* (1949). More recently, Wallace Stegner's *Angle of Repose* (1971) blends directly historical materials, actual family records, with fictional action that indirectly reflects the patterns of history, as the narrator attempts to establish a satisfactory home in modern California. Besides works such as these, which draw on the home-founding journeys of history more or less directly, a great many novels and other materials adopt home-founding patterns that reflect the shape of American history.

Like the exploration and the escape, the home founding is a forward-looking form, a venture from the familiar to the unfamiliar. It is this future-centeredness that clearly and obviously distinguishes the home-seeking journey from the homeward (returning home) journey far more common in world literature but far less common in American literature. The home-seeking journey often begins with escape, but its focus is the new home to be established and the associated benefits it will bring. The narrative may end with the arrival and the preparation of the home, or the actual journey may be only a preamble to an account of the difficulties and rewards of the new home itself, as it is, for example, in O. E. Rolvaag's *Giants in the Earth* (1929). In either case, the prevailing emotional tone is hope or confident purpose rather than rejection, as in the escape, and the time perspective, totally unlike the hymns to present beatitude of such nature communers as Thoreau or Cooper's Natty Bumppo, is the future. The great meaning of the West was opportunity,[1] a future-centered concept, and the home-seeking narrative, typically westerly, explicitly incorporates the standard directional values.

A recurrent incident conveying the qualities of hope and future-centeredness in the home-seeking journey is pregnancy and the first birth in the settlement. Crystallizing the settlers' aspirations for the future, the first birth is an occasion for celebration, even inspiration. In contrast, the death of a new-born infant or other child along the way epitomizes the adversities to be endured by the settlers if they are to "create a new life over this Endless Wilderness, and transform it into a habitable land for human beings."[2]

The arduous and preparatory nature of the journey itself is another typical, defining element of the migration narrative. The settler must struggle past obstacles to his goal of reaching the special place where he can begin to build his home. Often, especially in the Far West migration of the wagon train type, the terrain itself is the obstacle and is presented as such in incidents of difficult crossings, whether of river, peak, or desert. Such crossings are so characteristic as to be conventions. They are featured incidents in Guthrie's *The Way West* and Hough's *The Covered Wagon*, for example, and in the standard children's classic *Little House on the Prairie* by Laura Ingalls Wilder.[3] The conventional crossing is rendered comical in Caroline Kirkland's *A New Home* as the crossing of monstrous mud holes. In *The Ordways* (1964), William Humphrey appears to have taken a cue from William Faulkner's *As I Lay Dying* in developing his suspenseful narration of a crossing of the Red River into Texas. When the Ordway family's wagon is upset by an unexpected strong current in the narrow, muddy river, several kegs spill out that contain the disinterred remains of Thomas Ordway's ancestors. Such trials are never single or quickly surmounted; one crossing does not bring settlers to the Promised Land any more than the Red Sea crossing brought the Children of Israel there in the epic that always looms in the background of the pioneer migration. The pioneers must be steadfast through repeated trials before they can win their way to the expected homeland, a consummation that connotes salvation.

As the migrating pioneers persist in their arduous journey, the vehicle of travel becomes a featured narrative element. It is natural to expect that this would be so in any account of journeying. In the cowboy Western, for instance, his horse is the hero's means to that freedom he pursues, as well as a necessity of life itself in arid regions and often his dearest companion. But a particularly strong emphasis is placed on the mode of conveyance in the migration narrative. This emphasis is partly a factor of the structural importance of terrain as obstacle and trial, partly related to the necessity of equipment—household paraphernalia, tools, farming implements, and so on—which must be taken along for the establishment of the home at journey's end. (A recurrent incident in such narratives is the discarding of effects from the wagon when the way becomes more difficult than had been expected.) Such an emphasis on conveyance appears in all wagon train novels and films and in books of individual farmers' resettlement like Humphrey's *The Ordways* and Edwin Lanham's *The Wind Blew West*. Cooper similarly makes a great deal of conveyance, gear, and hired workmen in *Satanstoe* and of the cumbersomeness of Ishmael Bush's wagons in *The Prairie*. In Kirkland's *A New Home—Who'll Follow*? a light buggy unsuited to the boggy roads becomes a symbolic element in her development of the theme of false expectation and rude awakening.

Connotations of progress surround these vehicles and later, even more emphatically, railroad trains. An association of progress with railroads is evident, for instance, in Stephen Crane's attention to the trains of "The Bride Comes to Yellow Sky" and "The Blue Hotel." But in "The Blue Hotel" the easterners who arrive by train on the business of commercial pioneering find that the raw western environment and the moral anarchy it lets loose are too much for them. In Paul Horgan's *Main Line West* (1936), railroads are symbols of the nation's restlessness, which proves a stronger force than the urge to domesticity. Irma, the main character, rides the train to California in the expectation of making a home. Later, having been abandoned by her husband, she takes her son on itinerant preaching jaunts until she dies on a hot train in Arizona. At the end, the boy continues the tradition of restlessness by hopping a freight. Here, the image of the train is at the ironic center of the shift from homeward journey to mere wandering.

More typically, the migration or individual journey of home seeking is characteristically a comedic form centered on unification and arrival in the long-envisioned dwelling place. To use Northrop Frye's terms defining the "zenith, summer, and marriage or triumph phase" of myth, it concerns "apotheosis," the "sacred marriage," and "entering into Paradise."[4] To be sure, it can be manipulated to other effects, as we have seen. The home may never be found, or it may prove disappointing even to the degree that the home search may blend into the retreat, generally to the East. Such a treatment of the form occurs in Conrad Richter's *The Sea of Grass* (1937) and Horgan's *Main Line West*. An even more particularized version is Edith Wharton's *The House of Mirth*, in which Lily Bart's socially circumscribed efforts to establish herself by marriage involve a pattern of geographic movement that becomes more frenetic and far-flung as she becomes more desperate and haphazard; she lapses into a journey of wandering until her effort ends in a lonely death. Generally, however, when we read a novel of the journey to found a home, we expect that after due tribulations the special place will be found and marriages, births, and new social order will ensue. That expectation is usually rewarded.

The emphasis on the development of a social order is another defining element in the home-founding journey. Unlike the individualistic, alienating quest, it is always to some degree collective, even if only to the degree of being familial. Though the pioneer may feel an impulse to escape from established society to the unsettled wilderness, generally a journey east to west, there is still a sense of society in the background, whether it is a sense of his being a part of the larger social process of migration or of his building a society to come. This quality of collectiveness is evident to some degree in all of the examples we have mentioned, and, together with the necessity of a worthy purpose, is demonstration of how the original home-founding voyages of the Puritans have served as a shaping myth for the form. This collectiveness of the home-founding narrative, moreover, is the reason why it often approaches the epic.

That the effect of collective social movement can be achieved even in the story of a single character or pair of characters is well demonstrated, however, by Stephen Crane's "The Bride Comes to Yellow Sky." The bride who comes to a raw frontier town and averts violence represents the female principle of domesticity and order arriving at the heretofore male dominated wilderness state. Her transformation or taming of it merely by her presence figures the inauguration of a new historic era in the West by the taming presence of settlement or civilization.[5]

The story presents historic processes of unification (marriage) and the moderation of extremes (the easing of the groom's violence and the bride's shyness). It is possible for a single wedding journey to represent this vast historic process because it so well embodies the elements of that history: its westerly direction, its recurring change from frontier state to settled order, and its emphasis on expectation for the future and the crucial role of the female and domesticity in effecting these changes. Because it so well typifies these processes, Crane's "The Bride Comes to Yellow Sky" can serve as a plausible, crystallizing parable of the national epic of westerly migration.

The question of motive or purpose impelling the epical search for a new home is a concern in virtually all serious home-founding narratives and becomes a basis for evaluating the search as told. Again, this question is related to the societal quality of the form in that the founding of a better society is shown as a worthy goal, whereas individual footloose westering commonly appears within a home-founding narrative as rootless, irresponsible, and shallow. Cooper, for instance, admired pioneering of a forward-looking, proprietary kind, but distrusted the common pioneer who hoped for immediate profit involving, as Cooper saw it, no responsibility, planning, or stability. Such mobility was especially bad if it involved "squatting." Hawthorne too, in *The House of the Seven Gables*, distinguished between worthy and unworthy home seeking by paralleling the motives for several moves. The original Pyncheon's home founding, based on pride and achieved through guile, was unworthy, as was the later Judge Pyncheon's prideful acquisition of a suburban home for purposes of selfishly expropriating all possible material comforts for himself. Flight from harsh truth (the Judge's death presence) leads to destruction: a ruined church and a ruined house. Hawthorne was harder pressed, however, to formulate the right motives for relocation, and the fact that the ending of *Seven Gables* has so often dissatisfied readers is largely a matter of his inability or refusal to clarify the question of right motive.

The importance of a righteous purpose impelling the search for a new home is one element of the American home-seeking tradition that clearly relates it to the archetypal founding journeys. The question of motive was crucial in the early fathers' interpretation and evaluation of their own migration experience. William Bradford insisted that the Pilgrims in Leyden began to think of "removal to some other place" not because of restlessness or irresponsible escapism but because of their estimable founding purpose. As he put it, "not out of any newfanglednes or other such like giddy humor. . .but for sundry weighty and solid reasons."[6] He regarded this sanctified migration in a far different light from the individual drifting away to available land "remote from all society" that began soon after the founding of Plymouth. Similarly, John Cotton systematically and with scriptural citations enumerates seven purposes which justify "removeall." He warns, "we may not rush into any place, and never say to God, By your leave; but we must discerne how God appoints us this place."[7]

The early Puritans purposed no less than the establishment of the perfect church and, consequently, the perfect godly society, which they firmly expected to serve as a model for the rest of the world. Their purpose, narrow as it sometimes appears to us, actually involved a conviction of serving the divine will on a vast scale. It cannot be doubted that much of this same sense of mission permeated ideas about Manifest Destiny in the nineteenth century.[8] Such a rationale understandably exaggerates the despicability of undertaking the Western enterprise flippantly or, as in the case of land speculators, crassly. This concern with serious, constructive purpose is in large measure the source of the elevated tone that tends to pervade narratives of home founding.

The experiences of the Pilgrim and Puritan settlers exemplify and indeed prefigure all of the characteristic elements of the home-founding journey that we have enumerated. Their twin motives of escape from the oppressions and corruptions of the Old World and of determination to found their own godly community in the New are inextricable. The perilous passage, during which an unworthy member is purged from the group, culminates in the emotionally stirring arrival at a sacred, or at least a redeemable, land. Provision for a social structure had been made even before arrival. But the same arrival that fulfilled the founders' home-seeking journey initiated their impulse to turn and retreat. In Bradford's account of this sudden and altogether significant shift, no sooner had the Pilgrims "arrived in a good harbor, and [been] brought safe to land," for which they "fell upon their knees and blessed the God of Heaven who had brought them over the vast and furious ocean," than they looked about themselves and perceived that the Promised Land now appeared as "a hideous and desolate wilderness" and the ocean no longer a perilous obstacle to reaching the new home but "a main bar and gulf to separate them from all the civil parts of the world."[9] The resulting impulse to escape the new-found homeland has figured in numerous fictions of the eastward return.

In much the same way as we turn to the Puritans for the original pattern of the American settling experience, we turn to Cooper for the primary rendition of such national themes in early fiction. He was not the first to treat the recurrent native themes. James Kirke Paulding's frontier epic *The Backwoodsman*, for instance, was published in 1818, two years before Cooper's uncharacteristic first novel and five before he found his frontier matter in *The Pioneers*. More significantly, John Filson's fictionalized account of Daniel Boone had appeared in 1784. But Cooper was the first to capture the frontier theme in effective myth and to achieve a widespread popular impact. Later writers have followed and reworked his models—and also rebelled against him, thus by denial evincing his importance—just as they have the early historic models.

In Cooper's two chief settler novels, *The Pioneers* and *The Prairie*, the question of right motive is crucial. The earlier novel, *The Pioneers*, is by no means structurally a journey narrative, though it is a lengthy preparation for Natty Bumppo's departure on a journey west at the end. However, the novel does concern itself with the aftermath of resettlement, society in the transitional phase between raw frontier and established order. It is apparent from Cooper's presentation of such attributes of the settlement as its unsightly stump-littered clearings, its crude and tasteless buildings, and its bumptious manners that Cooper regards the migrants to the frontier in a dubious light. Lacking the long-range, constructive purpose of Judge Temple, the new town's most influential citizen, they have regarded only quick personal advantage. The reader inclined toward materialistic plain speaking might protest that what these settlers really lack that the judge possesses is money, that and the ambition to build a personal empire.

It is a similar situation to that in Cooper's *Satanstoe*. In that novel, the home-seeking journey Cooper celebrates is the young hero's "all-important journey" (VIII, 318) to locate a huge tract of land purchased by his father, not for personal settlement, but as an estate or investment to leave for his descendants, who will be enriched and, it is implied, socially distinguished by the holding. Corny's is a journey to establish a landlord's domain. Far different are the home-seeking journeys of the common pioneers, who are depicted as being generally a shiftless, narrow-minded lot who expect rapid aggrandisement for the least expenditure of effort and the least money or none at all. Going to the frontier without plans, equipment, or adequate finances, they lack a proper regard for the rights of those who have made such investments and who naturally expect to exercise control of their legally purchased property.

Another irresponsible home-seeking journey occupies center stage in *The Prairie*. The Ishmael Bush family are also adjudged unworthy migrants because they are squatters, thus violators of the laws of property and seemliness, and because their motive for journeying is, as Cooper sees it, purely negative, neither a far-seeing vision of stable social development nor Natty Bumppo's lone communion with the primitive, but a rude and selfish desertion of social order. The Bush clan learns, somewhat fuzzily, that in the absence of pure virtue (such as Natty's), order is inescapably necessary and, without the larger sanctions of established society, burdensome to apply. They turn back, leaving the prairie to old Natty, whose journey has ever been harmonious with the natural order of things.

It is important to distinguish here between the characteristics of Natty's westerly journey and those of the home-seeking or migration form. Natty's departure at the end of *The Pioneers* is archetypal as a westerly flight to the primal wilderness, but it is lone rather than collective and devoted to present (or rather, timeless) satisfaction rather than future progress. Such a purpose is by no means tainted with the settlers' shortsightedness, however, because Natty's motive is never exploitative but submissive to nature. Such is the quality of his nomadic life in *The Prairie* as well. His manner of life and movement corresponds to the cyclic patterns of nature and thus exists on a plane quite other than the social plane of aspiration, building, and progress.

Cooper, then, for all the mythic quality of his concern with the themes of wilderness, flight, and masculine comradeship,[10] is not characteristic of American writers in his attitude toward the theme of home seeking. His atypicality may in part be related to his time: he lived and worked before the period of the massive wagon train migrations to the Far West, which have been used more often than any other in fiction, at any rate in popular literature. We can only conjecture how the vastness of that social spectacle might have touched his imagination. Perhaps, given the nature of his social convictions, not at all.[11] We are on much firmer ground in seeing his lack of sympathy for the ordinary settler's removal to the frontier as a reflection of the polarized quality of his imaginative responses. As an advocate of hierarchical order and, in his more lastingly influential work, a celebrator of lone communion with the un-"improved" primitive, he straddles, as it were, the position of the subsistence frontiersman or the adventurer. Cooper's real importance here is that he did, at an early stage in American fiction, identify the search for a home as an important theme.

Hawthorne too, as we have seen, regarded resettling with considerable ambivalence. His treatment of the theme, as any reader of his subdued fictions would expect, is quite miniaturized and not a little ambiguous. In *Seven Gables*, migration means one small family's removal to an inherited house just at the edge of town. The qualities that elicit Hawthorne's approval of their move remain unclear, but seem to involve a kind of privative innocence, the absence of those positive ills which he had condemned in the earlier Pyncheons' home founding and in Hepzibah and Clifford's flight. To be sure, Phoebe and Holgrave show a spirit of loving kindness in their acceptance of old Uncle Venner, a candidate for the poor farm, and their two pallid relatives into their home. But chiefly their move is characterized by passivity, mere inheritance and an acceptance of what the "will of Providence" brings—hardly the qualities that opened and settled the West.

The basis of Hawthorne's misgivings is chiefly his affinity for the past. Despite his pronouncements about its crippling weight in *Seven Gables*, *The Blithedale Romance*, and various short stories and sketches, he was unable to approve any abrupt break with tradition. In *Blithedale* he expresses both grave doubts and ridicule of the innovativeness of his collection of reformers, who had detached themselves from society to set up a communal home based on the Brook Farm experiment. Still, in true Hawthornian fashion, his misgivings about Miles Coverdale's failure to persevere in the new settlement are as great as his misgivings about whether Coverdale should have embarked on so flighty a scheme in the first place. In *The House of the Seven Gables*, Hawthorne's disapproval of rapid change is conveyed in railway imagery in the episode of Hepzibah and Clifford's futile attempt to escape their past. The train's rush has a quality of violence and breach with the past and continuity as, through its windows, villages seem to have "grown up around them" in a breath and then "vanished, as if swallowed by an earthquake" (Centenary Edition, p. 256).[12] It is significant that the miniature migration at the end of *Seven Gables* is not a move to a new house or a home to be, but an acceptance of an old one. Phoebe and Holgrave's move into the future seems almost a regression to the past; in affirming "pioneering" (of a very limited kind) Hawthorne would prefer to be affirming a backward movement of integration into existing society.

Many of the texts that have defined the mode of the home-founding journey must remain nameless, lost in the jungle of ephemeral novels and film. However, two particular novels that are of great interest here as defining examples have been very well known and highly praised, though not examined explicitly as examples of the form we are now considering. These are O. E. Rolvaag's grand novel of Norwegian immigrants on the frontier, *Giants in the Earth*, and John Steinbeck's epic of the Okies, *The Grapes of Wrath*.

It is a commonplace observation that the experience of the first settlers on the strange continent is in a sense recreated in each new wave of settlers. Such an observation is well illustrated in Rolvaag's novel. Elements of the Puritans' primal encounter, as well as other motifs that have become conventional in the migration narrative, appear in sharp focus here. The ocean crossing and first landing appear in the recollections of Beret, the homesick and frightened pioneer woman. She recalls her response to that landing as a question and answer: "Was this the Promised Land? Ah no—it was only the beginning of the real journey" (p. 39). After landing, they "pushed steadily westward, over plains, through deserts" (p. 39). The biblical context indicated in "Promised Land," a context which was of course particularly significant for the Puritans, is quite strong in *Giants in the Earth*. The first locust swarms are quickly identified by the settlers as "one of the plagues mentioned in the Bible" (p. 343). Yet when the settlers who have not yet beheld the annual plague of locusts first arrive, they think, "Beautiful out here on the wide prairie—yes, beautiful indeed! . . . The finest soil you ever dreamed of—a veritable Land of Canaan!. . .the new Promised Land into which the Lord was leading the poor people from all the corners of the earth!" (p. 350). The first pastor who visits the settlement preaches about "the history of Israel. . .applying the parable to those who stood before him; they, too, had wandered in search of a Land of Canaan" (pp. 372-73).

Other characteristic elements of the home-founding journey as we have defined it also appear in the novel. Beret is pregnant when they make their journey toward "Sunset Land" (p. 6). Her delivery is a promise for the future; Per Hansa names the child Peder Victorious. Indeed, the entire narrative, to the extent that it follows Per Hansa's point of view, is victoriously future-centered. He goes to Dakota Territory intending to "take up land and build himself a home; he was going to do something remarkable out there, which should become known far and wide. No lack of opportunity in that country, he had been told!" (p. 5). Various chapters are given to the detailing of first occurrences: the first building of sod huts, breaking the prairie sod for the first time, catching the first fish, the first cutting of hay. Among these and others, the first birth is the most important. The arrival of the Hansas' son fixes Per's attention even more insistently on the future, which now becomes specifically his son's future. Continually he dreams of the "mansion" he will build some day. Seed grain seems to him "the good fairies that had the power to create a new life over this Endless Wilderness, and transform it into a habitable land for human beings" (p. 295). Per's friend

Tönseten, who shares his preoccupation and his confidence, "pictured the future to [all Norwegians who passed trailing west] with a fervour that was prophetic" (p. 163). Even when the settlers feel discouraged, they distract each other by "discussing the question of how this place would look in two years, or maybe in four years" (p. 284). Their hopes are to develop a society, not to live in a wilderness.

But to Beret, Hansa's wife, the West is a destroyer of life. She looks to the past rather than the future and to Europe rather than to the vacant land. The new settlers whom the others greet with excitement and exhortations she regards as "poor folks" who have "gone astray" (p. 157). At the harsh ending of the book, the question of the true nature of the westward journey is left in a tense balance. In an image partly suggestive of continuing aspiration and hope, Per Hansa is last glimpsed "sitting there resting while he waited for better skiing. . . .His eyes were set toward the west" (p. 465). But he sits frozen to death, destroyed at last by the harsh environment and by his wife's fears, for it was she who had sent him out in a blizzard to fetch the pastor for their friend's deathbed confession. The West may mean, after all, only death. In its ending, then, as well as in the tension between Per Hansa and his wife throughout, the novel fully manifests that familiar ambiguity in the connotations of the West that we have seen before.

Though it is concerned more with the trials of the actual home founding than with the details of the preceding journey, *Giants in the Earth* in many ways epitomizes the form we are considering. John Steinbeck's *The Grapes of Wrath* can also be considered a defining example of the form, especially in the way that the home founding grows out of an initial journey of escape.

Steinbeck's justly celebrated (however muddled) novel of the Okies derives its power from its reverberation of American history, or more precisely, from the emotions that surround American history,[13] combined with the humanitarianism with which it depicts its particular material. As Walter Allen notes in *The Urgent West*, Steinbeck's Okies evince "a principle of recurrence in American experience, recreating the experience of their forbears" who crossed the Atlantic and then, in covered wagons, the prairies.[14] It is this reverberance, as well as their own courage and persistence, that gives the Joads the dignity they retain even in the face of incidents that seem designed only to make low comic figures of them[15] and passages of embarrassingly "poetic" sociomystic philosophizing. Still, despite being overdone and intrusive, the rhetorical passages of the novel do, as F. I. Carpenter argues in his influential article "The Philosophical Joads," further ally the novel with American traditions by their echoes of Emerson and of William James.[16] This resonance of intellectual precedents reinforces the sense of a recapitulation of American history.

The novel proceeds from a return home (Tom's return from prison) through a flight or escape impulse (the Okies' expulsion from their land) to a search for a new home. Motion is stressed throughout. The introductory section of Tom's return and the Joads' preparations plus the accompanying so-called interchapters opens with two paragraphs describing the drought. Then the first reference to human life, initiating a paragraph that stresses "moving things," is, "In the roads where the teams moved. . ." (p. 4). Tom first appears "walking along the edge of the highway," and his first action is to lay his hand "on the shiny fender" of a truck (p. 8). Modes of conveyance are, as we expect in a homeward journey, an important element in the entire novel.

The introductory section is linked to the larger action of the novel through the device of the land turtle, which Tom finds as he "plod[s] along" toward home.[17] The turtle, hence the turtle's persistence, is linked to Tom himself by similarities of descriptive detail: the land turtle's heavy toenails and Tom's thick fingernails, its hard legs (the front ones are called "hands" on p. 21) and Tom's thickly calloused hands. When released, it plods insistently to the southwest, prefiguring the Joads' persistent southwesterly trek and eliciting Tom's pointedly thematic comment, "They're always goin' someplace. They always seem to want to get there" (p. 60).

The Okies' journey, shown in a typical eviction, begins in escape, lacking any clear goal. They ask each other, "But if we go, where'll we go? How'll we go?" (p. 46). In chapter twelve, a paeon to Highway 66, "the mother road, the road of flight," the dispossessed tenants appear as "people in flight from the terror behind" (pp. 160-66). Again, in chapter fourteen, they are "in flight out of Oklahoma and across Texas" (p. 222). But their flight modulates into defined migration when they experience "the beginning change" from *I* and *my* to *we* and *our* (pp. 204 and 207) and when they yield to the rhythm of the road and find a new life pattern, forming a society:

Two days the families were in flight, but on the third the land was too huge for them and they settled into a new technique of living; the highway became their home and movement their medium of expression. (p. 222)[18]

After that change, they "took the migrant way to the West. . .they talked together; they shared their lives, their food, and the things they hoped for in the new country." Camping at night, they "pioneered the place and found it good," shifting the care that previously "had gone out to the fields" onto "the roads. . .the West" instead (pp. 264, 267).

Except in their unreasoning haste to depart the first night, however, the Joads are not shown as people in flight. From the beginning of their journey, their goal is a home, which they envision as a little white painted house among the fruit trees of California. Ma clings to this hope until the end. It is to be both a continuation and a transformation of their old home, with the truck as transitional home. On the last evening before their departure from Oklahoma, the two, home and truck, are visually hallowed as in the last light of the setting sun the house becomes "luminous as the moon is" and the truck "stood out magically" in this "most important place" since it is "the active thing, the living principle" (p. 135). Once they leave, their attention is directed forward, onto the journey. Al, driving, is "one with the engine" (p. 167), and Ma, despite her private fears that they shouldn't have gone, insists that they deal with each day as it comes and not look back. Together they wonder "what's it gonna be like when we get there" (p. 168). Essentially their trek has become a journey toward, not away from, something.

Critics have often complained that the novel weakens after it brings the Joads to California. Indeed, that is the case, though it is hard to conceive how Steinbeck could have avoided such a dissipation of the narrative's linear force without giving it either a quick happy ending or a terminating disaster and in either case cheapening the work to blatant melodrama. If the argument is made that the late incidents in the book are melodramatic as it is, one must observe that at any rate they are presented as the reasonable outgrowth of the novel's social ideas and are therefore convincing.

Sources of the diffuseness of the final section are easy to see. The Joads' movements become mere short-term responses to external pressures, rather than their own volitional search, and of necessity they become circuitous, so that the steady force of the unswerving march onward in a single direction is lost. Nevertheless, the journey does not lose its identity even when it lapses into frustrated feints. Even to the last way station, when the Joads are squatting in a railroad car (the very image of movement instead of stability), they continue to hope for a true home. Ma says, for instance, "Maybe nex' year we can get a place" (p. 577). In the final disaster sequence, the flood and the loss of Rosasharn's baby are apocalyptic inversions of two recurrent elements of the home-seeking narrative, the river crossing and the first birth.

Through its resonance of these familiar patterns from American fiction and history, the Joads' search borrows a reflected glory from its precedents. Among these precedents is the biblical story of the Israelites' migration, a prototype implicit in American migration narratives but explicitly paralleled in *The Grapes of Wrath*.[19] But in the "interchapters," with their expository discussions of social conditions and their narration of typical, not particularized, incidents, Steinbeck makes it clear that his subject is larger than one family's journey. The Joads participate not only in a tradition but in a simultaneous mass movement as well. The novel gains the status of epic.

It is important to recognize that the strain in American fiction that the novels mentioned here and similar works, chiefly of the great westward movement, so clearly represent appears more diffusely in many other works. These could not be considered defining works, but fictional structures that in one way or another bear the mark of the American concern with home seeking. William Dean Howells's *A Hazard of New Fortunes* (1889), for instance, is in part a novel of home seeking. It is a novel of other things, too, and it is not typical of the home-seeking mode. Howells, unlike most of the writers we have mentioned in this connection, was more concerned with social structures than with space. But, as we have said, a sense of society is more integral to the migration than to other kinds of journey narratives. (The immigrants of Rolvaag's *Giants in the Earth*, for instance, are very eager to develop an orderly, populous Norwegian society on the plains.) In addition, the journey of *A Hazard of New Fortunes* is neither westerly nor, in the usual sense, individualistic. The Basil Marches' journey is to New York City, America's center of civilization if not of "culture." In that their hopes are pinned on the success of a new publishing venture and involve some reform in the customs of the publishing establishment, the story is future-oriented, but not by any means in the sense of building a new society or even of duplicating a previous one. Their aim is to establish themselves within the complexities of the existing, dense society they find in New York. Their home-founding travails are not the primal struggles to build a new home, but the comparatively trivial ones of locating "eight rooms and a bath in a good neighborhood" for $800 a year.[20] The search is detailed through seven chapters.

The Marches' domestic predicament and their helpless confusions as they try to solve it are gently comical. Howells causes us to smile at the Marches with sympathy. But at the same time, we take their bumbling search seriously because it is emblematic of the search for a useful niche in the social structure, a way of life, or, in other words, an identity. A similar, though more poignant response is drawn by the predicament of Professor St. Peter in Willa Cather's *The Professor's House* (1925). St. Peter's real home seeking is a refusal to "journey" to the new home, a house he and his wife have built in the same small town where they have always lived.[21] He walks back and forth between the new house and the old, where he continues to make his study in a littered attic. The two houses represent two divided aspects of his life, and he refuses to unite them from a sense that moving his study would mean capitulating to crass practicality and trivial socializing.

Basil March, St. Peter, and St. Peter's protege Tom Outland, whom he identifies with the austere life of the mind, share the cry of one of Hawthorne's shadowy allegorical figures, a young man in the sketch "The Intelligence Office" who rushes into the office from the street distractedly crying out, "A place! a place!" The word means, of course, not a geographical place but in essence a job, or more broadly a life work or career, a place in the universe, an identity. In *A Hazard of New Fortunes* and *The Professor's House*, these values are assigned to place, geographically speaking. Boston and New York represent differing modes of life and differing degrees of engagement with social needs; so, to some degree, do the various apartments the Marches examine. The professor's old study "represents" his integrity as a scholar, the downstairs of the old house his domestic involvements. For years he had juggled the two, "managed. . .to live two lives" (p. 28), but now the new house represents social climbing and he feels unable to reconcile that with his scholarly aspirations. Similarly, the Indian cliff dwellings locate, for Tom Outland, the values of cleanness, unselfish identity, permanence. The son of "mover people" who died in his infancy when "crossing southern Kansas in a prairie schooner" (p. 115), Tom finds himself in his archeological exploration of the cave dwellings. In Washington, where he goes to seek government money for a scientific excavation, he has no function and is shuffled uselessly from one office to another.

Literary identification of values with places is not, of course, peculiar to these novels. One thinks of *Huckleberry Finn*: town means one thing, the raft another; the widow Douglas's house means one kind of life, Pap's shack another. If Huck can find a satisfactory place, he will have found a satisfactory kind of life and so will have found himself. It is a technique, or more accurately a way of thinking, that we have been discussing throughout. Finding a right home means finding a right life. Certainly it means that for Thomas Sutpen, driving slaves, material, and French architect through the swamps and woods to build a dream in *Absalom! Absalom!* Unfortunately, it is not easy to find such a place. Home seeking in novels, like the home seeking of pioneers such as the legendary Boone, sometimes dissolves into wandering.

For a great many rather tenuous reasons, a few of them perhaps literary but most of them societal, it is the journey of wandering that is the characteristic form of journey narrative in our time, as the journey of home seeking was, perhaps, of the nineteenth century. Our characters do not often find a "place," in both senses; at best, they find, in Wallace Stegner's phrase, an "angle of repose," a tolerable stopping place. The contemporary novel of aimless or futile journeying will be discussed in chapter six, but at this point we can look briefly at a novel that manages to encompass and perhaps even to reconcile the two forms, the home-founding journey narrative and the journey of lostness.

Edward Abbey's *The Monkey Wrench Gang* (1975) is an interesting, if not altogether successful, book for a number of reasons, among them its relation to the settler and Indians Western. That generic issue, moreover, is closely involved with the generic question of the book's relation to the home-founding novel. The Gang of the title is a collection of four social misfits *cum* visionaries who, first individually and then collectively, take as their mission the liberation of the West (that is, the rugged West of the Western, the great spaces of the dry western states) from industrial and recreational exploitation and thereby destruction. Like other dissenting social activists throughout history, they use violence to achieve their goal. Their violence, however, takes on a peculiarly benign cast because all four members of the gang (with the possible but deceptive exception of George Hayduke at his times of outburst of temper) are revolted by violence against living beings. Their target is the monster of the modern world, the machine. As the members of the Gang traverse southern Utah and northern Arizona on their quest to restore their world to its lost savage purity, they are pursued by various representatives of the established, but in this novel malevolent, social order. Needing both to conceal their own identities and to signal their identity as a source of resistance, they take to leaving cryptic messages or signatures at the scenes of their havoc, which generally suggest rather vaguely that they are a splinter group of Indians. At any rate, they are aware that their messages will be so interpreted and, despite some rational disaffection from the vestiges of the Indian tribes as they now exist, the members of the Gang are pleased to accept this label. George Hayduke takes to signing himself Rudolph the Red, suggesting both dis-

sension, through the hint of communism, and the Red Man.
Figuratively, the Gang becomes a band of white Indians. It is a
well chosen figure, projecting their sense of being untrammeled,
primitive, close to the rugged land, and in some ways the outcast, the persecuted.

The Indian motif lends itself to various echoes as well as parodies of popular literature, particularly the Western. Like Indians, the Gang members are hunted down by white men with
the law on their side in a Western badlands setting.[22] Like Indians, they use stealth and tricks, including the old trick of
walking backwards or in their own footprints. Like the Indian,
they have learned to survive in an inhospitable environment,
and they have well concealed caches of food buried here and
there that they can find again with an uncanny sense of direction. In an inversion of normal Western values, it is, of course,
the "Indians" who are the heroes of the piece. Accordingly, the
familiar cast of that popular classic The Lone Ranger appears
with reversed roles. The "Indian" George Hayduke is the hero,
while a masked white man referred to only as Kemosabe is his
sometime sidekick. Most important of the Indian-related motifs
is the question of the Gang's mobility in the Western landscape
as it relates to their sense of being at home, where they belong.
Like the nomadic Indians of the rugged, dry territories of the
West, for whom wandering a given area was being at home,
during most of the novel they roam about with little fixed reference point to call home and no goal where they mean to stay.
Yet because they are, nomad-like, able to live out of their vehicles
or their packs, and because they have so complete a sense of
being where they belong, their wandering is not the recurrent
fictional motif of being *lost* and wandering. They have not lost
their social orientation, as the urbanized westerners of Larry
McMurtry have; they are attempting to decreate, and thereby
re-create, a social orientation as they go.

Because of this purpose of re-creation, the thrust of the story
is finally home founding. When Dr. Sarvis and Bonnie Abbzug
are most nearly at home in the prevailing order at the outset of
the book, they spend their free time wandering around the Albuquerque area on a mission of ridding the landscape of signboards. When the fourth Gang member, "Seldom Seen" Smith,

appears at the start of the book, he too might superficially be said to have a home—a "jack Mormon," he has three wives, therefore three homes!—but he is then the most truly homeless. His home town of Hite, Utah, has been submerged by a man-made lake so that he can never go back, he has no decided preference among his wives or "homes," where he is indeed "seldom seen," and he is first encountered preparing a short-term river expedition. In the course of their journeys of creative destruction the four are a group unit, a social nucleus (especially Doc and Bonnie), not the proud loners of the traditional quest, albeit their journey does have the fixed visionary purpose of a quest. Furthermore, their mode of travel, an abbreviated caravan of two or three vehicles that at one point become physically linked together, recalls the settlers' wagon train.

At the end, all four are firmly established in homes, with secure social roles, yet all four maintain a quality of freedom and secret dissent while being at home. Doc and Bonnie have married and established their home on a riverboat, a form of domicile offering the maximum in freedom.[23] Furthermore, following the traditional meaning of a home, they have a secure place in society, in the form of their medical service to a remote area. In sign of this social commitment they are even expecting a baby—the conventional sign of the establishment of a new society. Smith, at the end of the final chase sequence, comes to realize where his true home is; that is, he chooses one wife. The other two divorce him, and he settles down with his Susan (who, in true home fashion, farms) within walking distance of Doc and Bonnie. Hayduke too moves from a position of alienation to a place in society, a job. Accordingly, he has given up his Indian role; it was Rudolph the Red, he says, who was killed in his apparently fatal last stand against authority—actually, a stuffed dummy, one of the oldest tricks in the Western book. Reborn after that figurative death to a new life with a new name, he assures Doc of his real continuation: "Come on up here and feel the wounds."[24] For all of them, though, the new home combines maximum freedom with sufficient stability. Their quest to save the West from industrial exploitation has been redirected to a mining operation from within, and their wandering has led them home.

Abbey's novel is by no means literature of the first order. It is often verbally slick, sometimes trite, and occasionally clumsy (to the point of resorting to so worn-out a quip as "Rudolph the Red knows rain"). Yet, as we have seen, popular literature can serve ends and reflect traditions larger than itself. Viewed from the outside, so to speak, as a structure of conventional motifs (sometimes in parody) and thematic concerns operating within a recognized generic form, the novel becomes an interesting and indicative work. *The Monkey Wrench Gang* is a recent variant of the old and continuing fictional pattern of the escape merged into the home-founding journey.

NOTES

1. Louis B. Wright mentions the emphasis on the West as opportunity in the McGuffey textbooks in *Culture on the Moving Frontier* (1955; rpt. New York: Harper and Row, 1961), p. 220. Nicholas Karolides states, "The progress of organized society, democracy, and opportunity for the individual form the basic theme and impulse behind the overland trail novels." *The Pioneer in the American Novel, 1900-1950* (Norman: University of Oklahoma Press, 1967).

2. O. E. Rolvaag, *Giants in the Earth* (New York: Harper and Row, 1927), p. 295.

3. The role of children's literature in reflecting and defining the prominent features of social history is only recently being appreciated. Children's literature and the materials generally grouped together as "popular culture" or "popular literature" often convey in relatively clearcut form the ideas given more complex exploration and development in the texts we customarily call, simply, literature. Also, such materials provide another dimension in which to perceive the breadth of prevalence of an idea, motif, or concern.

4. Northrop Frye, *Fables of Identity* (New York: Harcourt, Brace, and World, 1963), p. 16.

5. James K. Folsom points out in *The American Western Novel* (New Haven: College and University Press, 1966) that this is a theme that descends from Cooper. Women on the frontier are "emblems for the necessity of some kind of law" (p. 53).

6. William Bradford, *Of Plymouth Plantation 1620-1647*, ed. Samuel Eliot Morison (New York: Knopf, 1952), p. 23.

7. John Cotton, "Gods Promise to His Plantations" (1634; Ann Ar-

bor, Mich.: University Microfilms, 1975; Early English Books, 1475-1640, reel 1375).

8. Wright connects the two in *Culture*, pp. 240-41.

9. Bradford, *Of Plymouth Plantation*, pp. 61-62.

10. Cooper's position in these respects is admirably discussed, though in what are at times idiosyncratic terms, by Richard Chase, *The American Novel and Its Tradition* (Garden City, N.Y.: Doubleday, 1957); Leslie A. Fiedler, *Love and Death in the American Novel* (1960; revised ed., New York: Stein and Day, 1966); and D. H. Lawrence, *Studies in Classic American Literature* (New York: T. Seltzer, 1923).

11. It is interesting to note that in spite of his identification with western material, Cooper, according to Louis B. Wright, was not read on the frontier as much as Scott. See *Culture*, p. 209.

12. Cooper's misgivings were very similar. In *Home As Found*, American civilization fails to have a "regular and methodical" advance, instead "start[ing] full-grown into existence," with no nourishment by a continuous past.

13. I disagree emphatically with Bernard Bowron, who argues in his article "*The Grapes of Wrath*: A 'Wagons West' Romance," *Colorado Quarterly*, 3 (1954), 84-91, that Steinbeck used a tired, mechanical convention as the basis of his "literary engineering" in *Grapes of Wrath*, with the result that the reader's response is not only conditioned and unthinking but also, so Bowron's tone implies, unintelligent. It is clear that Bowron regards the novel, not as an enrichment of the form and its tradition, but as a parodic cheapening of it.

14. Walter Allen, *The Urgent West: The American Dream and Modern Man* (New York: E. P. Dutton, 1969), p. 217. The earliest serious recognition of the historical background of the novel was Frederic I. Carpenter's article "John Steinbeck, American Dreamer," *Southwest Review*, 26 (1941), 454-67.

15. For example, Pa's exhortation to John to "get in a good las' one" before they leave the flush toilets of the government camp at Weedpatch. John Steinbeck, *The Grapes of Wrath*, with Introduction by Charles Poore (New York: Harper & Brothers, 1951), p. 490. This uses the plates of the first edition, Viking, 1939.

16. Frederic I. Carpenter, "The Philosophical Joads," *College English*, 2 (1941), 315-25.

17. Kenneth Burke discusses the linking function of the land turtle in *The Philosophy of Literary Form*, 3d ed. rev. (Berkeley: University of California Press, 1973), pp. 81-82. Its parallels with the Joads are analyzed by Howard Levant in his study *The Novels of John Steinbeck; A Critical Study* (University of Missouri Press, 1974), pp. 101-3. Lester Jay

Marks notes in *Thematic Design in the Novels of John Steinbeck* (The Hague and Paris: Mouton, 1969), p. 70, that the land turtle "symbolizes the heroic persistence of the migrants to keep moving against overwhelming odds."

18. Marks comments on the dual nature of the migration, as it partly is "necessitated by circumstances" and partly is "a dynamic means to a better life." *Thematic Design*, p. 69.

19. The biblical parallels have been discussed most thoroughly by Peter Lisca in *The Wide World of John Steinbeck* (New Brunswick, N.J.: Rutgers University Press, 1958), pp. 169-71, and Joseph Fontenrose, *John Steinbeck, an Introduction and Interpretation* (New York: Barnes and Noble, 1963), pp. 75-78.

20. William Dean Howells, *A Hazard of New Fortunes*, ed. Tony Tanner (Oxford: Oxford University Press, 1965), p. 48.

21. Willa Cather, *The Professor's House* (New York: Knopf, 1925), p. 28.

22. The chase motif is a convention of the Western deriving from Cooper's novels, chiefly, because of its popularity, from *The Last of the Mohicans*. In Cooper, it is usually the virtuous whites who are pursued by the bad Indians, though sometimes the Indians by the whites, the two in alternation. In *The Monkey Wrench Gang*, it is always the "Indians" pursued by the whites.

23. Their home is so free that even their garden is not fixed in place. Bonnie grows marijuana on a little raft that she can allow to drift downstream on a long rope if the Law comes around.

24. Edward Abbey, *The Monkey Wrench Gang* (Philadelphia: J. B. Lippincott, 1975), p. 350.

4
The Return:
Innocence Abroad

I had traveled halfway across the earth in search of some kind of
salvation. . . .And I kept thinking of the new sun coming up
over the coast of Virginia and the Carolinas, and how it must
have looked from those galleons, centuries ago, when after
black night, dawn broke like a trumpet blast, and there it was,
immense and green and glistening against the crashing seas.
—William Styron, *Set This House on Fire*

Mother England! Home!
—Sinclair Lewis, *Dodsworth*

As we have seen, the journey of home founding has been a
congenial form for the American imagination. The homecoming,
the return to a known or familiar home, has not. Except when
it is cast as a return to the cultural home in Europe, the homecoming occurs with remarkable infrequency in American literature. Our heroes have more typically moved out than back.

When the tale of homecoming does occur in American literature, its tone is strikingly different from the exultant restora-
tions of its ancient predecessors, the return of the Israelites from
Babylonian captivity, the story of the Prodigal, Odysseus' return

Babylonian captivity, the story of the Prodigal, Odysseus' return to Ithaca and Penelope. In American literature, the return home signifies defeat, frustration, the giving up of freedom. At best it is a disappointment. One thinks, for instance, of Cooper's wry *Home as Found* or Robert Frost's deeply ambiguous poem "Directive." The homecomings of Hamlin Garland's *Main-Travelled Roads* are frustrated attempts to recapture something outgrown or outworn; except for Mrs. Ripley's grim homecoming in the most famous of the stories, they simply don't work, and escape is preferable. Similarly, in Glenway Wescott's *Good-bye, Wisconsin* (1928), the homecoming is used as a frame justifying the central stories of escape. In the opening story a homecoming ends in renewed flight; in the closing one it ends in frustrated surrender.[1] Holden Caulfield's circuitous homecoming in J. D. Salinger's *Catcher in the Rye* remains, at the end of the book, uncertain and cheerless. It is as much a betrayal of his authentic self as it is a confirmation of identity.

As all of these works make clear, to the American imagination the return has signified retreat. The great ventures are westward, following the direction of freedom and the advancing frontier, the hope that just over the next ridge one will find the true America. (Find, not make it; it is conceived as a natural boon, a "given" awaiting discovery.) Conrad Aiken wrote of the westering hero of his "Little Travelogue" of linked poems *The Kid* that he was

in many respects the true prototypical American: ancestor alike of those pioneers who sought freedom and privacy in the "wide open spaces," or the physical conquest of an untamed continent, and those others, early and late, who were to struggle for it in the darker kingdoms of the soul.[2]

Westward movement means conquest and expansion. Easterly movement, in contrast, conveys timidity, constraint, retreat; it is back-trailing, the defeated rebound from the pioneering venture.[3] As Aiken expresses it in the eighth poem of *The Kid*, "The Last Vision":

Said Railway Willy, O carry me back
on the golden engine and the silver track,

carry back east in a tall caboose
this broken-down body that's no more use.

F. I. Carpenter terms the easterly back-trailing journey a "return" that is "usually an admission of spiritual defeat," and, carrying the association further, imaginatively links the "back-trailer" from the frontier with "genteel" writers and their styles.[4]

Resort to Europe is back-trailing on a grand scale. Whatever the positive values that might be discovered in the cultural pilgrimage—and a long line of American writers and artists have made that pilgrimage[5]—in fiction it is typically presented with an admixture of retreat or reduced expectation. The American tourist may approach Europe as a new experience of his own, but as a symbol Europe means the past, hence abandonment of the future-centered American ideals of progress and social perfectibility. He is encountering, too, what has traditionally served in the American tradition as an emblem of frivolity, social injustice, dissipation, and other negative values contrasted with innocence and the positive values associated with the West. Such a scheme of moral values is at the heart of the sentimental novel, the primary belletristic form of the young nation's literature from the late eighteenth century through the second third of the nineteenth. In this scheme, there is a moralistic opposition of country (West) to city (East), with the evils of the decadent, cruel city being cast as a parallel to those of Europe. A like value structure of opposition between the sophisticated city and the virtuous countryside or the desert of purgation pervades the other literary form of greatest influence in early America, the sermon. It is a trope established at the outset of the American tradition in William Bradford's enumeration of the Pilgrims' reasons for leaving Europe and in John Winthrop's contrast of the corrupt city with the city set on a hill. The contrast of innocent America and decadent Europe, then, is inherent in the American myth. A Cotton Mather or a Jonathan Edwards might be surprised to find himself thrust into the company of frivolous novelists. Yet insofar as the geographic projections of their moral terms—the value-laden opposition of rural and urban scenes—overlap, there is a concurrence of these two traditions in American letters, the religious peroration and the sentimental novel, that creates a powerful precedent for nineteenth-century fiction. Its effect is evident at all levels of literary sophistication, from the dime novel to the domestic chronicle such as Catherine Sedgwick's *Clarence* (1830) to Henry James's *The Golden Bowl*.

Nevertheless, attitudes linking Europe with moral decadence are complicated by a nostalgia for the Old World home. This too is a long-established cast of thought. According to Bradford, no sooner had the Pilgrims reached their longed-for godly refuge than they perceived it as a "hideous and desolate wilderness" and the ocean not as a road to freedom but as a "main bar and gulf to separate them from all the civil parts of the world."[6] If the West has been the natural and prevailing direction of the American's journeying, the East, specifically the eastward voyage to Europe, has been its natural complement, even its natural rebound. Europe has been the necessary destination, the place where the American or the American imagination has had to go in order to define itself by reference to an other.

Fiction of return from America to Europe is freighted with the irony of conflicting motives and attitudes. The Old World is approached with distrust, diffidence, and nostalgia, the sense of returning to a lost home.[7] When positive attitudes such as veneration for the cultural past predominate, the journey becomes a pilgrimage. When the emphasis is negative, a vision of the staleness and conventionalism of the European past in contrast to the youth and openness of America, the journey is a retreat.

The pilgrimage to Europe has been the characteristic journey of the American artist, either fictional (Roderick Hudson, T.S. Garp) or real (Story, Greenough, Irving), or the student of history (Henry Adams). In this form, the artistic and cultural treasures of Europe together with its storied places assume the position of the sacred places of veneration in the traditional religious pilgrimage: they are its sought-after treasured goal, expected to fill some lack that the voyager feels in himself. In Mark Twain's *The Innocents Abroad* (1869), the congruence of visits to art museums in Europe with visits to sacred places in the Holy Land reflects this association and, indeed, conveys an elevation of cultural-aesthetic values to sacred values. Accordingly, Henry Adams finds in *The Education of Henry Adams* (1918) a vision of history and of America's brittleness in the beauty of Europe's cathedrals; art and "culture" provide a quasi-religious awakening.

The journey of Henry Adams illustrates the difference between the pilgrimage and the quest, a distinction of great importance in dealing with the journey to Europe as a formal tradition. Adams's pilgrimage to Europe was dual in a very obvious way: it brought him to two great shrines defining the polarity of values that he explores in his noted chapter "The Dynamo and the Virgin." These are, of course, the cathedrals and the exposition where he saw the dynamo. However, his journey was also dual in a less obvious way, the relation between its motivating impulse and its fulfillment. Adams found both what he had meant to see, the sites (sights) to which he had made his pilgrimage, and something he had yearned for but not anticipated, a vision of historic process. This difference is the key to a pair of definitions crucially important in clarifying the motives and the final significance of American journeys to Europe. The pilgrimage is a journey toward a foreknown, fixed goal; the quest, a journey of search for an envisioned but not clearly known or located goal. Although both kinds of journey are undertaken for spiritual benefit, the goal or aspiration of the quest is generally more abstract than that of the pilgrimage. Henry James's *Portrait of a Lady*, for instance, in which Isabel Archer goes in search of a quality of life and of self, may well be treated as a quest romance. Melville's *Redburn*, in that young Redburn's motives are at first to relieve himself of intolerable pressures and deprivations and to visit the places his father had visited but later become broadened to include education and experience in themselves, combines the escape, the pilgrimage, and the quest. Similarly, Henry Adams undertakes his pilgrimage to the monuments of a past culture, a spiritually centripetal culture, as a specific part of his "education." But in a materialistic, spiritually diffuse culture, for Adams at any rate, this educational process is the only possible spiritual awakening. The sole spiritual enlightenment available to him is the full realization of why he cannot achieve spiritual enlightenment. The process by which Adams achieves this unforeseen state of awareness, or education, is in part projected narratively in his pilgrimage to Europe, which thus, because its scope is broadened beyond its originally foreseen and defined object, becomes a quest.

In *Innocents*, of course, Twain mocks the pilgrimage by denying its efficacy for any kind of enlightenment at all. Indeed, *The Innocents Abroad* occupies a curious niche in the history of the journey narrative. It is not a novel any more than Charles Dudley Warner's roughly contemporary *Saunterings* (1872) is a novel; they are travel books.[8] Nevertheless, *The Innocents Abroad* claims an association with fictional literature not accorded most travel books. Partly that is owing to Twain's eminence and his status of novelist, but it is also because of his donning and doffing of the comic mask, so that his narrative voice in the book assumes much the quality of a fictional *persona*, with a projected drama of shifting moods—that is, a created character. Indeed, part of the interest of *Innocents Abroad* is the tension created by the shifts of "Twain's" moods between obvious mockery (the predominant tone) and true pilgrim-hood. It is a broader and certainly simpler version of the irony of Henry James, who often uses the word "pilgrim" in writing of the American in Europe (in *The American*, for instance, as well as in essays), but uses it with varying shades of meaning. His pilgrims are pilgrims to Culture, and they are capable of displaying the same ignorance of culture, the same sober doggedness in sightseeing, the same rapaciousness, as Twain's burlesqued pilgrims. James, however, more deeply venerates their object, the ideal of the cultured life and its accompanying artifacts; hence his irony is more deeply felt and less strident than Twain's.

As we have said, the conception of the journey to Europe as a retreat is the opposite of the European pilgrimage and quest, with their affirmative connotations of aspiration and expansion. Retreat is, in general, the connotation of American homecoming narratives, because they imply the surrendering of the great venture into the unknown. However, in the journey to Europe—and, in general, in that form only—the homecoming is at times presented as the satisfaction of a feeling of nostalgia or loss. It was natural enough for the early colonists to think of a journey back to England as a return home. How long such an attitude persisted in any literal way is open to question; certainly there is a ring of affectation in Cooper's mid-eighteenth-century col-

onists' references to England as "home" in *Satanstoe* (1845).
Nevertheless, the urge to return to the security of a figurative
home, whether ancestral, racial, or spiritual, has remained a
strong counterstrain in American literature even into the present
century. (Witness the great popular acclaim evoked by Alex Hal-
ey's *Roots*.) Such an urge was particularly evident in the nineteenth-century novel of journey to Europe, and indeed in the
mentality of the period in general.

Nathalia Wright recognizes the nineteenth-century urge to
return home in commenting upon the artistic pilgrimages to Italy
of many prominent American literary figures:

Figuratively speaking, nearly all these authors discovered in Italy another native land—a home of the spirit or intellect. . . .They were, like
other Americans in this youthful period of their nation's history, in
quest of a cultural Heritage. . . .Most of them felt for that country a
unique attachment, quite unlike what they felt for their own.[9]

Nathaniel Hawthorne said of Italy that "the intellect finds a
home there,"[10] and signified the same impulse with regard to
England by titling his book on that country *Our Old Home*. This
sense of coming back to something old with which one feels an
instinctive affinity is very strong in fiction of the American's
journey to Europe, but at the same time the American is encountering something new. The result is an emotional duality,
an effect of bewilderment. Such a bewilderment is clearly evident, for instance, in Henry James's own difficulty in deciding
what place—Italy, France, or England—he would choose as
home. It appears throughout James's fiction as his Americans
attempt to reach an understanding of the European subtleties
that they are newly encountering. The problem is in fact more
complicated even than that, since the American generally brings
to the encounter an innate distrust or even disapproval.

The American journey to Europe, then, is a composite of several clearly distinct patterns of journey narrative—the escape,
the pilgrimage, the homecoming, the retreat. It is also, in the
twentieth century, a locus of the novel of directionless wandering. James Baldwin captures this latter tone precisely in *Giovanni's Room* when his narrator-protagonist, longing to "go

home. . .home across the ocean, to things and people I knew and understood" in America, cries, "I saw myself, sharply, as a wanderer, an adventurer, rocking through the world, unanchored."[11] Nevertheless, despite being a composite form, the fiction of the American's journey to Europe is a recognizable, distinct form, possessing its own tradition and continuity. Clearly, the form reached its fullest development in Henry James's international novels. But it took its characteristic moral shape much earlier with Hawthorne, who opposed American innocence to European dissipation, American cultural deprivation and rigidity to European richness and tolerance, within narrative structures of journeys to Europe. The work of the three most important American writers of the nineteenth century—Hawthorne, Melville, and James—defines the form and its characteristically ambiguous appropriation of the terms of a homeward journey. It was these three, not James alone, who shaped the international novel and developed its patterns of opposition.

Hawthorne's American artists in *The Marble Faun* (1860), the first major international novel in American letters, share the author's own urge, most evident in his prefaces, to find a more congenial aesthetic atmosphere than that afforded by his homeland. It is an urge to find an aesthetic home. In his preface to *The Marble Faun*, Hawthorne complains of

the difficulty of writing a romance about a country where there is no shadow, no antiquity, no mystery, no picturesque and gloomy wrong, nor anything but a commonplace prosperity, in broad and simple daylight.[12]

His Hilda and Kenyon likewise seem to have come to Italy to find the right chiaroscuro, a matter very specifically of darkened lighting effects, of old buildings and narrow streets, as well as the shaded mental cast, and to study their art and experience the rich museum hoards of a place where "objects, antique, pictorial, and statuesque. . .fill the mind everywhere" (Preface, IV, 3). Their journey, then, has been the artist's pilgrimage familiar throughout the history of American art and letters. It is strongly implied, too, that they have been motivated by another recurrent element in American artists' gravitation toward Europe: the desire to locate themselves within a community of congenial fellow artists, to find a kind of aesthetic home and family. In both respects, they seem to find their journeys rewarded, though Hawthorne insists that the experience is perilous in other ways.

It is clear from Hawthorne's *French and Italian Notebooks* that the Continent did not satisfy his own aesthetic urges. He complains of adverse weather, street filth, and tiresome museums. The novel, however, is not a mere transcript of the notebooks, fitted to a creaky plot, as critics have often implied, but a very conscious reshaping of the author's tour records. Unfortunately for present purposes, that reshaping involved so total a concentration upon Rome and its environs that the larger journey movement (Hilda and Kenyon's trans-Atlantic voyages to and from the Continent) is simply excluded. What we have is the result of their voyages. The journeying actually depicted within the novel occurs within Italy itself, chiefly between Rome and the country seat of Donatello's ancient family. This journey projects onto a symbolic geography a cluster of concerns with civilization and the primitive, guilt and innocence. Hawthorne's position, ambiguous as ever, seems to be that historic Rome provides at once a needed awakening for his naifs and a symbol of moral turpitude, the countryside is at once an Eden and a privative escape from significant experience.[13]

Because it is so ambiguous, Rome cannot serve as the true home of Hawthorne's virtuous Americans, though for a time it has served satisfactorily as their aesthetic and temperamental home. Kenyon, "startled by her agitation" at his speculations on the ambiguities of sin, exclaims in dismay, "O Hilda, guide me home!"[14] And indeed she does, though hesitantly and with what seems a more literal interpretation of the word than Kenyon's: "We are both lonely," she replies, "both far from home!" Except for an ill-advised "Conclusion," added to forestall readers' objections to the unresolved perplexities of his plot, Hawthorne ends the novel with Hilda and Kenyon's return to America to establish a marital home. His narrative comment is overtly affirmative: "And, now that life had so much human promise in it, they resolved to go back to their own land" (p. 461).

They have survived and learned from their encounter with

the evil, but beautiful, Continent, and we must believe that their final homeward journey could never have been made, not with the same implications of an educated imagination and a matured emotional capacity, had the first journey not occurred. At the same time, their return "home" to America has about it the aura of a retreat to an easier, thinner moral atmosphere. Kenyon is essentially a passionless creation, and in asking Hilda to "guide him home" from his speculative wanderings, he is giving up some real insights. Hilda herself is a pallid, privative saint, afraid either to launch out upon new seas of artistic endeavor (she is a copyist) or to fulfill her friend Miriam's need for a supportive audience and sharer of her sense of guilt. Sending these two back home to America is not entirely affirmative, either for them or for the nation.

Hawthorne dealt with the American's journey to Europe more elaborately, though by no means so satisfactorily, in the uncompleted late romances published as *The Ancestral Footstep*, *The Dolliver Romance*, and *Dr.Grimshawe's Secret*. (These titles, however, are not retained in the recent and authoritative Centenary Edition.) The evidence of these generally inconclusive manuscripts is clear that the journey to England, at any rate, held connotations of homecoming for Hawthorne. His own notes for "the arrangement of the Romance" (*The Ancestral Footstep*) dated May 19, 1858, lead from his own period as consul through comments on "how my countrymen used to be put out of their senses by the idea of inheritances of English property" to the introduction of his hero's "search for his hereditary home."[15] Etherege, in the fragmentary Romance,

sought his ancient home. . .as if he had found his way into Paradise, and were there endeavoring to trace out the signs of Eve's bridal bower, the birth-place of the human race.[16]

At several points in the confused fragment, which starts and stops in varying and conflicting versions of the one basic story idea, Hawthorne makes it clear that Etherege's search for his ancestral estate, or "ancient home," has about it the sense of a return to the past, an effort to join his existence with its origins. But at one point (the section dated May 10), Hawthorne presents the search as an escape—from "the fierceness of political contests in our country" (XII, 51). Essentially, Etherege's journey is a projection of Hawthorne's own urge to retreat from the turbulence of American life in the nineteenth century to a more stable, secure mode of life, generally to the past. It is a troubled dream of return to an approximation of pre-lapsarian existence. For that reason, Etherege's search for his ancestral home is explicitly compared to discovery of "Eve's bridal bower, the birth-place of the human race and its glorious possibilities of happiness and high performance" (XII, 3). His journey to England to search out his origins is like "awakening to a former reality" (XII, 148); with "rapture" he exclaims, "Oh home, my home, my forefathers' home! I have come back to thee! The wanderer has come back" (XII, 260).

Hawthorne's intellectual honesty, however, does not let him pass off such regressive impulses as valid possibilities; the retreat is marred by past crimes and ominous warnings such as a gunshot. Showing his misgivings about the regressive urge, Hawthorne terms Etherege's impulse a *"foolish* yearning for a connection with the past" (XII, 149, emphasis added). Hawthorne's yearning for the past cannot be reconciled with his democratic principles, and his fictions are, as he himself was, in fact, uneasy in the Old World. It is finally to the widening of this split in Hawthorne, this split and others, that we must attribute his inability to find a firm artistic center for his late writings. They provide, indeed, a distressing spectacle of failing control that knows itself to be failing. Hawthorne might well have called his late attempts at Romance "beggarly."

Actually, of course, the term was applied by Melville to his own *Redburn*, a work that many readers have found to be not beggarly at all. Melville's *Redburn* was published in 1849, somewhat less than ten years before Hawthorne would struggle ineffectually with his own romances of the American's approach to England.[17] Melville, the younger of the two, was just hitting his full stride when he came to the subject—*White-Jacket* and *Moby-Dick* followed in 1850 and 1851; Hawthorne was far past his prime, which we can confidently date as having occurred in the years 1849 through 1852. Like Hawthorne, however, Melville would continue to hover over the subject of the American's encounter with the Old World through the years of his own decline—if decline be the correct term, for in these years he produced from his fixation on the subject *Israel Potter, Clarel,* and *Billy Budd.* The reason for his success, where Hawthorne had failed, is perhaps impossible to determine. But it seems to be the result of a greater personal vitality and a fuller acknowledgment, and therefore a fuller resolution, of his own neuroses. In addition, to return to demonstrable technical reasons, Melville, unlike Hawthorne, was able to find appropriate personae through which to project clearly defined tonal variations.

Hawthorne's Middleton, or Etherege, in *The Ancestral Footstep,* is an ambiguous figure. He is innocent at an age that might be expected to obviate innocence, yet also at times curiously world-weary, politically sophisticated and uncommitted. Hence, his nature blurs the theme of New World innocence opposed to Old World sophistication. If achieved in the course of the novel, such a blurring might become that sense of equally feasible possibilities that marks Hawthorne's finest work. As a point of departure, it merely shows confusion of purpose. In *The Marble Faun,* of course, Hawthorne had used the clear contrast of innocence and sophistication, but his innocence there is merely privation.

Melville's Wellingborough Redburn provides a more useful vehicle for the story of the American's journey to Europe and his resultant growth in maturity and sophistication because he is at the outset purely naive. (He is naive to the point that students often find him painful and declare that they dislike him.) His naivete is, furthermore, appropriate to his youth. Because he is young, he has life and its learning experiences all before him. And indeed in the course of his voyage and his stay in England he does learn a great deal, most of it unpleasant. Thus the journey narrative form fulfills its strongest inherent value, journey as experience or education, and provides a particularly appropriate form for the theme of American innocence (the need to learn) and European sophistication (experience, knowingness). To some degree this appropriateness is inherent in the form, but it is consciously developed by Melville. He accentuates the learning function of the form in his subtitle: it is Redburn's *First Voyage.*

The voyage is, of course, Melville's basic metaphor throughout his work. Man sets off from the shore of deadening reality onto the sea of the unknown to search for the prize of knowledge, both of self and of the world. Melville's is an emblematic world (for example, the lee shore in *Moby-Dick*), a world shaped for quest. In Redburn, the quest motif is less clearly defined than in most of Melville's other works, partly because Wellingborough Redburn's journey to Europe is in part a journey into the past (he attempts to recapitulate his father's trip of long ago), and hence in some ways a return rather than a search, and partly because Redburn lacks clear purpose. He is not so much following a "lure"[18] as escaping hardship; the voyage is thrust upon him by force of economic necessity. It is also not a chosen but an inescapable voyage in the sense that it serves as a figure for the growing up process. Redburn travels from callow youth to informed (disillusioned) maturity and, correspondingly, from young America to old Europe. His journey "works" perfectly as figure even while it is perfectly convincing as "fact."

Yet Melville does not adopt any simplistic design of exaggerated contrast between innocence/youth/rural American and discovery/age/urban Europe. In Redburn's mood of disillusionment, in the shipboard life of cruelty and dissipation, and in the vividly seen and therefore absolutely believed social evils of Liverpool, Melville shows us the reality of the scheme of contrasts with which he is working. At the same time, he demonstrates that this scheme is inadequate as a representation of the full truth. Redburn's life in rural America has been no happy idyl, and his first encounters with cruel snobbery and villainy occur, not in England or on the voyage, but on the Hudson River and in New York City. The system of contrasts that Melville sets up and vivifies he at the same time undercuts by a system of insidious similarities between England and America. The voyage of education is not, therefore, a thin allegory; if it were, it would be a one-way trip from which Redburn could not return.

Less allegorical than either *Redburn* or *Billy Budd* (a far more allegorical work than *Redburn*, for all the critical debate it has occasioned) is Melville's slight and certainly uneven but nevertheless estimable short novel *Israel Potter*. Yet, paradoxically, *Israel Potter* is also less realistic than *Redburn*. Certainly flawed though probably more neglected than it deserves to be, it is a book of compelling scenes that occur in flashes of devastatingly bare writing. Scenes such as the naval battle, the spare details of Potter's poverty, and the miserable crowds crossing London Bridge like an "endless shoal of herring"[19] have an integrity that not only makes them impressive in themselves but also makes them precisely appropriate to Potter's bleak despair. Melville is at pains to show Israel Potter's journey to Europe as a figurative descent into hell. The Thames runs "balefully through the Erebus arches"; London crowds are like "tormented humanity" on the "thither side of Phlegethon"; the city is a "cindery City of Dis" (211-12). Yet Potter's life in America, both before and after the years of his exile, is equally bleak and harsh.

The import of *Israel Potter* then, like that of *Redburn*, is that the harsher truths of reality are very much the same regardless of geography. The American's encounter with Europe is adopted as a form that provides tentative insights of a recurrent kind— that is, the primitive innocent's discovery of sophistication and evil. But beyond these insights, meaning is only tentative, and the total import of the novels reveals the inadequacy and indeed the artificiality of the contrast. The final effect of Melville's exploration of the international theme is a subdued irony, as his journeys to Europe become discoveries of sameness as much as difference.

A similar irony or wisdom is evident in Henry James's mature international novels. Like Hawthorne's *Marble Faun*, James's fictions of the American in Europe are not so much narratives of the process of journeying as examinations of the results of journeying. His interest is in the traveler's social experiences and impressions after he or she has decided to venture out and has arrived at a European destination. In *The American*, for instance, we first encounter Christopher Newman three days after he has arrived in Paris, and his summer tour of other European countries is given, in brief summary fashion, for the dual purposes of showing a contrast in sensibility between Newman and the dutiful Babcock and of allowing his impression of Claire de Cintre to ripen. The linear, episodic quality of the road narrative is quite abandoned, and the journey itself is reduced to an implied context for discovery, surviving in the text in mere vestiges such as references to Newman's arrival shortly before *The American* opens. (Similarly, in *The Ambassadors*, James begins with Strether's landing, with its sense of high anticipation.)[20]

It is clear that James fulfills a tradition in his handling of the American's journey to Europe. His characteristic motifs of American innocence confronting European subtlety and of cultural youth experiencing the European artistic wealth are, as we have seen, the prevalent motifs in that tradition. Though Constance Rourke certainly overstated the Americanness of *The American* in her essay on that novel in *American Humor*, she is quite correct in viewing it within the context of American concern with "the European relationship." The American's sense of dissatisfaction and need to find a congenial place, particularly evident in *Portrait of a Lady* and *The Ambassadors*, reflects the homecoming impulse of that tradition. Particularly in his early international novels, where the cultural contrasts are strong and very nearly absolute in the alignment of their moral values, James indeed fulfills the possibilities of a mature form. He shows us, not so much the hazardous dynamics of the international journey, but the fullest potential for moral significance in its completion. Ultimately, however, he does not rest in the form, but shows us its inadequacies as well as its possibilities.[21] Perhaps that is only to say that he does what the master artist always does with an established form.

The late novels move out of the pattern of the international novel, which, however fruitful it had been for James, had by that time in his career become a confinement. In these works the emphasis is not on contrasts between stable opposites that confront each other on European soil, but on the growth in one character's sensibility. Particularly in *The Golden Bowl*, contrasts of nationality are little more than a convenient metaphor for the real contrasts of temperament and moral stance, but even these are finally of far less importance than the growth of awareness experienced by both Prince and Princess—who were initially parties of the opposite terms of the contrast. As numerous critics have observed, following James's own lead, the ethical clashes could almost take place anywhere, though Europe is the convenient, the apposite setting: they are not the standard clashes of the American's Europe.

The difference between James's rich fulfillment of the form

and his final testing of it is well demonstrated in the contrasts between *The American* (1877) and *The Ambassadors* (1903). In the earlier novel it is fully significant that Christopher Newman is an American. He is, one may say, the archetypal American: a westerner, a self-made man, sturdily independent. His journey is the typical American's journey, though backward: just as the American traditionally presses westward toward the unknown, Newman presses forward toward an old world which is new to him.[22] The irony of the novel derives from his attempt to treat as new that which is old and fully formed. But it is not an irony that leads to any questioning of the ethical framework of the novel. Newman is indeed the new man, morally untainted, and the Bellegardes are indisputably the villainous old order of moral murkiness and artificial subtlety. Newman's journey to Europe, or rather, the resulting circumstance of his presence in Europe, is the essential kernel of the novel's conception as James describes it in his preface to the New York edition.

In *The Ambassadors*, heroes and villains are not so neatly sorted out. An obtuse complexity (the Bellegardes) has become a very real richness and ambiguity (Mme. de Vionnet). No longer are the moral contrasts drawn along strictly national lines. Chad Newsome (his initials signal his pairing with Christopher Newman) is not altogether innocent, nor is Mme. de Vionnet altogether corrupt—not by any means. The hero, Strether, is not a national type but a fully individuated man of the imagination. His journey and the resultant European situation are not at all the conceptual kernel of the novel, which according to James was rather his quality as an observer. It is not that the journey is irrelevant to the story, but rather that it is relevant purely (or almost purely) as symbol. James calls Strether a belated man of the world; Europe most plausibly represents the world of which he comes to be a man. It represents richness of experience. James's comments make it clear that *The Ambassadors* is not another treatment of his theme of American innocence confronting European duplicity. In his preface to the novel, he termed the European scene

. . .itself a minor matter, a mere symbol for more things than had been dreamt of in the philosophy of Woollett. Another surrounding scene would have done as well for our show could it have represented a place in which Strether's errand was likely to lie and his crisis to await him.[23]

One might demur from his word "mere," and indeed James stresses the rightness of the symbol: it was "the *likely* place." But the emphasis is not on national type but on what happens in the sensibility of a most untypically imaginative and liberal person. The fact that Strether journeyed makes little difference in itself, but is necessary as symbol. The sense of spatial distance conveys the growth in Strether's self, or rather the liberation from the determinants of custom and circumstance essential for transformation.[24]

The Ambassadors is colored by a pervasive irony growing out of the contrast between James's deepening of the form and his perception that its significance is only quite tentative. It is a balanced irony, one which proceeds from a clear perception of contrary richness and produces, not a sense of moral irrelevance, but a sense of moral possibility. Nevertheless, it prefigures the far deeper irony at the core of Ernest Hemingway's fictions of the American's journey to Europe, in which the revelation is that he might as well not have come and the final emotional effect is an oppressive ennui.

The journey to Europe as a fictional form reached its zenith with James. Since then, though the form has continued in the work of such novelists as Sinclair Lewis, Hemingway, and F. Scott Fitzgerald, it has become largely repetitive and drained of meaning.[25] In *Dodsworth* (1929), for instance, Lewis seizes upon the themes and conflicts that in James's novels are so subtle and resonating and makes them obvious, heavy-handed, and indeed tedious, as Dodsworth and wife go repeatedly through the motions of the American's discovery of European culture and discuss the same issues again and again without making any real discoveries. Lewis asserts that their journey has a deeper meaning, the traditional discovery of self: "So, after months given more to exploring themselves than to exploring Europe, they came in April to Berlin."[26] But his assertion does not ring true; Fran never explores herself at all, and Dodsworth's self-conscious ruminations have none of the dynamism that the parallel of the journey would suggest. For these modern novelists, the journey reflects not so much a return home as a search for a satisfactory home.[27] It is a projection of their disaffection from American society. The European locus is chosen not so much for a viable set of values as for a rejection of America and of modernity, thus, at times, of reality itself. In the poetry of Pound and Eliot, the journey to Europe comes to mean a turning away from present reality and a delusory search for the past—delusory because the Europe of the dramatized encounter is itself a part of the frustrating present.[28]

The journey to Europe was a vital, signifying fictional form in the nineteenth century. In the twentieth, much of its meaning has been drained away by ready communications and easy travel, with the consequent loss of inherent strangeness. The strange has become the familiar, or at any rate more nearly the familiar, and the possibilities for contrast that were the essential element of the form have been, to a great extent, diluted. As a result, the value of the European journey as a symbol is less easily accessible. The journey is no longer inherently significant; it must be *made* significant.

An example of what still can be done is William Styron's *Set This House on Fire*. The contrast of America with Europe is not inherent in Styron's narrative. Indeed, conflict arises chiefly between American and American on European soil; the characters have taken their tension and their evil with them. Even more, conflict is internal, between the self and the abstract essence of evil. Naturally, this clash could occur anywhere; indeed, it is often presented as an intrusion upon an idyllic landscape. Yet the European setting here is never irrelevant and seldom merely exotic. The simple fact that it is presented as a different, a foreign setting—even if no qualitative difference were apparent—would make it useful for projecting a shift from ordinary relationships and ordinary consciousness to the unfamiliar. Further, Styron heightens his presentation both of spontaneous delight and of poverty in the Italian village, which is the chief setting of the novel and emphasizes the effects of war, the primary resource of the modern novelist who wants to preserve a sense of difference in a European setting.

Naturally, the European setting of *Set This House on Fire* allows Styron to exploit the historic pairing of Old and New Worlds as symbols for change in consciousness. It is because he goes to Europe and acquires memories which he prefers to forget that Cass can longingly project himself into discovery of a vital and innocent America, "immense and green and glistening."[29] That discovery does not convey an escape to innocence for Cass, but a discovery of possibilities for mellowness and serenity. So once again going to the Old World is a means of immersion in sordid experience, guilt, the past, the "old self." After that immersion, Styron's voyager is released to discover America for himself.

NOTES

1. An exception to this typical pattern, however, is the insistent and lyrical homecoming urge of William Goyen's fine first novel, *The House of Breath* (1950).

2. Conrad Aiken, Author's Note to *The Kid* (1947; rpt. New York: Oxford University Press, 1970), p. 6.

3. Ferner Nuhn ponders the directional connotations in *The Wind Blew from the East: A Study of the Orientation of American Culture* (New York and London: Harper, 1942), p. 24: "It is interesting to speculate why it should always have been a Western star that meant adventure of the wild, not an Eastern one. . .there might be good solar reasons. . . . So at least it has been."

4. F. I. Carpenter, *American Literature and the Dream* (New York: Philosophical Library, 1955), pp. 38-39.

5. Among American creative artists who made the troubling but enlightening journey abroad: Washington Allston, William Wetmore Story, Washington Irving, James Fenimore Cooper, Margaret Fuller, Ralph Waldo Emerson, James Russell Lowell, Thomas Eakins, Henry Adams, T. S. Eliot, and numerous others. Both in individual critical biographies and in general studies such as Alan Holder's *Three Voyagers in Search of Europe* (Philadelphia: University of Pennsylvania Press, 1966), and Nathalia Wright's *American Novelists in Italy. The Discoverers: Allston to James* (Philadelphia: University of Pennsylvania Press, 1965), a considerable amount of scholarly attention has been devoted to these encounters with Europe. Willard Thorp's essay "Pilgrim's Return," in the *Literary History of the United States*, 3d ed. rev. (New York: Macmillan, 1963) is an excellent summary of the "great Exodus" to Europe that occurred in the period 1850 to 1900.

6. William Bradford, *Of Plymouth Plantation, 1620-1647*, ed. Samuel Eliot Morison (New York: Knopf, 1952), p. 25.

7. The conflict in American attitudes toward Europe is summed up by Christof Wegelin as an "image of Europe as the locus of America's cultural past. . .balanced by a counterimage of the social dead hand of the past." *The Image of Europe in Henry James* (Dallas: Southern Methodist University Press, 1958), p. 13.

8. The conventions of the travel book genre and something of its impact on American literature are discussed by James Jubak in his article "The Influence of the Travel Genre on Melville's *Mardi*," Genre, 9 (1976), 121-33.

9. Wright, *American Novelists in Italy*, p. 34.

10. Quoted by Wright from an unpublished letter to James T. Fields, *American Novelists in Italy*, p. 140.

11. James Baldwin, *Giovanni's Room* (New York: The Dial Press, 1956), p. 91.

12. Nathaniel Hawthorne, Preface to *The Marble Faun*, *The Centenary Edition of the Works of Nathaniel Hawthorne*, 14 vols. (Columbus: Ohio State University Press, 1968), IV, 3.

13. Cf. the geographic and moral poles of Robin's journey in "My Kinsman, Major Molineux."

14. *The Centenary Edition of the Works of Nathaniel Hawthorne*, IV, 461.

15. *Centenary Edition*, XII, 87.

16. *Centenary Edition*, XII, 3. In the Fireside Edition, George Parsons Lathrop rendered this passage "the site of Eve's bridal bower."

17. The dates of Hawthorne's work on these abortive narratives, as well as their complicated editorial and publication history, are discussed by Edward H. Davidson and Claude M. Simpson in an "Historical Commentary," *The Centenary Edition of the Works of Nathaniel Hawthorne*, XII, 491-521.

18. Milton R. Stern, in *The Fine Hammered Steel of Herman Melville* (Urbana: University of Illinois Press), uses the pejorative term "lure" (for example, pp. 15-16) in developing his argument that "Melville always presents the quest as futile" (p. 11).

19. *Israel Potter; His Fifty Years of Exile*, *The Works of Herman Melville*, Standard Edition, 16 vols. (London: Constable, 1923), XI, 210.

20. E. M. Forster comments of this episode that for James "poetry and life crowd round a landing." *Aspects of the Novel* (New York: Harcourt, Brace, & World, 1954), p. 221.

21. As one critic has commented, James "never lets his dialectic become a static contrast of opposites suitable for partisan polemics." Cushing Strout, "Henry James and the International Theme Today," *Studi Americani* (Rome), 13 (1967), 285.

22. R. W. Butterfield observes in his essay *"The American"* that Newman is "in many characteristic respects, a Westward-stepping pioneer merely turned about." *The Air of Reality: New Essays on Henry James*, ed. John Goode (London: Methuen and Co., Ltd., 1972), p. 5.

23. Henry James, *The Art of the Novel* (New York: Charles Scribner's Sons, 1946), p. 316.

24. Strether's journey, then, is not a primary element, but neither is it irrelevant as is the journey to Europe in, for example, Katherine Anne Porter's *Ship of Fools* (1945), where the ocean crossing is not a real journey at all but only a device for isolating her microcosm.

25. It has continued too in the popular war novel and film, where it is generally only a framework for adventure and melodrama—the European setting, then, only the trappings of glamour. The journey is thus drained of its thematic significance. Oscar Cargill notes the difference in remarking in *The Novels of Henry James* (New York: Macmillan, 1961), p. 46, that "a foreign setting gives merely a romantic interest" in Hemingway's novels.

26. Sinclair Lewis, *Dodsworth* (New York: Harcourt Brace, 1929), p. 225.

27. Malcolm Cowley comments authoritatively that the young American writers in the early and middle 1920s "went to Paris, not as if they were being driven into exile, but as if they were seeking a spiritual home." *A Second Flowering: Works and Days of the Lost Generation* (New York: Viking Press, 1973), p. 53.

28. Alan Holder, *Three Voyagers in Search of Europe* (Philadelphia: University of Pennsylvania Press, 1966), p. 268.

29. William Styron, *Set This House on Fire* (New York: Random House, 1960), p. 500.

5
Search and Encounter: The Quest

Sail forth—steer for the deep waters only,
Reckless O soul, exploring, I with thee, and thou with me,
For we are bound where mariner has not yet dared to go,
And we will risk the ship, ourselves and all.
                    —Walt Whitman, "Passage to India"

                                        yes, Walt,
Afoot again, and onward without halt,—
Not soon, nor suddenly,—no, never to let go
    My hand
            in yours,
                Walt Whitman—
                        so—
                    —Hart Crane, *The Bridge*

The quest has been so often invoked as a descriptive label, particularly with the influence of mythological criticism, that it has become a kind of excuse for noncriticism. The term "quest" has been applied to narratives involving journeys of all sorts or no spatial journeys at all, as if the mere word were an explanation:

this or that character is "on a quest" or "in quest of" something. The critic assumes that his term is clear, well understood, and final; often, one surmises, he also means it to be dignifying, and indeed it is generally received that way. But greater precision is needed here. At the risk of belaboring the obvious, we need to develop a clearer definition of the quest as narrative pattern if we are to apply the term usefully to specific works and arrive at an assessment of the history and importance of the quest as a form in American literature.

The quest is, first, a journey of search, a pursuit of the unknown. Its goal is both radically uncertain and radically significant, beyond definition or rational assessment—a whale embodying ultimate truth and ultimate mystery, a fleece of wondrous and magical gold. Equally uncertain is the route that the quester must follow; his journey is a perilous search, fraught with great danger. A golden fleece may be known to hang from a branch, but the precise location of the tree and the realm within which it stands are likely to be in doubt. Worse yet, the fleece is guarded by formidable preternatural monsters, so that the hero's approach to the prize will either destroy him or prove him more than mortal.

The goal of the quest may be either proximate or ultimate—proximate in the sense of a materially real, obtainable object, however magical or totemic; ultimate in the sense of an abstraction such as Truth. In either case, it is deeply involved with the self-realization of the questing hero, who proves and finds himself in the course of his journey.[1] The hero of a quest narrative, though he may be accompanied by a supporting group as Jason is by the Argonauts, is essentially, even unnaturally, alone. He has none of the "office and place in a politico-historical context" of the hero of epic, a form often mistakenly identified with romance.[2] Daring to undertake a great search, he sets out with a sense of solitary exhilaration and expansion and persists in his commitment with an extraordinary and isolating devotion. It is this stress on the loneness of the hero and its sense of consuming or even compulsive aspiration that make the quest the quintessential romantic form.[3] The chief defining quality of the romantic as distinct from the romance, quest is its even greater emphasis on the theme of self-realization or self-discovery; its goal is primarily, rather than secondarily, a "psychological search for identity."[4]

In respect to its emphasis on the solitary nature of the undertaking, the quest is clearly distinct from other journey forms we have been considering. The home-founding journey is questlike in that it involves a search, but its terms are social; it is a parable of the founding or reshaping of society. The American's journey to Europe can be questlike (as it is for Isabel Archer in James's *Portrait of a Lady*), and indeed the journey to Europe can adopt other forms as well, but, again, its terms are more social. It is a journey from a relatively isolated place to a sense of social and historic density and is typically used as a vehicle for cultural contrast, so that the individuality of its characters and their longings tend to be blurred into the representation of types. The escape is a lone journey, but negative or propulsive in impulse; whatever it may become as it develops, it is primarily a journey away-from. But the quest is primarily a journey toward, a journey of aspiration rather than rejection, presenting the lone hero and solitary endeavor in an aura of fierce celebration.

The geography of the quest, even in the outward quest for a "real" object, is not the world of reality so much as a patterned, emblematic landscape presented in terms that point to its essential or affective quality rather than its perceived components. It is, as Gibbs points out in his study of Middle English romances, a "world of strangeness and fantasy" or a "dreamland quite outside geography," providing an "excellent setting for adventure in the nearly abstract."[5] The morally emblematic setting of Hawthorne's "Young Goodman Brown," with its eery gloom imaging the gloom and moral peril into which the traveler plunges, is a perfect example. Another, somewhat less familiar, is the wild, surrealistic landscape through which the narrator of Charles Brockden Brown's *Edgar Huntly* (1799) pursues his quest for truth.

In the more fully internalized romantic quest, setting becomes a projection of the mind of the quester, and the outward and forward motion of the questing journey becomes metaphoric for the inward search of self-discovery. The spatial dimension as a whole, the motion of journeying and the boon being sought as well as the landscape, becomes collapsed into the mental dimension.[6] The narrative is released from everyday external reality, as the quest reaches beyond specific conditions toward absolute and eternal meanings. The epitome of this impulse toward the eternal is Ahab's obsessive desire, in *Moby-Dick*, to "strike through the pasteboard mask" of material nature to get at whatever transcendent meaning lurks beyond. This reaching toward absolutes or essences gives the quest its tendency to be prolonged or endless, as, for example, Taji's voyage at the end of Melville's *Mardi* appears destined to go on forever. Plot incidents, manifesting this same release from ordinary reality, are likely to be at least to some degree bizarre or mystifying or, in more realistic narratives, horrifying (a similar effect, since horror contains astonishment at the presence of the revolting or fearful event and an impulse to deny its reality).[7] It is with this internalized quest form, reflecting as it does the romantic emphasis on the conquering imagination and the artist's discovery of self, with which the journeys of American literature (which has been predominantly a romantic literature) have their strongest affinities. Todd Lieber rightly comments on a tendency in American romanticism to "make the heroic journey the dream of the creative self."[8] The American quest tends to appear as a symbolic journey of the creative artist toward full understanding of himself and his art.

The quest, then, tends to be a mental journey; its "real" spatial dimension tends to recede or lose substance and its symbolic import to become dominant. This is why many critics use the word quest to designate any prolonged or elaborated effort toward abstract or spiritual goals even if it is not projected into geographic movement. Certainly there is a rationale for such a use of the term. Even in a relatively external quest, the searcher tends to pursue his goal-emblem with an intensity of yearning altogether disproportionate and implausible unless it is taken as a totem or symbol. (A good example is Taji's singleminded pursuit of the maiden Yillah, in *Mardi*; to any realistic view, she appears altogether insipid.) Nevertheless, using the designation quest for a purely mental yearning and effort is a muddling of terms. Even though the spatial journeying of a romantic or postromantic quester may be only the thinnest figurative pattern, that minimal spatial pattern should be the essential requisite, the sine qua non, for labelling any fiction a quest. A hope, inquiry, or discipline having no projection into the spatial dimension as journey should be called something else.

A parallel development to the shifting of emphasis from the spatial surface toward thematic concerns in the romantic quest is the tendency for emphasis to be shifted away from the goal of the quest toward the process of questing itself. Paradoxically, the quester pursues a goal with compulsive devotion, but the very act of pursuing it becomes his primary value, surpassing the goal itself. The paradox, however, is not so absolute as it first appears. Because the goal of a quest tends to be absolute or ultimate, it comes to appear, in a limited and sceptical world, impossible to attain. Yet aspiration for the unattainable is in itself an exalted moral condition, worthy of the hero's aspiration. Hence the questing process becomes both means and end. Whitman's injunction that we "farther and farther sail" on a "perpetual journey" is characteristic of American Romantics—which is very much to say that it is characteristic of American literature.

A sub-species of the quest developing its tendency toward abstract goals, symbolic action, and the reach toward absolute enlightenment is the inner journey of the soul or the "night journey." In this form of quest, familiar in world mythology and very important in American fiction, the loneness of the hero is accentuated and the perils of his journey magnified to the dimensions of a descent into a hell or underworld and an encounter with secret or atavistic guilt. Except in stories of signal heroes or gods, who prove the fullness of their being in these encounters and return in apotheosis, the goal or reward of the descent is tenuous or even absent. The dimensions of the night journey narrative, which is far less displaced toward realism even than other quests, are well and simply stated by Joseph Campbell:

The usual pattern is, first, of a break away or departure from the local social order and context; next, a long, deep retreat inward and backward, backward, as it were, in time, and inward, deep into the psyche; a chaotic series of encounters there, darkly terrifying experiences, and presently (if the victim is fortunate) encounters of a centering kind, fulfilling, harmonizing, giving new courage; and then finally, in such fortunate cases, a return journey of rebirth to life.[9]

Campbell's definition points to the chief distinction between the expansive outward quest, however symbolic, and the intensive soul journey: the center or hero of the inward journey may persevere through trials just as the quester does, but his journey is not so controlled by his conscious volition. He feels himself carried along by a great undirected force and may be said to endure his journey of trial rather than undertake and pursue it. One thinks of Brockden Brown's *Edgar Huntly*, in which the narrator at times wills his search but at other times is literally carried away with no conscious volition to endure the most harrowing, morbid, and bizarre trials. Or, even more definitive, the narrator's surrender to his whirlpool journey in Poe's "Descent into the Maelstrom."

The history of the night journey and quest forms in American literature reads like a roll call of our major writers. Brockden Brown, our earliest significant novelist, was also our earliest writer of the night journey, with *Arthur Merwyn* (1799), *Ormond* and *Wieland* as well as *Edgar Huntly*, all of them stocked with sequences of weird, compulsive journeys to guilt-laden discoveries. Much influenced by Brown were two lesser but nonetheless interesting writers working in the same vein in the earlier nineteenth century, Robert Montgomery Bird and George Lippard. Bird's curiously influential Western *Nick of the Woods* (1837), as well as *The Hawks of Hawk Hollow*, demonstrates his fixation on horror and unreasoning repugnance, qualities that link his work with Brockden Brown's. The influence of Bird and of Melville, with his great haunting beast, is clearly felt behind so recent a work as Richard Brautigan's *The Hawkline Monster* (1974), well described by its author as being (like *Nick of the Woods*) a Gothic Western. George Lippard's horror novels such as the famous *Quaker City; or, The Monks of Monk Hall* (1844) regularly employ nocturnal expeditions down rivers, along dark streets of mysterious cities, or through subterranean passages, at the end of which waits some horrific encounter. Among Bird's and Lippard's greater contemporaries, Hawthorne produced definitive miniature versions of the night journey in "Young Goodman Brown" and "My Kinsman, Major Molineux." Both end with their heroes' discoveries of their own participation in the external evil into which they have ventured and thereby successfully convey the oneness of the inner and the outer dimensions of the fiction. Melville, too, worked in the night journey form as well as the outward quest in "Benito Cereno" and specific sequences of *Redburn*, *Moby-Dick*, and especially the little-read *Pierre*.

It was Poe, however, who took the night journey to its fullest and least displaced development in *The Narrative of Arthur Gordon Pym*. The work epitomizes the use of spatial travel through a weird or disorienting geographic region to project the even more harrowing exploration of submerged levels of the psyche. Further, in its lack of a sense of triumph or regeneration and the absence of any traditional kind of superlative heroism surrounding Pym himself, it illustrates the difference between the night journey and the expansive heroic quest. To be sure, Pym appears more than mortal in his survival ability and probably in his insatiable curiosity but not in virtue or might. Nor does his journey accomplish any redemption of society.

Pym's adventurous journey conveys instead the magnitude as well as the perversity of man's desire to know and the destructive and guilty darkness of the knowledge to which that desire leads. It is crowded with elements of nightmare and atavism: strange and unreasoning fears; an uncannily hostile dog and unaccountably deceptive primitives; sequences of immurement resembling burial, darkness, and diving or falling to great depths; pairing with a misshapen and sinister human-like being; violence and the breaking of taboos, including the taboo of cannibalism. Pym himself begins his adventures as an apparently sane, well-educated youth given to irrationality only to the degree that one might expect, romantically and stereotypically perhaps, of youth; that is, he is unnecessarily reckless, insufficiently prudent, and bent on escaping social restraint. From that relatively sane character and stable, modern social environment, he ventures out on a voyage that moves him ever deeper into savagery, improbability, and apparent madness. Particularly in the events on the island of Tsalal, with its black/white reversals, he encounters the kind of inversion of external, rational existence that often characterizes the inward voyage into the hidden and unacknowledged self. In other, though certainly not contradictory, terms, the Tsalal episode is a descent (including an abrupt physical descent, a fall into a gorge) into an underworld or hell, a parallel to the descents of Odysseus, Aeneas, and Dante. Unlike these heroic descents, however, that comprise only limited phases of larger quest journeys, Pym's descent does not provide him the self-plumbing, integrative fullness of being which the earlier mythic heroes' descents provide them. After the Tsalal underworld, Pym rushes onward to the famous terminal encounter with an immense white being:

But there arose in our pathway a shrouded human figure, very far larger in its proportions than any dweller among men. And the hue of the skin of the figure was of the perfect whiteness of the snow. [10]

The passage carries overtones of color and directional symbolism, but unfortunately—for it renders the work not richly ambiguous but merely confusing—the identity of the figure, as well as the import of the surrounding whiteness and the polar direction, is never made clear, any more than is the overall intention of the narrator, who remains not so much lone and obsessed, like the questing hero, but alienated and frenzied. The passage is generally interpreted as an encounter with death,[11] and as such it is, of course, perfectly consistent with the traditional implications of the night journey tradition. If not marking a break with death, Pym's encounter with the white figure at the end of his journey at any rate marks a break into a new level of consciousness, along with a new and fantastic geographical realm. In that sense, too, it follows the chief convention of the form, that the geographic dimension be a projection of an inner dimension.[12] Again, we are given no indication that the break into a new level of consciousness in this instance is in any way integrative or restorative, either to Pym or to society. To be sure, Pym does survive to tell his story, but that may well be only a fantastic and most illogical convention of narrative strategy.

Pym is not only the most discussed in terms of the night or nightmare journey of any American work, but it is also our most thoroughgoing, most unrelieved extended example of the form. Poe's "King Pest," "The Man of the Crowd," "A Tale of the Ragged Mountains," and "The Cask of Amontillado" are equally unrelieved night journeys among his shorter fiction. At least two of these, "The Man of the Crowd" and "The Cask of Amontillado," are more successful aesthetically than *Pym*, which for all its sporadic intensity and susceptibility to critical play, is as a whole strained.[13] Indeed, it is at least arguable that for any writer the successful work operating exclusively as night journey, uncombined with other formal patterns, will necessarily be short. The demands that an extended night journey narrative places on a reader's willingness to suspend disbelief are such that something we might call success—credibility plus aesthetic finish and an air of serious meaning—is much more likely to be achieved in a long work if the night journey or inner horror journey comprises only a sequence within a larger structure or is one of the suggested implications of a highly displaced, multidimensional structure. Among the most brilliantly successful nightmare journey stories are certain of Hawthorne's tales as well as Poe's, Melville's "Benito Cereno," Faulkner's "The Bear," and Richard Wright's "The Man Who Lived Underground" (1944)—all of them relatively brief works. Hemingway's "Big Two-Hearted River" derives its power not only from its compression and its clipped style, but from its quiet understatement of the soul journey. Faulkner's *As I Lay Dying*, Bellow's *Henderson the Rain King* and James Dickey's *Deliverance* are examples of longer works that combine elements of the night or soul journey, with its physical as well as mental horrors, and other patterns of journey narrative in complex, multidimensional structures.

In the more inclusive quest form, the monumental work is of course *Moby-Dick*. Like *Huckleberry Finn*, *Moby-Dick* has so often been discussed in just these terms—as journey and as quest— that a wise economy here requires us to direct only a brief summary and a few observations toward America's behemoth of quests. The prominence of journeys in Melville's work springs only partly from the fact that he was himself a restless voyager. This biographical voyaging and its relation to his fictional journeys are examined in a considerable body of scholarship. Given Melville's own and his family's experiences in seafaring, it is scarcely surprising that in his extensive reading he would often turn to books of travel and exploration. From this reading springs a related but nonetheless separate source of the journey forms of his narratives. In accordance with his usual and well documented practice of consulting and paraphrasing the authorities on whatever subject was at hand, as well as interesting writings on subjects not at hand, Melville utilized travel books and guidebooks both as points of departure and as generic models for his fiction.[14] Indeed, his attraction to this kind of material, much of it having no more than a curiosity or antiquarian value, goes far to account for the travelogue flavor and hence the journey forms of much of his work.

Melville's journeys are always to some degree symbolic. An uncertain symbolism is present even in the relatively one-dimensional adventures of *Typee* and *Omoo*. In *Mardi*, a virtually unreadable book of great importance to Melville's development, the enrichment of incident with thought becomes, as Charles Feidelson says, "fanciful and allegorical."[15] This urge toward broad symbolic enrichment is anchored in fact and expressed largely through structure and through meditation first in *Redburn*, then in *White-Jacket* and *Moby-Dick*. The exploration of an emblematic landscape, a technique or more properly a mode of vision mastered in *Moby-Dick*, dominates *Pierre* and "The Encantadas," and the equally masterful use of the ship as microcosm of *Moby-Dick* recurs in *The Confidence-Man*. A much slighter piece but remarkable and indeed startling in it use of motion through an emblematic landscape is "The Tartarus of Maids."[16] It is perhaps because symbolism and surface narrative had become so perfectly fused in *Israel Potter*, and because the surface narrative itself had become so spare, that the book has been regarded as an inferior and uncharacteristic work.[17] In every novel Melville wrote, he relied on travel for his plot and made that travel represent more than itself.

Criticism of *Moby-Dick* has frequently been concerned with the significance of the traditional patterns in the work, either the quest (Ahab's) or the escape (Ishmael's). Both approaches are correct; the book plays off the two journeys against each other. More important, it examines and redefines the two. Ahab's quest, for all its nobility, becomes an antiquest because its goal is solely destructive. In his perseverance and his refusal to accede in simple answers or easy acquiescence to what he regards as ultimate injustice, Ahab achieves heroism. But his urge to strike through the mask of an illusive universe is less an urge to find an enlightenment beyond it than a determination merely to strike, to break, to reveal the malicious nothingness of which he is certain. As this destructiveness of motive becomes more dominant in Ahab and more clear in the narrative, the positive heroism of Ahab's quest is perverted and his journey becomes an antiquest. Concurrently, Ishmael's journey of escape becomes redefined as the authentic mythic journey of the mind. Like all heroes of the night journey, whether mythic or displaced toward realism, Ishmael confronts alone ultimate questions (hence chapters such as "The Masthead," examining through imaginative symbols the alternatives of philosophical idealism and philosophical realism), perilous trials, and death itself. His journey takes him to the underworld, imaged in sequences such as the black mass of the harpoon socket communion (chapter 36), the blasphemous baptism of newly forged harpoons in blood (chapter 113), and the trying out of the whale at night (chapter 96), when the smoke from the blubber "smells like the left wing of the day of judgment" and the "pagan harpooneers" become "Tartarean shapes."[18] In surviving to be picked up by the cruising *Rachel*, then, Ishmael has returned from death. Like the mythic hero who harrows hell and returns, he has assimilated the forces of death and evil and henceforth carries them as part of the survival and strength of his character. In emblem of this assimilation, he is borne up by Queequeg's coffin, the image of the ultimate darkness. Queequeg too, the friendly dark, has been symbolically absorbed by Ishmael in his achievement of wholeness.

The quality of Melville's own response to questing has been examined by Milton R. Stern in his suggestive book *The Fine Hammered Steel of Herman Melville*, where he argues that Melville rejected quest as a delusive waste.[19] Such an argument is necessarily based on the demonic character of Ahab. Stern does not regard Ishmael's journey as a quest at all. Yet, as we have seen, elements of the quest are incorporated in the narrative as it is Ishmael's story, and the ending of the book is to some degree an affirmation of Ishmael as emblematic character, as is the closeness of Ishmael's point of view to the third-person narrator's— they share the wisdom of the book. The question can never be wholly or unequivocally answered. In many and obvious ways,

Moby-Dick is too inclusive and complex a work for simple or one-sided answers. Specifically, the duality of the hero figure complicates the problem of critical judgment, since Ahab, the antiquester, bears the narrative powerfully before him by his fierce and assertive heroism, while Ishmael, the escaper who becomes the affirmed quester, has the relatively unexciting role of the moderate, the septic, the dry wit. Yet the moderate is able to retain his balance in a way that the fierce hero is not. He does not look too long in the fire. The question of Melville's verdict on questing—to assume for the moment that he must have given such a verdict—continues through *Pierre* and *The Confidence-Man*, in both of which his tone is yet more septical than it is in *Moby-Dick* and in *Clarel*, the inadequately recognized major work of the closing half of his life.

The same formal issue that we have noted with respect to *Moby-Dick*, the generic question of whether the central journey is formally an escape or a quest, arises in the consideration of the other chief journey narrative of the nineteenth century, Twain's *The Adventures of Huckleberry Finn*. Again one can regard the work as an amalgam of two journey narratives in two different forms, one Jim's and one Huck's, again sharing a common vessel. Such a solution is no happier here, however, than it is in Melville's great work, since again the two cannot be so clearly assigned to distinct characters. Elements of both forms are involved in the travels of both characters: Huck's journey can as well be seen as an escape from Pap and the widow Douglas (as indeed it is; he wants to "get so far away that the old man nor the widow couldn't ever find me any more" chapter six) or as an independent thinker's search for a just society; Jim's as well be interpreted as a quest for freedom as an escape from slavery. If, instead of an amalgam of two heroes' journeys, the structure of the novel is conceived as an amalgam of two spatial patterns, the one linear (embodied in the flow of the river) and the other a back and forth, shore to raft pattern, the two, escape and quest, again overlap. The linear, down-river movement provides Huck and Jim's escape and the path toward the goal of freedom or the desired, but never found, ideal. The second pattern, the alternation between raft and shore, establishes the novel's social criticism. Social life on shore is always fraught with injustice and corruption, which are blessedly absent when Huck and Jim with-draw to their floating sanctuary. Is the action, then, an escape from a corrupt society to solitary beatitude? Or is it, as it repeats the pattern of exploratory ventures ashore, a search for a right-eous society? Both. Escape and quest are related in any event, the difference arising from the question of which motivation is stronger, the repellent force or the attracting goal. Twain simply does not care to distinguish the two, in part, perhaps, because a painstaking concern for traditional form would violate his pose of writing a simple boys' tale. Actually, of course, though the work bears the imprints of the traditional quest and the escape, it more nearly approximates the picaresque adventure than any other single form. And in its concluding turn to the untrammeled West it enacts the central movement of the American experience.

The structural inconsistencies of *Huckleberry Finn* have given rise to the greatest bulk of the critical commentary on the work, most of it either negative or excessively defensive. There is no blinking the lack of structural integration in the novel, great as it is. Still, it is the interplay of these diverse threads of narrative, all of them heavily laden with the associative significance of the American journey, that has made *Huckleberry Finn* so lastingly influential on generations of readers.[20] In what he called merely "another boy's book" Twain captured the diverse crux of literary Americanness. *Huckleberry Finn*, *Moby-Dick*, and the poems of Walt Whitman, particularly "Song of Myself," are the three cen-tral and defining works of American literature in the nineteenth century. All are centrally concerned with quests.

In the twentieth century, perhaps because of a modern scep-ticism regarding the possibility of achieving absolute enlight-enment, the narrative of quest has come to be typically curtailed or fragmented. It is a pronounced change from earlier times, and particularly from the quest narratives of religious myth, when the hero returned from his voyage enlightened, bringing his redemptive knowledge to bear on society. His perilous voy-age had an inner dimension, to be sure, but the discovery of the secret depths of the hero's self was complemented by and indeed related to social dimensions, and the denouement of the quest (in itself a linear journey)[21] was a circling back to the point of origin. The hope or assumption implied by such a structure was that the hero could indeed survive his ordeal, plumb the perilous depths, inner as well as outer, and complete the redemptive cycle. That is, the quest which is completed in a return manifests a confidence that there is in fact a redemptive talisman and that it can be found and shared. Such a hope no longer inspirits our writers of quest narrative.[22] Nick Adams journeys to an encounter with a kind of absolute in Hemingway's "Big Two-Hearted River," but remains locked in an ambiguous half-enlightenment when the narrative breaks off with the nonking still fishing. The businessmen canoers of James Dickey's *Deliverance* survive (some of them) their three-day descent into hell, and those who do, manage to return, but they bring no message, no talisman, only bad dreams.

Not only are our quests incomplete, but they are also, more typically, not narratives so much as pieces of narratives. Modern literature is replete with fragmented snatches or images of the quest or the night journey. Again, this fragmentation, as well as an apparent willingness to see the horrific as part of the experience of all men, may well be an indication of a pessimistic temper of the times.[23] Certainly it is evidence of the influence of poetry and poetic techniques on novelists of the impressionist and postimpressionist period. But the recurrence of fragmentary quest motifs may also indicate our post-Freudian, post-Jungian awareness of the buried mysteries of the psyche. Todays's writer expects his audience to have some familiarity with mythic and psychological iconography and therefore feels free to manipulate this iconography and its typical structures of incident in a kind of shorthand that does not require full narrative development. Such techniques of fragmentation go far to account for the relative density as well as the temporal stasis characteristic of modern fiction.

A further development in modern versions of the quest, closely related to its tendencies toward incompleteness and fragmentation, is the modulation of journeys of quest into journeys of wandering. As we have seen, the transcendent and inherently unreachable goals toward which questing heroes often reach naturally result in journeys that can have no real end. Therefore, the narrative forms in which these journeys occur are necessarily to some degree nonclosural. However, the generic modulation discussed here goes beyond this formal reflection of a prevailing sense of inconsistency between transcendent aspirations and a limited world. More precisely, it is an accentuation of that sense. In a disheartened and disheartening social atmosphere, a society of anomie, uncertainty, and scepticism, the questing hero may find not only that he cannot reach transcendently noble goals but also that he cannot formulate goals at all or that he loses sight of those he has formulated. When this occurs, the quest, like the escape and other journey patterns that have been characteristic of the American literary tradition, becomes absorbed into the pattern, or nonpattern, of the journey of wandering, the journey of the lost hero. Scepticism about the possibility of quest leads, too, to a comical treatment of those who undertake heroic journeys—in Faulkner's *As I Lay Dying*, for instance, or Bernard Malamud's *The Natural*.

When combined with a genre that has traditionally been serious or tragic, such comical tone raises generic questions that cannot easily be resolved. It becomes one more factor contributing to that generic mixing that has become evident in the twentieth century. The result is a kind of thematically determined quasi-genre, a loose fictional pattern that can be observed to recur in works of widely differing form, that has become the dominant mode of the fictional journey in current literature.

NOTES

1. A. C. Gibbs, *Middle English Romances* (Evanston: Northwestern University Press, 1966), p. 8: "The great theme of the chivalric romance is self-realization." Use of the masculine gender in discussing the questing hero is historically justified. Literature has produced very few female questers. Full consciousness of this fact and the need to break out of a restrictive pattern is reflected in the name of Doris Lessing's heroine Martha Quest.

2. Gibbs, *Middle English Romances*, pp. 5-6. Gibbs adds that the quester's journey "serves no practical reality at all."

3. Cf. Robert Scholes and Robert Kellogg, *The Nature of Narrative* (New York: Oxford University Press), p. 212: the fundamental "romantic" plot in fiction is "desire to consummation." That phrasing might be altered to the more quest-like terms of aspiration to achievement.

4. Harold Bloom, "The Internalization of Quest," Scholes and Kellogg, *The Nature of Narrative*, p. 237.

5. Gibbs, *Middle English Romances*, pp. 4-10. Charles Muscatine, "Locus of Action in Medieval Narrative," *Romance Philology*, 17 (1963), 115-22.

6. Joseph Campbell, speaking not of a literary but of a scientific quest, celebrates the moon flight as "an outward journey. . .into ourselves." He concludes, "our depths are the depths of space." *Myths to Live By* (New York: Viking Press, 1972), pp. 239, 266.

7. Alan LeMay's classic Western *The Searchers* (1954) capitalizes on horror to achieve effects of the preternatural.

8. Todd M. Lieber, *Endless Experiments: Essays on the Heroic Experience in American Romanticism* (Columbus: Ohio State University Press), p. 243. Lieber adds—erroneously, I believe—that this tendency "reaches a culmination" in the works of Wallace Stevens. A more plausible candidate to single out in this way would be Hart Crane.

9. Campbell, *Myths to Live By*, p. 202.

10. *The Complete Tales and Poems of Edgar Allan Poe*. Introduction by Hervey Allen (New York: The Modern Library, 1938), p. 882.

11. Sometimes the shrouded figure is seen as a redeemer. That interpretation solves the problem of credibility raised by the retrospective first person narration, but it does not reflect the atmosphere of menace and doom surrounding the work as a whole and in particular the concluding sequences. A similar problem of narrative probability occurs at the end of Larry McMurtry's first-person novel *All My Friends Are Going to Be Strangers*.

12. Pym's journey has often been interpreted as a virtual allegory of either biographical or political concerns of Poe, particularly the question of race in the South. See, for instance, Leslie A. Fiedler, *Love and Death in the American Novel*, rev. ed. (New York: Stein and Day, 1966), pp. 397-400.

13. A defense of the work, as well as the most valuable concise analysis I know of, is the chapter "Poe's Imaginary Voyage" in Patrick F. Quinn's *The French Face of Edgar Poe* (Carbondale: Southern Illinois University Press, 1957), pp. 169-215.

14. Classic critical works that take this approach are Howard Vincent, *The Trying Out of Moby-Dick* (Boston: Houghton Mifflin, 1949); Willard Thorp, "Redburn's Prosy Old Guidebook," *PMLA*, 53 (1938), 1146-56; and the more general basic study Merton M. Sealts, Jr., *Melville's Reading: A Check-List of Books Owned and Borrowed* (Madison: The University of Wisconsin Press, 1966).

15. Charles Feidelson, Jr., "Introduction" to *Moby-Dick* (Indianapolis:

Bobbs-Merrill, 1964), p. xi. James Jubak's essay "The Influence of the Travel Narrative on Melville's *Mardi*," *Genre*, 9 (1976), 121-33, examines this problem of genre and meaning with great discernment and good sense.

16. The figurative representation of female sexual structures and processes in this sketch is obvious and has been fully recognized in criticism, as has been the social dimension. The complementarity of the companion sketch, "The Paradise of Bachelors," has been examined by W. R. Thompson in his essay " 'The Paradise of Bachelors and the Tartarus of Maids': A Reinterpretation," *American Quarterly*, 9 (1957), 34-45. The settings, however, are more complementary in their ana-tomical figurativeness than Thompson suggests.

17. Richard Chase, *Herman Melville: A Critical Study* (New York: Mac-millan Co., 1949), p. 176, unjustifiably dismisses *Israel Potter* as a "light-hearted" book.

18. Quoted from the Feidelson edition, published by Bobbs-Merrill in 1964. At least until the long anticipated Northwestern-Newberry *Moby-Dick* appears, this remains the most useful edition.

19. Stern's thesis that Melville's work is unified by condemnation of "the inhumanity of quest" in *The Fine Hammered Steel of Herman Melville* (Urbana: University of Illinois Press, 1957) is a minority view. The debate continues.

20. The influence of Twain's *Huckleberry Finn* scarcely needs dem-onstration. Hemingway's tribute is renowned, and the influence on Faulkner's *The Bear* is clear.

21. The two basic shapes of the journey, within the biblical/romantic tradition, are the circular return home and the linear quest. See M. H. Abrams, *Natural Supernaturalism* (New York: Norton, 1971).

22. Hence, partly, the distinctiveness of that literary sport of the twentieth century, J.R.R. Tolkien's *Lord of the Rings* (London: Allen & Unwin, 1954-55, Pt. 1. *The Fellowship of the Ring*; Pt. 2. *The Two Towers*; Pt. 3. *The Return of the King*), a quest narrative in three volumes complete with triumph, return, and social regeneration.

23. Paul Zweig attributes the "fragmentary forms" of the "memo-rable works of fiction" in the post-1950 era to a general loss not only of belief in the possibility of coherent forms that can reflect and explain reality but also of willingness to see pattern as a desirable thing. "It is not the end which is important," Zweig writes, "but the episode; not the form, of which the end is the final clarity . . . but the illumination itself, unruly and momentary." See Paul Zweig, *The Adventurer* (New York: Basic Books, 1974), pp. 247-50.

6
Lost and Wandering

"Sal, we gotta go and never stop going till we get there."
"Where we going, man?"
"I don't know but we gotta go."
—Jack Kerouac, *On the Road*

In American fiction of the twentieth century, the motif of the journey has insistently recurred in the amorphous form of homeless wandering. Our characteristic journey has become the journey of uncertain destination or duration, the journey to no end. The traditional journey narrative patterns were based on a relatively secure set of social and moral assumptions or goals that found expression in particular works by means of associated aesthetic patterns readily available for fulfillment or variation. As these assumptions and goals have been modified or even discarded, the literary patterns through which they were expressed have been emptied of value. As we reached "the end of America," as Louis Simpson puts it, and found that the old injustices of a stale society were still with us, we found less purpose in continuing to express the hopeful notions that motivated the home-founding journey. As the technological optimism of the preceding few generations exploded at Hiroshima or dissipated in environmental decay and as hopeful assumptions of society's progress foundered on Hitler's holocaust, there appeared to be little possibility that a transcendent hero could even exist, much less successfully pursue a quest for some supernal truth. The old optimism that launched journeys of discovery has (with the notable exception of space exploration) been sunk in a prevailing social mood of futility.

Mood is a tenuous enough quality to define for an individual, let alone for a society; nevertheless, it is real, and it has an effect on literary history. A deepening mood of futility in the United States has been noted by a variety of social observers and deplored in political rhetoric, popular journalism, and sociological comment. Its discernible impact on literature extends not only to the more direct expressions of tone but to variations in the traditional formal structures of literature. (Witness, for instance, such transformations of the novel as Philip Brautigan's or, at an opposite extreme, Truman Capote's.) Only if traditional forms are considerably modified—for instance, as the quest is rendered idiosyncratic by Saul Bellow in *Henderson the Rain King*—can they remain viable in a literature produced out of and for the current fractured sensibility.

Generally, two processes of formal evolution of the journey narrative can be observed. First, the traditional patterns or myths rendered in journey fiction (the redemptive quest, the migration to form new societies, the pilgrimage to a place of central value and importance, the escape from repression to freedom for self-discovery) are fragmented, so that we seldom encounter a completed journey of any one kind but rather a mixture of uncompleted journeys that approximate the conventions of more than one form or a sequence of repeated, incomplete journeys. To be sure, in any more or less realistic fiction, as the novel has been, there is always a degree of multivalence and fragmentation. However, the discussion here is of a more radical abandonment of sequential development. Second, the traditional narrative patterns, once fairly distinct from one another, have tended to blur together and overlap as the sense of purpose motivating them has dissipated. Extended narratives of journeys are not only less common than in the fiction of earlier periods but, when they do occur, are also more likely to appear as an amalgam of patterns subsumed in a general lack of direction or terminal point and a sense of being lost. More often than in earlier fiction, our characters tend to travel either idly or compulsively but not purposefully.

The motif of the undefined journey or journey of lostness is not in itself a new or unfamiliar symbolic action. Its ultimate source is the biblical story of the forty-year wandering of the Children of Israel in the wilderness. In American literature, a spatial disorientation both actual and symbolic occurs as early as the point in Bradford's *Of Plymouth Plantation* when the Pilgrims step onto American soil and abruptly decide that they have arrived, not in the New Promised Land, but in a hideous desolation. In the nineteenth century, the motif appears in Hawthorne's *Blithedale Romance* in Coverdale's confused vacillations between town and country and in Melville's *The Confidence-Man* in the devastating uncertainty in which the novel ends, a prospect of being endlessly lost.

The thematic import of sequences like these is clear to the reader because it is thoroughly conventional; when the Israelites wander in the wilderness, they have lost their spiritual direction. Variants of the archetype utilize a trope whose ramifications are easily accessible to the general reader. When Christopher Newman, for instance, in James's *The American*, gives up his purpose of marriage to Claire de Cintre yet remains too emotionally distraught to formulate other goals for his life, he wanders restlessly between France, England, and America, unable to feel at ease anywhere. Like the aimlessness of the Israelites, his movements in space reflect his inner lack of purpose. Edith Wharton similarly projects her heroine's emotional state onto her spatial movements in *House of Mirth* (1905). As Lily Bart becomes more insecure and distracted by anxiety and less certain of a social base of operations, she travels more widely with less coherent purpose to places that do not comport with the social milieu within which she has hoped to move. Her geographic movements become continuous and erratic rather than defined and deliberate. Fitzgerald uses virtually the same motif in *Tender Is the Night* in conveying Dick Diver's inner deterioration. Diver loses purposeful direction of his spatial orientation until, at the end of the novel, in a thoroughly dissipated and professionally disreputable state, he is supposed to be "almost certainly in that section of the country, in one town or another."[1]

The distinction we are noticing in these novels is that between controlled and erratic movement, but it also involves a difference between hopeful, destination-directed movement and hopeless, futile movement. It is this futile, monotonous motion that becomes characteristic of the fiction of the aptly called Lost Generation and after. Hemingway's *The Sun Also Rises* (1926), in many ways the definitive novel of its decade, demonstrates the motif with particular clarity. Here, random wandering is no longer a small segment of a larger narrative (as it is in *The American* or in other novels we have mentioned), introduced to convey a character's lapse from inner direction or purpose; it is the controlling pattern of the novel. Hemingway's disillusioned and dissolute characters,[2] trapped in a self-imposed exile, ramble from cafe to cafe or from country to country as momentary impulses move them and their bank accounts permit. But despite the larger action of constant motion, even adventure, in its specifics their activity is depressingly unvarying. Wherever they are, they drink, smoke, make love idly, and fall into squabbles with no hope that they are progressing toward any decisive action or any stable relationship—toward any goal at all. One place is much the same as another; they are, in effect, lost in a moral landscape of monotony with no ability to make significant distinctions or to choose a direction. The brilliance of the novel lies in its complete unity in the delineation of this single dominant effect. The oppressive sense of futility or incapacity for decisive action is developed in every element of the novel, notably in the calculated monotony of its dialogue, and is epitomized in Jake's reàl and symbolic impotence.

The world-weariness of *The Sun Also Rises* is the characteristic tone of the fiction of the 1920s, though nowhere else is it conveyed so definitively, and it is typically projected through the same kind of frenetic motion that we have noticed here. The midwesterners of Glenway Wescott's *Good-bye Wisconsin* (1928) escape to Europe, return, and escape again. Fitzgerald's disheartened socialites in *The Great Gatsby* (1925) and *Tender Is the Night* (1934) rush back and forth endlessly from party to party in a kind of numb, aimless urgency. The Divers of *Tender Is the*

Night are most comfortable together in a railroad diner, where the proprieties of the smart set insulate them from the emptiness within. John Dos Passos's *Manhattan Transfer* (1925) and John O'Hara's *Butterfield 8* (1935) present montages of frustrated New Yorkers in endless motion. In these two very similar books, both of them brilliantly innovative in their structural design yet deeply representative of their period, the structural principle at work is not causation but a thematically laden simultaneity with structural links created through random encounter. Images of transport and motion are insistent. *Manhattan Transfer*, for instance, opens with the arrival of a ferry and ends with the departure of Jimmy Herf (the most nearly central of the book's many characters) from New York by ferry and by thumbing a ride on a truck. At the end of *Butterfield 8* the focal character is killed by being mangled in the machinery of a ferry, an incident that is thematically as well as dramatically climactic. It is significant that the kind of conveyance featured in both of these important novels is the ferry, which shuttles people back and forth to temporary destinations. It is an appropriate kind of passage for the characters in these novels, who do not know where they want to go. Repeatedly, Dos Passos insists on their substitution of motion for direction. "All we can do is go round and round in a squirrel cage," one character says.[3] Jimmy Herf, unable to decide on a career, walks the streets "doggedly" or "desperately," with "nowhere in particular he wants to go" (pp. 236, 366). At the end, when the truck driver who gives him a ride asks his destination, he replies, "I dunno. . . .Pretty far" (p. 404).

His reply is closely echoed thirty years later in 1955 in what is probably the quintessential novel of compulsive wandering, Jack Kerouac's *On the Road*. Asked "Where we going, man?" Kerouac's hero Sal replies, in words very similar to Jimmy Herf's, "I don't know but we gotta go."[4] To be sure, the novel continues the tradition of zest for motion itself that we have observed throughout American literature. There is often a sense of footloose fun to the book, and Sal tries to maintain a pitch of exhilaration in his journeying. He insists that he and his companions were "leaving confusion and nonsense behind and performing our one and noble function of the time, *move*" (p. 133). They pattern their lives on "the white line in the holy road" (p. 138) and in moments of emotional highs affirm that "the road is life" (p. 211) and the "whole country like an oyster for us to open; and the pearl was there; the pearl was there" (p. 138). However, their zest for the unlimited journey is insistently challenged by expressions of discouragement and a sense of futility. When one of the group asks himself, "Where go? what do? what for?" and longs for sleep, he finds the "foolish gang" still "bending onward" (p. 167). They go "rushing through the world without a chance to see it" (p. 205), making no discoveries. One place looks much the same as another.

> I looked down Market Street. I didn't know whether it was that or Canal Street in New Orleans; it led to water, ambiguous, universal water, just as 42nd Street, New York, leads to water, and you never know where you are. (p. 172)

With no basis for differentiating one place and its associated experiences from another, the less intoxicated of the group realize that their frenetic travelling is pointless: "What I accomplished by coming to Frisco I don't know" (p. 177). The final image of the novel's life of wandering is not exhilaration or heroism or even escape from the "confusion and nonsense" of the surrounding culture, but helpless imprisonment in "the hell of it, the senseless nightmare road" (p. 254). *On the Road*, the definitive fictional expression of the Beat Generation, clearly displays a No Exit sign. It suggests that in the modern closed-in world of alienation and irrationality, motion deteriorates into a "frantic" zigzagging between arbitrary terminal points on linear reaches into emptiness.

It is clear that the circuitous, endless wandering these writers present as the primary mode of spatial motion in their fictional worlds conveys an oppressively somber social view. There exists no social structure, no common and viable value system that can provide a goal or orientation for their characters. Lacking both a home and a destination, they can do nothing else but wander through aimless sequences of empty experience. No hope is offered that their roads will lead them to places of stability or meaning, and since the spatial dimension is so easy and

conventional a metaphor for the temporal dimension, the implication is that there is also no hope that time, their lives' duration, will bring them to any integrated understanding of
experience. Theirs is a paradoxical and destructive condition of
footloose freedom that is actually a helpless imprisonment in a
randomly drawn maze.

The realization conveyed in a novel such as *On the Road* is well
summarized in the thoughts of the travelling salesman in Eudora
Welty's short story "The Hitch-Hikers" as he passes through
one of the many towns in his territory:

. . .none of any of this his, not his to keep, but belonging to the people
of these towns he passed through, coming out of their rooted pasts
and their mock rambles, coming out of their time. He himself had no
time. He was free; helpless.[5]

The travelling salesman, with his random encounter with senseless violence, is Welty's Modern Man. Like many other modern
writers, she uses his automobile as her symbol of a society that
carries people helplessly away from all sense of purpose or
meaning in their lives. The image of the automobile appears to
very similar effect in Welty's story "Death of a Travelling Salesman" and in her novel *Losing Battles* (1970), in which, after a
series of auto mishaps involving various comically obtuse or
distracted characters, the couple who are the book's center of
value are shown, not driving, but walking barefoot in the dirt.
The effect of deep nostalgia here is a note that one hears often
in postmodern fiction.

The themes of divorce from the past, rootlessness, and disorder that we have seen associated with the motif of the journey
of wandering appear in a distinctive and peculiarly plausible
way in a distinct sub-species of modern fiction, the Hollywood
novel. Probably the definitive novel of this latter-day fictional
"tradition" is Nathanael West's *The Day of the Locust* (1933). The
basis of the Hollywood novel in reality—specifically, the basis
of its characteristic satiric stance—is the widely assumed view
that Los Angeles, or Southern California as a whole, constitutes
a social world of its own that is peculiarly disordered, speeded
up, and artificial. The popular idea (substantiated to a degree

by historians) is that because California was for so long the special end point of the westering dream, the pot of gold at the end of the rainbow hopes of countless pioneers, it has received more than its share of restless visionaries and misfits and is therefore a more intensely neurotic version of the neurotic life of modern America. Accordingly, the Hollywood novel offers the social flux of Los Angeles and, in particular, the celluloid subculture of Hollywood as a symbol of a deplorable sort of modernity. Often the hectic, shallow life presented satirically in such novels assumes narrative patterns of purposeless motion. Two relatively recent Hollywood novels that particularly develop this motif of frenetic geographic motion as a controlling structural pattern through which to examine the California idea are Alison Lurie's *The Nowhere City* (1965) and Joan Didion's *Play It As It Lays* (1970).

Lurie's novel, somewhat like Edward Abbey's *The Monkey Wrench Gang*, combines the journey of home seeking with the journey of wandering, but does so in a different way than Abbey's. *The Nowhere City* (the city, of course, is Los Angeles) begins as a standard, if updated, novel of the search for a home. Paul Cattleman, an ambitious young easterner partway through his course of study for a Harvard Ph.D. in history, comes to Los Angeles to accept an unconventional but lucrative job in corporate history writing. He finds California somewhat startling, but he has an openness to change that enables him to adapt to its peculiarities and laxness, even to adapt with enthusiasm. In part this is because of his thoroughgoing acceptance of the optimistic American historic myth of the frontier, with its corollaries of progress and perpetual newness: "He liked to think of this city as the last American frontier."[6] By contrast, his wife Katherine resists newness. Having preferred that he "take one of those shabby jobs back East," she literally shudders at the plastic garishness and the indecorous confusion of the seasons in "awful" Los Angeles (pp. 5-11). The conflict between her Eastern preconceptions and his unthinking immersion in the westering myth produces a heavily ironic reversal, as both of them find their assumptions invalidated by experience. It is Paul who discovers that his California adventure brings only disappointment, disillusion, and estrangement from his wife and who finally retreats back East. In image of the overwhelming of his California dream by shabbiness, the city of Los Angeles, viewed from his departing airplane, "had disappeared into a bowl of smog" (p. 276). Katherine, on the other hand, so thoroughly reverses her earlier notions that she abandons her old self altogether. Remade from the repressed and whining character she possessed at the opening of the novel (disagreeable enough) into a shallow, unfeeling party-goer, she becomes an anonymous copy of hundreds of other California women, including movie starlets, as they are glimpsed in the novel, even to her hairdo, clothes, and sunglasses. Rather than founding a new home in California, the two have lost the inner "home" of their sense of identity. In an important bit of symbolic action, Paul fails even to recognize his wife at a party: "the girl, laughing at some joke that had been made, turned her face full in his direction. He realized that it was Katherine" (p. 274). Exploring their feelings for each other in the weeks before he leaves on his journey of return, he concludes that "even her voice had changed: it was. . . not Katherine's voice at all. Somehow his wife had disappeared" (p. 274). Their journey of home founding has modulated into a retreat for him and, for her, a vaguely realized readiness merely to fool around in California, to drift.

Lurie's *Nowhere City* is not finally a successful novel. The terms of its satire of the Los Angeles scene are too obvious and the import of this satire and the theme of personal metamorphosis too uncertain. For instance, it is difficult to say whether Katherine's change is for better or for worse. At the outset she is certainly an unsympathetic character; as the novel goes on she is probably the injured party and possibly the more open to discovery of the two; but at the end she has been remade into a lifeless plastic doll. This uncertainty is voiced explicitly in Paul's belief that "if she would only come back East with him. . .she would turn into herself again" and her reply, "Yes, I know. . . .That's what I'm afraid of" (p. 275). The reader can't be sure which would be better, because Lurie seems not to know either or possibly not to care. The significance of the book's structural pattern is equally elusive. Is Lurie saying that the old pioneering dream was an illusion, or only that it is now irrelevant? Or (with an involved business about Katherine's ugly heirloom furniture) that homing is a kind of stagnation? Or is she deploring a world in which home founding is impossible? If so, is it only "this phoney nowhere city" (p. 26) that thwarts modern pioneering, or is her satire a general indictment of modern America? The book does not afford answers to any of these questions. It offers a striking but finally uncertain parable of the lapse of America's traditional pioneering journey into a restless uncertainty.

Joan Didion's *Play It As It Lays* starts from a point of a less traditional action pattern than Lurie's but presents what is finally a more devastating, more inside, view of the Hollywood social world. It uses repeated images of cars and driving to suggest the nervous restlessness of a society lacking any stability or security. The central character of the book, Maria, is a minor movie actress who fears "empty sardine cans in the sink, vermouth bottles in the wastebaskets, slovenliness past the point of return"[7] and can forget her "dread" only when driving the Los Angeles freeways. She finds a fast lane and compulsively drives "the San Diego to the Harbor, the Harbor up to the Hollywood, the Hollywood to the Golden State, the Santa Monica, the Santa Ana, the Pasadena, the Ventura" (pp. 15-16). Driving the complicated interchanges allows her to focus her full attention on the road and forget the disorders of her life. Beyond this, she has no purpose in driving. Indeed, as she reminds herself repeatedly, no aspect of her life has any significance beyond itself. Accordingly, incidents lack continuity and her numerous parties, conversations with her agent and her former husband, and other contacts lead nowhere but to other inconsequential contacts. She arrives at a party with one person and leaves with another, a stranger, goes to bed with him, then steals his car for more aimless driving. Asked "what matters," she replies, "Nothing" (p. 202).

In the last chapter (or segment), she speaks from the mental institution where she guards her secret knowledge, which is to "know what 'nothing' means, and keep on playing" (p. 214). It is a circling ending, since the book had also begun with Maria's speaking directly to the reader from her asylum, explaining that "to look for 'reasons' is beside the point" since "NOTHING

APPLIES" (pp. 3-4). The action of the book essentially goes around in a circle in which we learn only that there is nothing to learn. (We, the readers, "learn" of course the felt impact of Maria's futility; we plumb it more fully than we can in an opening statement; but as far as the character herself is concerned, there is and can be no discovery.) The shape of the action is a cipher, just as Maria's circuitous, purposeless driving is a cipher; it means nothing beyond itself. Driving is a synecdoche of Hollywood life, which is itself, we surmise, a synecdoche of modern America. Here as in other novels, the journey of wandering contributes to the development of a bleak, essentially nihilistic world view in which maximum freedom (Maria is free to drive wherever she wants with whomever she wants) is actually the most abject bondage.

Another current writer who shares the concerns with the California scene, divorce from the past, and compulsive travelling that we have seen in these novels of Lurie and Didion is Larry McMurtry.[8] The theme of journeying as a symbol of departure from one's cultural roots runs throughout McMurtry's work. Widening spirals of wandering parallel widening breaches between his characters and their Texas past and indeed between McMurtry himself and his own roots in the West Texas ranch country. Starting with nostalgia for the old West and its heroic associations in his first novel, *Horseman, Pass By* (1961), he has increasingly turned for his material to urban scenes and rootless characters, until in his latest novel, *Somebody's Darling* (1978), the fictive world is Hollywood, the very epitome of rootlessness. A disaffection from any cultural heritage is manifest in the successively greater prominence of automobiles and circuitous, aimless wandering in McMurtry's novels. In *Terms of Endearment* (1975), one character literally lives in his car.

The youthful protagonists of McMurtry's two early novels, *Horseman* and *Leaving Cheyenne*, which chronicle the decline of the ranching tradition, keenly feel the urge to be off, to broaden their horizons. To them, journeying means adventure and initiation into the adult world. But this urge is tempered by an equally strong allegiance to values represented by their ranch homes and to the people—fathers or grandfathers—who have embodied those values. Only for characters who are identified with destructive change, specifically with the oil industry—Hud in *Horseman, Pass By* and Eddie in *Leaving Cheyenne*—is footloose journeying a way of life. These two characters are precursors of the wanderers in McMurtry's later novels.

In *The Last Picture Show*, the little town of Thalia has become a place to be escaped, and the dominant motivating force of all the main characters is restlessness. Sonny, another late-adolescent, who is the nearest in the book to being the central character, first appears in the opening chapter struggling to get his old pickup to run. It is a prophetic detail, for Sonny will never be able to escape. During the novel he and various other adolescents of Thalia travel to California, to Mexico, to Fort Worth, and continually back and forth between Thalia and Wichita Falls in their search for amusement. Even for athletic events their school team has to drive to towns "well over a hundred miles" away. Their circuitous travels, always ending in Thalia, are as futile as their frustrating sexual adventures, which typically occur in cars and trucks. Sonny, appropriately enough, earns pocket money driving a truck; he works for Frank Fartley, who, in a satirical thrust typical of McMurtry's earthy style, sells bottled gas.

By the end of the novel, a few of the young people have escaped, but Sonny, physically crippled by his past and emotionally dependent on an older woman, is left in dusty Thalia, inheritor of a pool hall and custodian of a mentally defective boy who had been cared for by Sonny's surrogate father. But Sonny is not allowed even the solace of continuing that protective role, for the boy is struck and killed by a cattle truck, the image of that tradition that in its passing has crushed those left behind. Sonny's last act is to start out of town in his truck, but finding nothing but emptiness all around, answering the emptiness within, he returns in fear. Doubly orphaned, he lacks a past that can provide him an identity and a role in his shabby present. The most visible sign of his regional heritage is the death dealing cattle truck. It is this lack of a meaningful past, present, or future that creates the restlessness increasingly evident in all McMurtry's adolescents. Lacking significant temporal orientations, they are thrown back onto a spatial search that is equally unsatisfactory because they are not equipped with the capacity to set goals or make distinctions. Thus they find all places much alike and much like Thalia; they wander.

In his next novels, *Moving On* and *All My Friends Are Going to Be Strangers*, McMurtry moves even further from the traditional cultural roots of his region. None of the characters in these two novels has any sense of a usable past, and none is purposefully directed toward the future. They inhabit the burgeoning cities of Texas with no apparent means of orienting themselves and nothing to engage them but endless, unsatisfying motion. They drive endlessly and pointlessly around the country, chiefly between Texas and California. The casts of characters in both novels are quite large, since as the main characters wander, seemingly for no particular reason, people drift into and out of their lives. Action develops in a pattern of encounter, involvement (often sexual), and estrangement. Danny Deck, for instance, narrator and hero of *All My Friends* is hopelessly subject to random emotional entanglements, all of which prove destructive as well as transient. He feels, he says, "dislodged" (p. 47), and stability in his personal relationships is as impossible to achieve as fixity in place.

None of the characters in either of these novels travels with fixed purpose; their wanderings are neither quests nor clearly motivated escapes. Rather, they travel out of a vague dissatisfaction with life as they find it and uncertainty as to what they want to do. When Jim of *Moving On* drives, not for the first time, to California, he suspects "almost the whole distance" that he is "going the wrong way" but cannot decide to turn back because "there was always a chance that the place he was looking for would appear somewhere ahead" (p. 643). Of course, it never does.

McMurtry's engagement with the California scene—which for him, as in the popular mind, is the epitome of transience—has culminated in his recent Hollywood novel *Somebody's Darling*. Once more the fictive world is a place of fleeting relationships and sporadic motion within which McMurtry affirms the value of personal commitments as the only source of order for people's lives. But in this nightmare version of the great California dream of American tradition, the characters depicted are so shallow, so fully occupied with fleeting amusements, that this potential principle of order is never fulfilled except momentarily.

McMurtry's use of the journey narrative, whether in passing incidents or overall stretches of action, as a structural principle places his work in the company of other serious fiction that allows social climate to be reflected and commented upon through both content and form. However, his extensive use of the journey of illusory freedom creates a serious formal problem. McMurtry's early novels were very neatly structured—perhaps, as he himself has suggested, too neatly structured. But as he moved away from their nostalgic subjects to treat contemporaneous materials, he began to construct his novels by what appears to be a principle of mere accretion. The four later novels, possibly excepting *Somebody's Darling*, lack cohesive form.[9] Perhaps he is suggesting that an art honestly treating the present-day social flux is foreordained to fragmentation. If so, he is offering a bleak aesthetic vision. The forms of his later novels are so perfectly imitative of the social flux he depicts and satirizes that they become dreary and unfocussed. The confusion of that world is not made into coherent art.

This sort of structural problem is in fact inherent in the use of the journey of wandering as a controlling narrative principle. Lacking the unifying emblems and motivations conventional in the quest and other traditional journey forms, or even the unifying satiric purpose of the loose picaresque, the journey of wandering offers little basis for structural cohesion. Narrative problems of emphasis and closure become particularly acute. In effect, this variant of the journey narrative may well be viewed not as a form but as a kind of antigenre, a principle of formal dissolution.

NOTES

1. F. Scott Fitzgerald, *Tender Is the Night* (1934; rpt. New York: Charles Scribner's Sons, 1951), p. 408.

2. Malcolm Cowley writes that the talented young Americans who survived the Great War were "not so much disillusioned as disaffiliated." *A Second Flowering: Works and Days of the Lost Generation* (New

York: Viking Press, 1973), p. 15. John W. Aldredge, in a review of Cowley's book in *Commentary*, 56, no. 5 (1973), 37-41, refers to the Lost Generation writers as being "physically so displaced—not only from home but from the past represented by home."

3. John Dos Passos, *Manhattan Transfer* (1925; rpt. Boston: Houghton Mifflin, 1953), p. 220.

4. Jack Kerouac, *On the Road* (1955; rpt. New York: Viking, 1959), p. 238.

5. Eudora Welty, *A Curtain of Green and Other Stories* (Garden City, N. Y.: Doubleday, Doran, & Co., 1941), p. 135.

6. Alison Lurie, *The Nowhere City* (New York: Coward-McCann Inc., 1965), p. 5.

7. Joan Didion, *Play It As It Lays* (New York: Farrar, Straus and Giroux, 1970), p. 16.

8. References to McMurtry's novels are to the following: *Horseman, Pass By* (New York: Harper, 1961); *Leaving Cheyenne* (New York: Harper & Row, 1963); *The Last Picture Show* (New York: Dial Press, 1966); *Moving On* (New York: Simon & Schuster, 1970); *All My Friends Are Going to Be Strangers* (New York: Simon & Schuster, 1972); *Terms of Endearment* (New York: Simon & Schuster, 1975); and *Somebody's Darling* (New York: Simon & Schuster, 1978).

9. In this last book, McMurtry has returned to the tripartite, three narrator scheme of *Leaving Cheyenne*, but without great success. In part this is because the characters are not strong enough to sustain the narrative focus he places on them, and in part because he attempts to impose so neat an external structure on so chaotic a fictive world. The two fail to cohere.

McMurtry himself has stated that he is more interested in textures than in structures. Reviewers, however, have complained of structural looseness. See, for example, Thomas Landess's review of *Moving On* in *Southwestern American Literature*, 1 (1971), 38-39, and William T. Pilkington's of *All My Friends Are Going to Be Strangers*, in the same journal, 2 (1972), 54-55.

II
DEPARTURES

7
The Profound Remove: Melville's *Clarel*

How can the prisoner reach outside except by thrusting through
   the wall?

—Herman Melville, *Moby-Dick*

Here is no water but only rock

—T. S. Eliot, *The Waste Land*

In recent years, scholars have agreed that *Clarel* is perhaps the
most unjustly neglected of Herman Melville's works and, especially since the appearance of Walter Bezanson's Introduction
to the Hendricks House edition in 1960, have been conducting
an energetic campaign of resurrection. Readers in general, however, have been content to let it lie. There is no doubt that *Clarel*
is a forbidding work that makes extreme demands on the reader's patience and attention. It is very long, especially for a verse
narrative, and its verse form (irregularly rhymed tetrameter) and
diction are often impediments to the success of the whole, though
at times they are brilliantly functional.[1] Nevertheless, *Clarel* is
probably, after *Moby-Dick* and "Bartleby the Scrivener," the single most important work in the Melville canon, both in its revelation of Melville's own state of mind in maturity and in its

complex and searching examination of its social and intellectual moment.[2]

As Newton Arvin remarks, it is "characteristic of Melville" that his characters should be "on the move."[3] *Clarel* both recapitulates and reshapes a long engagement with the journey narrative. From *Typee* on, with the notable exception of "Bartleby" alone among his genuinely important works, Melville utilized the journey as a symbolic action expressive of man's (mankind's, but also very specifically the male's) discovery of self and universe through venture and confrontation. Though his journeys are structurally varied, the form that most fully engaged his imagination was the quest.[4] *Clarel* reflects this engagement but demonstrates Melville's willingness to use other journey forms. If its closest affinity is with *Moby-Dick*'s quest for truth in an indifferent universe, it also recapitulates the allegorical voyage of education as it appears in *Redburn* and *White-Jacket*. The form of *Clarel* is complex in many ways. In addition to being a quest and a journey of education, *Clarel* is also an escape from the confusions of America and the bewilderments of academic study and an escape from the female and sexuality, to mention only the escape journey of Clarel himself.[5] At the same time, the poem describes a circular journey of futility. Like the Children of Israel, Clarel is lost in the wilderness.[6] Interwoven with all of these journey patterns, and perhaps basic to them all, is a shifting and to varying degrees ironic appropriation of the pilgrimage, the journey to a venerated place made from motives of devotion. As one critic has phrased it, *Clarel* is a "modern Canterbury pilgrimage made by victims of a faithless age."[7]

In Melville's day, the trip to Jerusalem and the surrounding Holy Land was well established as the chosen journey of those able to afford the pious veneer of a religious pilgrimage combined with the excitement of an adventure. Numerous popular memoirs and travel books produced by visitors to the Holy Land made the noted features of the area vicariously accessible to those who could not make the pilgrimage themselves. In Melville's journal of his own trip to Palestine, *Journal of a Visit to Europe and the Levant, October 11, 1856-May 6, 1857*, he followed the standard pattern of such memoirs by recording both his visual impressions and various meditative effusions triggered by the biblical associations of the places he visited. But beyond these predictable elements of the traveler's journal he included, as Bezanson phrases it, "explorations into the geography and events of his inner life."[8] The explorations made in these inner voyages, informed by a keen sense of the intellectual uncertainties and speculations of the age, carry over from the journal to *Clarel*. It is this willingness to elaborate upon the symbolic properties of the landscape and to extend them to their fullest intellectual ramifications that gives the work a complexity beyond that of its pilgrimage form. For the implications that Melville finds in his symbolic setting and structure of action undermine the assurances of the linear pilgrimage not only by transforming it from an approach to a known value into a search for an undetermined value, as in the quest, but actually by overthrowing its framework of assurance altogether and replacing it with uncertainty. The end-stopped pilgrimage form gives way to an open-ended spiral of possibility and doubt.

By superimposing an element of radical doubt upon the pilgrimage form, Melville created rich possibilities for irony. These possibilities had been anticipated in Mark Twain's ironic modulation of the pilgrimage published just seven years before the publication of *Clarel, The Innocents Abroad*. But where Twain's ironic treatment of the pilgrimage is predominantly comic and at times even flippant, Melville's irony is solemn and brooding. To borrow the excellently accurate phrasing of Kenneth Requa, appearing in a brief essay on *Clarel* entitled "The Pilgrim's Problems," Melville "more deeply and darkly than Mark Twain. . .contrasts the old religious certitudes with modern doubts," using the pilgrimage "ironically to reveal the quester's frustration."[9]

In its basic narrative line, the poem follows the journey of a young student, Clarel, who goes to the Holy Land in the hope of recovering his lost religious faith.[10] Taking that loss as a premise, the story begins with Clarel's arrival in Jerusalem. But the city is a place of barrenness, deadness, constriction; to Clarel, its religious shrines are not so much inspirational as merely shabby. Instead of a renewed faith, he finds in Jerusalem new motives for doubt.[11] Among residents of the city and other pilgrims like himself, he discovers a multiplicity of religious views, none of them fully convincing. The occasion for his exploration of these contending beliefs, doubts, and theories is an excursion down the Jordan to the Dead Sea, the monastery Mar Saba, Bethlehem, and back to Jerusalem, a standard tourist circuit on which he embarks because his new-found sweetheart, Ruth, is shut away from him in a ritual period of mourning for her father. Throughout his excursion, Clarel attempts to replace his waning spiritual and intellectual confidence with reliance upon love and the life of the affections. On his return, however, he finds that this alternative is closed to him; Ruth has died. This concluding event gives Clarel, not a discovery of the harsh facts of death and pain, for he has been aware of these all along, but a more pronounced and more personal sense of their impact. At the end, lacking answers, and lacking personal consolations, he is urged by the poet-narrator merely to persevere.

For Clarel, the journey of a few days is a "profound remove" (I.xliv.50) from questioning to settled doubt, from depression to gloom, from hopeful expectation of personal happiness to bereavement and loss of hope. Formally the poem itself is a "profound remove" from the pilgrimage tradition with which it begins to an idiosyncratic blending of symbolic narrative, character sketch, symposium, and verse essay, all strung on the linear structure of the journey. No one formal pattern adequately defines the form of the whole. *Clarel* is finally a meditative consideration of the social, intellectual, and emotional currents of a transitional time, developed through the intersection of several traditional narrative patterns, and presented in four structural divisions.

I

The first section, "Jerusalem," serves chiefly to introduce most of the major characters and to establish the somber emotional tone and the faith/doubt issue. Occupying a full quarter of the total length of the work, this first section is static and even diffuse in comparison to those that follow. Clarel's voyage from America to Palestine has occurred before it opens and the circuit out from Jerusalem and back does not begin until part two. Nevertheless, the journey as image-idea and as mode of experience is powerfully operative in part one, shaping our perceptions of the ensuing action in two chief ways: in Clarel's wandering of the city, and in the characterizing images and personal histories of the other characters.

Clarel himself is presented in terms of unsettlement, as one in transit. In the opening canto he sits in a room of an inn, beside his luggage, where "the dust lies, and on him as well—/ The dust of travel" (I.i.13-14). He has just experienced the excitement of landing (travellers to Palestine customarily entered at Jaffa by being ferried in rowboats from their ships) and has crossed the coastal plain, "Sharon's prairie land" (I.i.38), only to fall into depression upon entering the city:

> Like the ice-bastions round the Pole,
> Thy blank, blank towers, Jerusalem!
>
> (I.i.60-61)

He has hoped to shed his "cultivated narrowness" by leaving his collegiate "confinement" and roving "at last abroad among mankind" (I.i.103-110)—the spatial movement, of course, is figurative for the widening of mental horizons. But he finds himself wandering a prison-like city of blank walls and confined spaces, and lost in an equally confining figurative wilderness: "through brakes, lone brakes, I wind:/ As I advance they close behind" (I. ii.128-29). Disillusionment itself is a figurative shipwreck on "underformings in the mind" that suddenly become clear to the mental voyager on "time's vast sea":

> But little heed men that they wind
> Unseen, unheard—till lo, the reef—
> The reef and breaker, wreck and grief.
>
> (I.i.77-79)

Clarel hopes yet to avert that shipwreck. His inn is a figurative ship carrying its pilgrims over dark waters, and the Coptic Convent near the Church of the Holy Sepulcher, a lighthouse. But Clarel cannot find his way.

His sense of being lost and in search of something is heightened by a series of encounters in which the motif of long and generally fruitless voyage is continued. His first significant encounter is with the innkeeper, Abdon, a descendant of the Lost Tribes of Israel, a wanderer impelled by an unnamed personal loss to set his face toward Zion and death. (His tombstone is propped in one corner, ready for use.) The others that Clarel meets are also essentially displaced persons. Nehemiah, a devout millenialist first encountered near the Tomb, is a "wanderer" (I.xxiii.1). Because of his delusion, the old man feels himself at home in Jerusalem, but his house, appropriately enough, is beamed with "wreck-stuff from the Joppa strand" (I.xxii.30), and he breaks his bread with a "Crusoe air/ Of castaway on isle in sea" (I.xxii.65-66). Celio, a rebel against his received religion who has taken temporary refuge in a local monastery, identifies himself with the Wandering Jew of legend. Failing to communicate despite their spontaneous sense of kinship, Celio and Clarel are like ships foundering in a storm:

> Blue-lights sent up by ships forlorn
> Are answered oft but by the glare
> Of rockets from another, torn
> In the same gale's inclusive snare.

(I.xiii.1-4)

The storm is doubt. Though they might have weathered it together, they are denied that chance by Celio's death, and the two "ships" are parted:

> What speck is that so far away
> That wanes and wanes in waxing day?
> Is it the sail ye fain had spoken
> Last night when surges parted ye?
> But on, it is a boundless sea.

(I. xv 88-92)

Similarly, Nathan, the father of Ruth, is an American who has chosen to live in an alien land. Like his pilgrim forebears, Nathan had voyaged in search of a promised land but found that his ship had "erred, and on a wilderness" (I.xvii.6). The removal leaves his wife and daughter feeling permanently homeless. All of these wanderers and virtually all of the tourists encountered in the city approach Jerusalem in the expectation of some revelation or at any rate realization. However much their motives may vary, they are united in being far from home on a journey that they expect to be in some way momentous. But they endure the hardships of their long journeys for the sake of a vision which amounts finally to a mere "dizzying fable" in a "mummy land" (I.v. 221, 186).

Two pilgrims who will have particular importance for Clarel enter in the later cantos of the Jerusalem section. These are Vine and Rolfe, both Americans. Vine wanders about, observing and speculating. Rolfe, a figure of greater vitality, is by nature and by vocation a venturer:

> Trapper or pioneer
> He looked, astray in Judah's seat—
> Or one who might his business ply
> On waters under tropic sky.
>
> (I.xxxi.4-7)

As his hardy pioneer image suggests, Rolfe dares to pursue the challenges of conflicting and elusive possibilities. He predicts that mankind will never be content to wander but will always, in adverse moral weather, turn to the "haven" of "religion's ancient port" (I.xxxi.187-88). For himself, he will not turn into the easy port of received religion, yet still hopes for an answer: "Some lurking thing he hoped to gain" (I.xxxi.36). Thus all three— Rolfe, Clarel, and Vine—are "pilgrim men" (I.xxxi.298), travellers toward the sacred. But in an age of doubt, to be a genuine pilgrim means to be a searcher for uncertain, unlocated values. Whether the searchers will find their goal is impossible to say; Rolfe's story of the persistent mariner humbled by disaster suggests that the braver the search, the more savagely the voyager is rebuked by experience. Nevertheless, Rolfe persists in his own search, within a fictive world of dislocated travellers.

Rolfe's appearance in the narrative is so timed that he becomes a catalyst for the shift in Clarel's journey from a melancholy, peripatetic questioning to an active, strenuous search. It is this dramatic shift that gives coherent form to part one, which oth-

erwise becomes a mere tourist's guide to Jerusalem with inter-
polated character sketches. Seen from the vantage of the shift
in Clarel's journey, however, part one, though it certainly lacks
the dynamic force of the later books, is not without movement.
The apparent diffuseness in cantos i through xxx, preceding
Rolfe's appearance, springs from the great number of characters
introduced and from the circuitousness of Clarel's wanderings,
"slack and aimless" (I.v.45), about Jerusalem. These cantos,
however, function as a preparation or frame for Clarel's response
to Rolfe and his decision to reorient his journey by joining the
pilgrim excursion. From this point on, the narrative structure is
much tighter.

Melville stresses the traditional character of Clarel's sightseeing round in Jerusalem as he visits the usual sites of veneration.
But Clarel cannot feel himself a part of the tradition because he
is, as he imagines himself accused by the sounds of an overheard
liturgy, a "pilgrim-infidel" (I.vi.19). Traversing an allegorical
landscape of ruin and barrenness as a wanderer "without a
guide" (I.vii.79), he is "from joy debarred" (I.x.18). The dead
quality of the setting and the circularity of his aimless tour accurately reflect his condition of unresolved and reluctant doubt,
a state of spiritual aridity or lassitude. So long as he remains in
this state, neither breaking out of his vague scepticism nor pursuing its ramifications to some more boldly formulated position,
he is, in effect, merely wandering in dreary circles spiritually,
just as he is physically. He must, Melville urges, "migrate," take
a direction:

> . . . shall Clarel too
> Launch o'er *his* gulf, e'en Doubt, and woo
> Remote conclusions?
>
> (I.xli.76-78)

It is the example of the freely wayfaring Rolfe and the opportunity of the wider tour that give Clarel the impetus for a linear
movement beyond the limits of his indeterminate circling. If his
bolder migration is finally only another circle, it is nevertheless
a circle that includes more ground of investigation and deeper
self-knowledge. Part one ends with the narrator's assurance that

the tour of only a "brief term of days" will nevertheless be a "profound remove" (I.xliv.50).

II

In part two, "The Wilderness," Clarel and a party of other pilgrims leave Jerusalem on their tour. This thirty-nine canto section will take them northeast almost to Jericho, then southeast and sharply south to the shore of the Dead Sea, in all a distance of about thirty miles. With pauses and overnight stops, it takes them three days and three nights. The leisurely pace of travel here—somewhat, but not markedly, slowed from the typical tourist pace—allows Melville to make full use of the receptiveness of the road narrative form to extraneous matter. The sense of ongoing linear movement, of a literal journey, is easily maintained with intermittent references to the horses, the road itself, pauses for rest, and so on, leaving the bulk of the narrative for the "incidental" conversations and descriptions that are its real emphasis.

The entire sequence, of course, had its immediate source in Melville's own tour and journal. But it also bears the imprint of two powerful literary precursors, the Canterbury Tales specifically, representing the pilgrimage form in general, and the mythic archetype of the night journey or descent into hell. At different levels, the narrative moves within both traditions, and it is by playing one against the other that Melville creates the powerful ironies of part two.

The parallel with the Canterbury Tales is signalled in the opening lines of the first canto, as the "mounted pilgrims" ride out from Jerusalem. Melville explicitly invites us to consider the similarity but at the same time insists that these pilgrims are different:

> Not from brave Chaucer's Tabard Inn
> They pictured wend; scarce shall they win
> Fair Kent, and Canterbury ken;
> Not franklin, squire, nor morris-dance
> Of wit and story good as then:

Another age, and other men,
And life an unfulfilled romance.

(II.i.7-13)

Life is now, he says, impoverished to the point that the similarity
to glorious precedents is only tantalizing, not fulfilled in reality.
Yet he continues to invite our consideration of the parallel by
repeated use of the words "pilgrim" and "pilgrimage" and by
structural parallels such as the introductory character sketches of
the first canto. In these sketches, the travelling party emerge with
a variousness and universality like that of Chaucer's band of pilgrims and with a similar range of motives for making the journey.
But it will be evident in the following cantos that they are shrunk
from their Chaucerian models. The sensualists of the party, the
banker and his prospective son-in-law, are not so much licentious
as merely frivolous; the men of religion are neither staunch de-
fenders of the faith nor scoundrels, but merely a Pollyanna of the
cloth (Derwent) and a deluded old man (Nehemiah).

The usefulness of the parallel with the *Canterbury Tales* lies in
its many possibilities for irony. Once the parallel is drawn, it
can be maintained with little effort, and the reader continues to
entertain comparisons that turn into contrasts. The term pilgrimage, raising the possibility that the present journey should
be regarded as a traditional religious pilgrimage, is itself invoked
in order to be undercut. The "pilgrims" of *Clarel* ride out toward
some of the most fully foreknown, fully revered place symbols
of Christianity, places central to the faith, places that have provided inspiration to devout pilgrims for centuries. But these are
not, in any effective sense, devout pilgrims, even if some of
them wish they could be. The modern loss of faith, whatever
its cause (and Melville explores many causes as well as many
kinds of loss), has drained these spiritual shrines of their power,
so that they can now draw pilgrims only through empty custom,
a nostalgic wish for recovery of viable faith, or mere tourist
curiosity. An additional and considerably more subtle irony arises
from the travellers' actual pattern of movement. In setting out
on a "pilgrimage" that will take them to one of the two most
hallowed places of Christianity, the site of the Nativity, they are
leaving behind the other of the two, the Holy Sepulcher. They

are in effect moving backward from the culmination of the Gospel narrative to its beginning, as if groping for ever more distant roots. The implication is that this theologically culminating symbol of redemption has already proven inefficacious for them and that their essentially regressive pilgrimage is thus likely to prove futile.

The archetype of the night journey, however, is not ironic but directly and fully referent as a shaping tradition. It provides a tradition, a shape both from literature and from mythic experience, that expands and enriches the significance of the literal narrative. Essentially, the journey begins as a pilgrimage and grows into a "night journey" of confrontation with the forces of the underworld, both outer and inner. The transition, with the consequent interplay of the two forms, intensifies both the irony and the darker implications of the journey.

It is primarily the landscape itself, both as visual reality and as symbol, that allows Melville to transform his pilgrimage into a darker journey. The circuit made by Clarel and his party as they approach Jericho and the Dead Sea takes them through a wilderness not only in the sense of a relatively uninhabited or "wild" area but, especially as they cross the Siddim Plain near the Sea, in the sense of natural desolation, absence of life and fertility. Melville, like other visitors to the area, noted in his journal the region's "bleached" barrenness; it was a "desert," a *"mouldy* plain" encrusted with a "whitish mildew" like "leprosy" or an "encrustation of curses." "Nought grows," he commented, "but wiry, prickly bush."[12] The element of disease in his description indicates the sense of many visitors that the desolation of the place was so extreme as to be virtually unnatural. An almost superstitious recollection of the cities of this plain, Sodom and Gomorrah, appears to have colored the responses of most nineteenth-century vistors.[13] This sense of the unnatural colors Melville's journal description, which terms the area "black and funereal," "diabolical," the "Gate of Hell" (pp. 134-35). The actual landscape, then, very readily lends itself to development as a symbol of spiritual decay or aridity. Further, the hellish quality Melville found in the scene is sustained by the fact that travel from Jerusalem to the Dead Sea involves a dramatic and evidently oppressive descent. The archetype of descent to an underworld conceived as being literally *under* the plane of life finds here a peculiarly appropriate representation. Dominating the landscape at the lowest point of this long and symbolically appropriate descent is the Dead Sea. Accordingly, all through this section the travellers' conversations and the narrator's account as well are dominated by an awareness of death, both actual and metaphorical.

After the opening canto, establishing the "Cavalcade" of characters, a brief second canto poses, as a comic foil to the somber journey to follow, a glimpse of the frivolous Glaucon, the rich banker's prospective son-in-law, who sings a praise of pink ribbons and pretty girls. By his light heart, his "folly," Glaucon is qualified to be "good against the melancholy" (II.ii.35) but disqualified for any adequate response to the first stopping point, the Garden of Gethsemane. Here the pilgrims are on "the Mount of God," within sight of Jerusalem and with a view of the Dead Sea. Response to this richly significant landscape becomes at once a touchstone of character: Glaucon babbles about souvenirs, the banker refuses to hear any reference to death or the Dead Sea, Derwent reinterprets all solemn facts so as to make them reassuring, Mortmain (the hand of death) focuses on destruction and despair, and Clarel broods. Mounting, they follow the road to Bethany and the Adommin glen, the scene of the Good Samaritan story. The narrative, however, does not emphasize the Samaritan's mercy but a quality of threat in the landscape, which still provides a perfect ambush point for brigands. It is indeed a figurative hell—like "Acheron/Run dry" (II.ix.10-11).

The sense of a descent into despair, death, and hell intensifies as the party moves deeper—in both a horizontal and a vertical sense—into the Dead Sea region. Allegorically, they have entered a realm of open possibility. Though it is a hell, a place of death, the fact that the desert has traditionally been a place of withdrawal for meditation and purification gives it the potential for blessing:

> Waste places are where yet is given
> A charm, a beauty from the heaven

Above them, and clear air divine. . .

(II.xi.21-23)

This indeterminacy is itself oppressive:

> . . . forever floats
> Over all desert places known,
> Mysterious doubt—an awful one.

(II.xi.14-16)

The desert's openness of possibility allows Melville to pose it as the thematic equivalent of the ocean setting in *Moby-Dick*.[14] It is a realm of radical freedom and radical ambiguity:

> men here adore this ground
> Which doom hath smitten. 'Tis a land
> Direful yet holy—blest though banned.
>
> But to pure hearts it yields no fear;
> And John, he found wild honey here.

(II.xi.92-96)

More often, however, it yields desolation. The pilgrims will see a rainbow, an image of hope, but only the demented Nehemiah will find "honey" in the acrid Dead Sea water.

In Canto xii, all feel oppressed by the desolate landscape and sultry weather, and the entire party will either confront doubt or be revealed as unequal to the call of confrontation. Melville as narrator reminds us that the Kedron ravine winds through here (Kedron meaning either "anguish hard on death," as he poetically has it, or literally black, as Bezanson notes); without qualification, he labels the region a "rival" to Erebus, a "caked, depopulated hell" (II.xi.69-72). The sense of desolation forces the travellers apart to their separate confrontations; they ride "through solitudes" (II. xiii.44), "o'ercast,/ Estranged" (II.xiv.51-52). The frivolous Greeks (the banker and Glaucon) turn back. Mortmain, already obsessed by gloom, turns away from the party for his own descent into a hell both of self and of place, resolving to spend the night alone in the shadow of Quarantania, the Mount of Temptation. He will reappear on the shore of the Sea, utterly set apart by whatever vision has come to him in the "black dens" of the desolate ridges, and will seal his commitment to death in a symbolic communion, a taste of the bitter water.

In the meantime, while Mortmain is absent, the other characters experience their confrontations in a series of conversational exchanges. Released by darkness from the constraint of their daytime selves, they are able to explore issues and anxieties that they usually skirt. For instance, during their first night in the desert, they sit talking about the biblical associations of the place and proceed to a discussion of how intermingled are fact and fiction—even, that is, in Scripture. Nehemiah, however, is asleep to such questions; he literally goes to sleep. Derwent, equally inadequate to the rigors of darker explorations, persistently turns the conversation aside from sterner speculation to sentimental effusions. Readiness to participate in the night journey of confrontation becomes a test of character by which both of them, like the Greeks who turned back earlier, are found wanting. Indeed, no one in the party survives the test unscathed; they are all flawed in their own ways. But for the more admirable characters—Clarel himself, Rolfe, and Vine—the withdrawal to the desert is not a retreat but a strategy of reduction to essences. Here in the desert, where the accidents and distractions of society are sloughed off, they can ask the important questions. They explore the dimensions of religious faith and doubt in the post-Darwinian world. As so often is true for Melville, their free inquiry is associated with images of travelling or voyaging. But by that standard, too, the modern world has declined, since instead of the "primal band/ Of gipsy Christians" (II.xxi.78-79) in the early centuries, we see a divided, uncertain group of doubters encamped in a wasteland.

After a second night at Jericho, they ride on toward the Jordan, then turn south along the river to the Dead Sea. The deeper descent and nearer approach to the emblematic Sea takes them into deeper depression and confrontations with death. The day begins with mist, then a "vaporous rain" that conveys premonitions of disaster (II.xxiii.31). Mortmain's horse, being led by one of the others, ominously breaks away in sudden panic just before a band of armed Bedouins appears, threatening death. After the Bedouins accept a tribute of gunpowder and depart, the pilgrims pause beside the Jordan, where the "halcyon Teacher waded in with John" (II.xxiii.197), to rest. Here they sing a hymn and converse with another pilgrim, a Dominican friar who urges the necessity of maintaining religion in its traditional structures. The devotional interlude, however, amounts to nothing more than a "transient, an esthetic glow" (II.xxiv.63). It is the last companionable moment before the party moves out onto the Siddim Plain on their journey through hell, introduced with references to the Styx and "Pluto's park" (II.xxviii.1). It is a world of distorted topography, "pale hollows foully smeared" (II.xxviii.19), and blighted vegetation, the shrivelled Apples of Sodom. Even the fresh palms broken beside the Jordan are withered by the "bitter mist" (II.xxviii.42), and as soon as this happens the pilgrims catch sight of the Dead Sea, the lowest depth of their natural hell.

Arriving at the shore of the Sea, they look for Mortmain and settle down to wait and talk. Once again they circle the questions of faith and doubt, hope and despair, each taking his customary position and testing it by reference to both the desolate scene itself and a splendid rainbow that momentarily appears as a promise of a redeemed world, "a world made new" (II.xxix.128). Margoth, the scientific sceptic, mocks at all superstitions and customs alike; Nehemiah retreats in memory to a world of bucolic simplicity; ambiguous Vine first responds, then jests; Derwent avows confidence that the rainbow means "the rose upon the coffin lies" (II.xxix.151); Clarel longs for personal consolation but fears the worst. The rainbow vanishes, and they are left in a "dumb dejection" (II.xxix.17) confronting the sea, the image of corruption and death. Only Rolfe is willing to state openly and frankly the "ominous. . .horrible" quality they all feel in the scene, thus proving his fully informed courage in contrast to Nehemiah, who, because he is ignorant and deluded, sleeps blissfully and heedlessly under a "crag's impending block" (II.xxxi.89).

They find a camping place along the shore and wait for Mortmain, who silently appears just at dusk. He launches into a tirade on contemporary evils and the need for repentance, then stoops and tastes the bitter water despite the guide's warning that "never from thy heart shall haste/ The Marah—yea, the after-taste" (II.xxxiv.62-63). Like Persephone, who ate in Pluto's kingdom and was forever doomed to spend part of the year in the underworld, Mortmain has communed with hell and now can never escape it.

After Mortmain's dramatic gesture of communion, there is a one-canto pause, "Prelusive," which heightens suspense before the climactic night cantos on the shore. In this well-timed meditative pause, Melville once again indicates the inward focus of his outward journey, directing the reader's attention to the labyrinthine quality of the human heart, as projected by Piranesi in his engravings of shadowy, winding ruins. The implication is clear to all except those who, retaining "childhood's illusion" (II.xxxv.39), turn aside from the truth: like Piranesi's prints, Melville's spatial projections convey a nightmare truth. After this preamble, there follow several tableaux set by the Sea during the night, short dramatized scenes reminiscent of the "staged" chapters of *Moby-Dick*. First Mortmain, sitting on a camel's skull, gives a meditation on complex evil, or nominally on the sins of the Cities of the Plain, which according to legend are submerged in the poisonous water:

> . . .those malefactors stood
> Guilty of sins scarce scored as crimes
> In any statute known, or code—
> Nor now, nor in the former times:
> Things hard to prove: decorum's wile,
> Malice discreet, judicious guile;
> Good done with ill intent—reversed;
> Best deeds designed to serve the worst;
> And hate which under life's fair hue
> Prowls like the shark in sunned Pacific blue.
>
> (II.xxxvi.30-39)

The passage states, in as precise a way as any he ever wrote, Melville's view of the ambiguous quality of moral evil. It is this ambiguity that oppresses Mortmain. Transfixed by the baffling complexity of evil, he cannot see the even greater complexity of evil intermingled with good. Therefore, his vision is distorted, as blighted as the landscape. But if he is monomaniacal, he is at any rate stubborn in his refusal to evade what he sees as truth. It is this refusal that makes Mortmain, in contrast, say to Derwent, one of the heroes of the poem, though not one of its wisest heroes. Rolfe, who is one of the wise, sees both Mortmain's extremism and the heightened sensitivity which is its probable source:

> . . ."If mad,
> 'Tis indignation at the bad,"
> Said Rolfe; "most men somehow get used
> To seeing evil, though not all
> They see; 'tis sympathetical;
> But never some are disabused
> Of first impressions which appal."
>
> (II.xxxvii.55-61)

In his usual way, Derwent turns this acute characterization aside by dropping a vague hope for redemption of all and changing the subject.

After all the party have given up conversation and gone to bed, old Nehemiah wakes and, imagining the City of God to have descended to the water rather than the doomed cities to have, in effect, risen from it, walks into the sea and drowns. Totally disoriented, displacing reality with delusion and even in his delusion confusing evil with good, he pursues the ancient hope that death (the sea) is to be transformed into resurrected life (his vision of the transfigured city set among pure streams and centered around the sacred totem of the fleece from the lamb). In his delusion, all pain and evil are vanquished, and a "great voice" invites him into paradise:

> *Pain is no more, no more is death;*
> *I wipe away all tears: Come, ye,*
> *Enter, it is eternity.*
>
> (II.xxxviii.29-31)

Clearly, to imagine that such a paradise exists in this world is to invite disaster; it is as futile and as hazardous as preaching mercy to sharks in their feeding frenzy, as in *Moby-Dick*. The happy delusion beckons foolish old Nehemiah away to the bitter waters, no Jordan to cross to the great beyond but in fact a sunken pit of perdition. His corpse, found by the others in the morning, is the very image of death itself: pale, bleached by the salt and mineral deposits, surrounded by none of the customary trappings that hint at comfort and sleep, but instead by the Dead Sea.

The section ends with two natural manifestations marking Nehemiah's burial, a violent avalanche and a fogbow, a "counter object" (II.xxxix.151), perhaps, but evanescent, indicating the fragility of hope. At this point the descent into hell, the night journey *through* a natural and spiritual hell, is complete. The remaining journey will be, in its overall contours, ascending, but will continue to display motifs of descent and, more emphatically, of circularity, so that the underworld is never entirely transcended or left behind.

III

Part three, "Mar Saba," is essentially a pause in the journey, less clearly shaped than what has gone before by the dynamic pattern of the journey of search. However, part three presents the culminations of two motifs that characterize the physical movement of *Clarel* as a whole, an insistence on vertical motion and a contrast between memories of a verdant natural world and the present passage through the desert.

From the opening cantos of part one, patterns of physical movement are markedly halting and constrained, with emphasis on the rugged hilliness of the region, the narrowness and difficulty of paths, the sheerness of ascents and descents, and the pervasive presence of stone walls, both natural and man-made. Joseph G. Knapp, observing this halting, confined quality of motion, comments that part one follows "not the horizontal motion that denotes progression but rather a disconcerting up-and-down motion," and adds that in part two the "strange verticality of motion continues."[15] What is emphasized in part one, however, is not so much the ascending and descending of parapets and heights as the horizontal circularity of Clarel's wandering in the city. In part two as well, the significant pattern is not so much up and down as a steady descent to the Dead Sea. Even so, Knapp is correct in noting that a pattern of verticality begins in part one and gains significance in part two. In part three, verticality becomes the controlling physical pattern, while the pattern of winding circularity, which will reach its culmination in part four, is virtually suspended.

At the beginning of part three, the pilgrims ascend from the low point of their journey, approximating the lowest circle of hell, to the "high desert" of the arid uplands, where they will enter Mar Saba through its upper gate. This arid ridge, like the lower desert, is a morally ambiguous realm, lacking any defined quality except its very vacancy and disorder:

> Judah's main ridge, which horrors deaden—
> Where Chaos holds the wilds in pawn,
> As here had happed an Armageddon,
> Betwixt the good and ill a fray,
> But ending in a battle drawn,
> Victory undetermined.
>
> (III.i.40-45)

In this indeterminate space, overlooking the natural hell of the Siddim Plain but removed from it, the travellers pause and vainly debate the undefined religious character of the times, the ebbing of Christian faith and the impossibility of knowing what the ultimate outcome will be or what its effect on mankind:

> In one result whereto we tend
> Shall Science disappoint the hope,
> Yea, to confound us in the end,
> New doors to superstition ope?
> As years, as years and annals grow,
> And action and reaction vie,
> And never men attain, but know
> How waves on waves forever die;
> Does all more enigmatic show?
>
> (III.v.159-167)

Clarel himself is oppressed ("ungladdened") by the uncertainty, and Vine, whom he wants to admire and to know better, merely sits and throws rocks at his own shadow, taking no side in the debate. After long and inconclusive talk of doubt and of the desert-like austerities of the Judaic and Christian religions, the travellers hear the bells of Mar Saba, summoning them from desert (doubt, dispute) to refuge (a fortress of religion).

The fact that the pilgrims *ascend* to Mar Saba would seem to indicate its superiority to the depths they are leaving behind, the nearness of Mar Saba to heaven. Yet the pattern of vertical motion and relative height is more ambiguous than that. On the heights, just as in the depths, the travellers continue to en-counter reminders of death, both before and after they enter the actual monastery. They find that Mar Saba itself is not entirely situated on the heights but "soars" in winding layers from the "profound" Kedron ravine to the mountain top, so that those entering the lower gate "mount from Erebus to light" (III.x.14). Because of its comparative elevation and because it offers a pause after the Dead Sea hell, Mar Saba can well be regarded, as many critics have seen it, as the Purgatorio of a Dantean spiritual universe.[16] The parallel is somewhat misleading, however, since the monastery itself serves as a kind of microcosm, a brief, styl-ized restatement of the entire moral span.[17]

Together with two seafarers and a soldier of fortune, the pil-grims range up and down the levels of the monastery, discov-ering both its spirituality and its flaws (an insane hermit, a blind and slothful abbot). Their emotions range from frivolous re-velling, when they pass around the bottle as freely as they do songs and jokes, to "unaffected joy" in the beauty of the desert sunrise (III.xxi.36), to their separate despondencies. Their own moments of despair are mirrored in a masque of the Wandering Jew, "cut off. . .made separate" from all humanity and inhab-iting "the perilous outpost of the sane" verging on insanity (III.xix.61, 99). On the following day, separate and, except for Derwent, introspective, they make again a descent to the depths, the base of the Kedron, and climb back up the stone track, peering into a series of natural hollows or cells along the way and pausing to make their responses to the one green thing in the scene, a palm tree growing just midway (that is, at the consoling, human level) between the depths and the heights.

The main characters' responses to the emblematic palm are presented in a stylized tableau reminiscent (as virtually every critic writing on *Clarel* has noted) of the doubloon scene in *Moby-Dick*. The sequence draws together a series of references to a green bucolic world—often explicitly to rural America—beginning in part one. Such references at times indicate a lost Eden and at times a wishful evasion of truth, but in every instance it is desolation that is real, not the green world and the vitality it symbolizes. (One implication of the contrast, since the green world is repeatedly linked with America, is that the New World itself, like the world of simple religious faith, is now an opportunity lost, an Eden from which the characters of the poem are shut out.) This emblematic contrast of green memories with the bleak desert landscape culminates in the image of the green palm, growing from a crevasse in the dry rock on the side of a cliff, a ready symbol of Christianity as well as of natural vitality and succor. As they respond to this symbol, all of the major characters except Clarel reach the culmination of their development.

Derwent catches sight of the palm while ascending from the "hell" of the Kedron floor. He has made the descent with a shallow levity, confirming the self-revelation made in his complaint to Clarel, "Alas, too deep you dive" (III.xxi.312). As we have seen, Derwent characteristically turns aside from stringent realizations; in visiting an inner chamber of the monastery, for instance, a "place for discipline and grief," his "tarry" had been "brief" (III.xxii.17-18). Accordingly, his response to the palm is the most trifling of the five. He finds it "fair," wishes it may stand for a "millenium," and passes on.

Vine laments (in tones sounding much like Hawthorne) the isolation that he himself has caused—"And is it I. . .that leave the others,/ Or do they leave me?" (III.xxvi.9-11)—and confesses his affinity for the past:

> For my part, I but love the past—
> The further back the better; yes,
> In the past is the true blessedness;

> The future's ever overcast—
> The present aye plebian.
>
> (III.xxvi.15-19)

A man who prefers the past is shielded, of course, from demands for commitment or frank response. Vine, then, claims to yearn for human friendship, the "magnetic chain" of brotherhood, but evades the emotional commitment it entails, just as Melville believed Hawthorne to have evaded commitment to their friendship. He is essentially dishonest with himself. Vine's response to the palm is shaped by the same emotional evasiveness: he tells himself that he will merely "try an invocation" to the palm in order to "pass the time." He reveals his longing for "dreams of Eden," his fear of death, and a sense of historical decline from something like the Golden Age. But his address is finally just that: an address, a formal apostrophe. Cast in coolly formal, elegant verse, itself a kind of insulation from the concerns he is actually voicing, his response to the tree becomes an aesthetic gesture.

In contrast, both Mortmain and Rolfe address the tree in outcries of personal grief. Mortmain has just voiced a meditation on the personal torment of those who would "cling to His tree, and there find hope" (III.xxviii.13) but are prevented by temperament or by the "curse" of "knowledge." A challenge from a mad recluse, Cyril, brings a revealing encounter:

> . . .He heard,
> Looked up, and answered, "Well?" "The word!"
> "*Hope*," in derision. "Stand, delay:
> That was the pass-word for yesterday."
> "*Despair*." "Advance."
>
> (III.xxviii.30-34)

The two sequences together reveal Mortmain's state of mind as he approaches "the Tree," which to him is a "holy Palm" reminiscent of the lily carried by Gabriel when he announced to Mary the coming incarnation. Recognizing that the tree is a powerful symbol of the divine consolation he has never found in life, he appeals to it for the ultimate solace:

When the last light shall fade from me,
If, groping round, no hand I meet;
Thee I'll recall—invoke thee, Palm:
Comfort me then, thou Paraclete!
The lull late mine beneath thy lee,
Then, then renew, and seal the calm.

(III.xxviii.89-94)

Rolfe similarly expresses his deepest concerns as he invokes the tree. For him it is a symbol, not of the possibility of hope, but of the loss of Eden, "Puck's substantiated scene" (III.xxix.62) in the South Seas. Rolfe's reminiscences of his own South Sea idyl may be foolish, in a sense, but are not a mere indulgence of escapism, for they involve also an intense self-accusation, a recognition of personal responsibility. He does not merely wish for a lost bliss, but blames himself for losing it:

But who so feels the stars annoy,
Upbraiding him—how far astray!—
That he abjures the simple joy,
And hurries over the briny world away?
Renouncer! is it Adam's flight
Without compulsion or the sin?
And shall the vale avenge the slight
By haunting thee in hours thou yet shall win?

(III.xxix.73-80)

At last Clarel approaches the palm. A monk standing on the level just below the tree and feeding doves from his hands represents for him the best in Christianity, in contrast to the Classical world of "Venus' court/ Voluptuous with wanton wreath" (III.xxx.65-66). The scene is fitly ruled not by the myrtle tree sacred to Venus "but sole the Palm," the "martyr's scepter" (III.xxx.69, 72). Still, however intensely he responds to the integrity and serenity of the monk's life, Clarel is preoccupied with Ruth, and he voices to the monk his reservations about the loneliness of monastic life. For reply, he is given a book containing a misogynist tract and hymns in praise of "the vowed life austere," the "pure desert of the will/ Chastised" (III.xxx.123-24). This, too, is a plausible and very traditional view of the desert as a place of purgation and purity. But the poem as a whole undermines that view, showing the desert instead as a place of death and punishment and supporting the warmer human emotions more than the life of withdrawal and renunciation.

Looking down, Clarel sees in one vista Mortmain, Vine, and Rolfe, all looking at the palm tree. It is one of the obviously important moments in the poem, but the import is left unclarified. Henry Wells in effect throws up his hands before what he is certain is the profundity here: "Even in many pages it would be impossible to analyze in this fugue-like passage the nuances of the poet's symbolism."[18] Merlin Bowen finds an absolute unriddling significance in the placement of the three characters, Vine at the highest level because of his stoicism, Mortmain higher than Rolfe because he has just freed himself from regret, and Rolfe on a ledge far down toward the ravine because of his "inability to aspire beyond the natural" and his "nostalgic preoccupation with an outgrown life."[19] But Bowen's reading attributes a greater wisdom to Vine's coolness than Melville himself gives it and ignores the ambiguity of height and depth in Melville's world. Depth may indicate either a descent to hell, as in part two, or "diving," always a positive term for Melville, indicating something like plumbing the depths of meaning. The placement of Rolfe at the lowest point, then, may indicate either negative or positive judgment. At any rate, he, like Mortmain but unlike Vine, has looked within and pronounced judgment on his own moral responsibility.

This characteristic ambiguity in Melville's presentation of the symbolic setting finally disallows so schematic an interpretation as Bowen's. What is most important here is that Clarel is at the top, not because he is superior to the others, but because from that vantage he can *see* them. It is left to Clarel to sort through the three "messages" of their characters as he can best understand them and to find his own truth. But at this point in the poem (as, indeed, at its end) he is unable to arrive at that truth. The need to do so provides the impetus for the final state of the journey.

In the final canto of part three, the pilgrims, led by Clarel, find Mortmain dead, still facing the palm. Part three, then, like part two (and indeed, though it is not structured quite so dramatically, like part one), ends in an encounter with death and the renewal of the journey of search.

IV

The final section, "Bethlehem," demonstrates the futility of the traditional pilgrimage in the post-Darwinian age of technology and scepticism. This last phase of Clarel's journey, from Mar Saba to Bethlehem and then back to Jerusalem, completes the circle that the pilgrims' route has described. It is not a circle of completeness, but a circle of emptiness, a cipher. Nevertheless, Melville concludes with an affirmation of the pilgrim mentality.

At the end of the journey Clarel is no nearer an answer to his religious questions than he was at its beginning. Indeed, the fact that he is still following a doubtful road toward no clearly defined goal is presented at the key to part four (and indeed, as we see in the final narrative canto, the key to the entire work). Melville, speaking in his own person, offers this key in the opening lines of the first canto of part four by posing a contrast between his travellers and those earlier travellers also bound for Bethlehem, the scriptural Three Kings or Wise Men:

> They failed not, for a light was given—
> The light and pilotage of heaven:
> A light, a lead, no longer won
> By any, now, who seekers are:
> Or fable is it? but if none,
> Let men lament the foundered Star.
>
> (IV.i.13-18)

Again in Bethlehem, as in Jerusalem, the travellers view the sacred shrines with a sceptical eye; Melville implies that no other response is possible to intelligent modern men. More devastating for Clarel himself, however, is the continuing indeterminacy of debate among the pilgrims. They have talked their way through the trip, going over variations of the same issues again and again, and still no one position emerges as the most credible, most viable position. Clarel is as divided in mind as ever. In fact, he is more so, since new personages are now added who restate some of the old arguments and add new ones.

One of the three significant new characters is Agath the timoneer, who was introduced in part three but first gains powerful dramatic import in part four. In the first canto, as all pause on a high ridge, Agath sights Jerusalem in the distance and calls out, "Wreck, ho! the wreck—Jerusalem!" (IV.i.191). It is one of the genuinely memorable lines in the work, and serves to draw together the imagery of aridity, rubble, decay, and deadness associated with the city throughout. Although Agath is tattooed with the Jerusalem Ensign of the Crusaders, it is contrast rather than similarity that is conveyed by the sign, since Jerusalem is now only a "Stony metropolis of stones" (IV.ii.12). Its apocalyptic namesake, too, the New Jerusalem, is perhaps defunct:

> . . .Gleam
> No more, like Monte Rosa's height,
> Thy towers, O New Jerusalem?
> To Patmos now may visions steal?
> Lone crag where lone the ospreys wheel!
>
> (IV.ii.18-22)

Jerusalem reminds Agath of the death-like Galapagos Islands, where the giant tortoises make their life "pilgrimage" for "a hundred years of pain" (IV. iii.87-88). He is himself the relic of a life of pain and disaster, so worn that he cries out at the sight of a scorpion, but at least he survives. It is that quality, his stubborn survival, that is his lesson for Clarel and his importance as a moral symbol.

Part four also brings Clarel into confrontation with Ungar, a former officer in the Confederate Army, embittered by defeat, who restates Mortmain's argument that the world is in decay and disorder. Indeed, Ungar adds cogency to the pessimistic view because he is less distraught than Mortmain had been and is able to draw more fully on evidence from social history. Also, he adds to his pessimistic view a religious certainty that Mortmain had lacked, and thus, though he has a less comprehensive sensibility and a less open mind than his predecessor, he has a keener pertinence to Clarel's problem. Ungar's debates with Derwent and Rolfe during their stay in Bethlehem exacerbate Clarel's sense of being torn by conflicting views, all of them partly feasible and none altogether tenable.

Last, during the one night spent in Bethlehem, Clarel encounters a young man called merely "the Lyonese" and described as "a prodigal," whose impact is out of all proportion to his intellectual force or the length of their acquaintance. In contrast to Clarel's, the "pilgrimage" of the Lyonese is "casual" (IV.xxvi.11). He simply refuses to engage in speculation or debate; he disavows all concern with religious matters. What the Lyonese offers, then, is a possibility Clarel has not previously entertained, that of self-indulgence and unconcern.

Various commentators on the poem have seen the incident of the Lyonese as a revelation of a suppressed strain of homoeroticism or at any rate confusion in sexuality on Clarel's part. Certainly Clarel's response to the prodigal young man's faintly lascivious conversation and comely physique are surprisingly strong. He dreams that he is being offered a choice between a lush Persian setting, representing sensuality, and a desert of purity, and is held back by "clasping arms" (IV. xxvi.316) when he would choose the ascetic life. The arms may be Ruth's, but in context they may also be those of the Lyonese. When Derwent remarks that the young man's form is like the "sweet shape" of young Bacchus (IV. xxvii.24), Clarel starts. However, this "scare/ Of incredulity" (IV.xxvii.19-20) is plausibly explained by the controlling narrative voice as surprise that a minister would show himself so "paganish" or lascivious (IV.xxvii.36).

Interpretations of the Lyonese incident as a revelation of homosexuality finally rest on very little (though indeed teasing) evidence. They derive chiefly from a long tradition of critical search for evidence of such a conflict in Melville himself. The prodigal's account of his friendship with a certain "young Peruvian" sounds rather ardent; Melville himself could be ardent in his responses. But the Lyonese is overtly, at least, a ladies' man, interested in petticoats and veils (IV.xxvi.100) and other feminine allurements. There is little reason to conclude, as Bezanson does, that Clarel is possibly "afraid to return to Ruth because she may be dead, but also because she may not be" (p. 640). The Lyonese does, however, pose the temptation to Clarel to abandon his serious pilgrimage and become an irresponsible, unthinking sensualist.

That temptation, which never becomes altogether convincing, is conclusively vanquished in Clarel's culminating confrontation with death. Approaching Jerusalem, the party turns aside from the easy route to the gate, where it is assured of entry, and instead passes a series of portentous sites—the low Valley of Hinnom; Tophet, the place of fiery human sacrifice to Moloch; and Aceldama, the field purchased by Judas with his thirty pieces of silver, a burial place of wanderers and strangers. The somber associations of this approach to the city, as well as the earlier impact of Ungar, who was explicitly labelled an Ishmael, foreshadow Clarel's final lapse into lone wandering and his preoccupation with death. Approaching the Jewish cemetery, which they must pass to reach St. Stephen's Gate, they see a burial procession. Clarel discovers that the dead are Ruth and her mother. His response is a frenzy of grief followed by prolonged gloom. Entering Jerusalem on Ash Wednesday, he remains through Lent, Passion Week, and Easter, until Whitsuntide, the commemoration of the descent of the Holy Spirit in tongues of flame. On that day he is last seen as he walks down from Olivet and "vanishes in the obscurer town" (IV.xxxiv.56). There follows the epilogue, which has troubled so many readers with its seemingly unaccountable tone of hopefulness.

At this point the logic of *Clarel* is indeed difficult, but it does exist. The key to it is the relationship of the poem's insistent death awareness to the empty circularity of its pilgrimage form. It is clear that Clarel's pilgrimage is a failure, at least in terms of the expectations with which he embarked on it. He has tried to solve a personal crisis, rooted in the social currents of his time, in the impersonal terms of the intellect and hallowed traditional forms. But he lives in a world in transit; indeed, one of the real successes of the work is Melville's achievement of a sense of motion, both literal and figurative. In such a world, the old, fixed pilgrims' circuits no longer lead to valid answers. In following such a circuit, Clarel followed the worn ruts of unanswerable and essentially abstract quandaries. He tried to answer the wrong questions in the wrong way.

The real value of the journey was not its pilgrimage form or the shrines that Clarel approached, vainly hoping that they would cast a light of certainty into his darkness, but the travelling itself, the very endeavor of looking, and the human interactions along the way. The "answer" that these may provide is not a solution to the abstract theological issues that bothered him at the outset, but the existential question of how, given a world that poses such unanswerable questions, a person is to go about living. Ultimately it is death that poses, in ultimate terms, both of these questions: both *why*, if one is disposed to take the problem on the intellectual plane of causation and implication, assuming a preordained meaning, and *how*, if one takes it on the existential plane of a problem in personal response, assuming that a meaning is to be created or shaped. Clarel confronts the ultimate question, the ultimate meaninglessness, death, in every major division of the poem: Nathan's and Celio's deaths in part one, Nehemiah's in part two, Mortmain's in part three, Ruth's and Agar's in part four. In every case he elects to address the problem in the traditional, intellectual manner. Suppressing his personal grief (in the first four instances, at any rate), he asks *why* and pushes on in the rigidly structured pilgrimage of tradition. But when he completes that empty circle he finds the same problem confronting him, death. It is still meaningless, and indeed always will be; there is no possible meaning to emptiness. Yet it was right, Melville asserts, for so absolute a question to send him forth. He only needed to travel in his own way, on his own brave search, leading to his own possibilities of discovery, rather than follow a course laid down in the past, expecting fixed shrines of meaning to be revealed to him.

Clarel's prolonged vigil in Jerusalem following his final and most devastating confrontation with death is a period of transition from one mode of response to the other. Isolated, beaten down by grief and futility, he remains in the dead city throughout the traditional period of death in the Christian calendar.[20] Stubbornly, he persists in demanding that a meaning be given him. He continues to visit the hallowed sites around Jerusalem and to observe the rites of the Holy Week as if they could explain everything. But the way of tradition still leads to a void. Viewing a Palm Sunday procession of Armenian Christians, he is reminded only of the earlier "futile omen" of the Armenian Funeral (IV.xxxii.72). Good Friday brings him visions of all his dead, from Celio through Ruth and her mother, all utterly "estranged" and unreachable (IV.xxxii.99). In bitterness, he, or Melville for him, cries out for the absent Holy Spirit:

> Where, where now He who helpeth us,
> The Comforter?—Tell, Erebus!
>
> (IV.xxxii.104-5)

The Easter celebrations leave Clarel still questioning the meaning and absoluteness of death:

> The cheer, so human, might not call
> The maiden up; *Christ is arisen*:
> But Ruth, may Ruth so burst the prison?
>
> (IV.xxxiii.64-66)

At last, on Whitsuntide, when still no Comforter descends, Clarel concedes that no absolute answer will ever be handed down to him, that death remains the insoluble puzzle:

> They wire the world—far under sea
> They talk; but never comes to me
> A message from beneath the stone.
>
> (IV.xxxiv.51-53)

Following a vast throng of fellow "cross-bearers" (IV.xxxiv.43), who are now viewed as distinct individuals for the first time in the poem, Clarel turns away from the darkness of Olivet, here representing revealed religion, and, following the Via Crucis, immerses himself in what is, in a way, an even greater darkness or mystery, the "obscurer town" (IV.xxxiv.56).

In joining the crowd in the street, however, Clarel has finally made the right choice. In terms of the imagery of the poem, he has chosen present life, human involvement, over the isolated symbols of the past.[21] It is because he has made this choice that the narrator can address him, in the epilogue, with hope, exhorting him essentially to keep travelling that street in search of his own possibilities. Accordingly, the structure of meaning in the epilogue is a contrast between intellectual knowledge and existential possibility, between answers and modes of response. Melville, speaking directly and in an expanded five-beat line, begins by asking if intellectual history imposes absolute limits on the possible emotional responses to life's puzzles:

> If Luther's day expand to Darwin's year,
> Shall that exclude the hope—foreclose the fear?
>
> (IV.xxxv.1-2)

Plainly, the question is rhetorical and the answer is no. Choices of response (the Sphinx of stoicism, Despair with his nihilistic jibe, bleeding Faith) go on nevertheless, in spite of the intellectual "strife and old debate" that in and of themselves will "run forever" without reaching any conclusions (IV.xxxv.12,17). But the debate is not the whole story; life is larger than intellectual reasoning, and living means endless possibility. Strange things do happen.

> But through such strange illusions have they passed
> Who in life's pilgrimage have baffled striven—
> Even death may prove unreal at the last,
> And stoics be astounded into heaven.
>
> (IV.xxxv.23-26)

Melville's final pronouncement is not that the final answer *will* be any better than the "old debate" has shown, but that it *may* be. Keeping the pilgrim mentality, then, means recognizing that the answers are not all in and continuing to search on the existential plane of experience (the heart) rather than the abstract plane of the intellect and tradition. Melville exhorts Clarel to persevere in the choice he has made: "Then keep thy heart, though yet but ill-resigned—/ Clarel, thy heart" (IV.xxxv.27-28). The implication is to continue, too, but in freer terms, the journey begun in the poem. Characteristically, for Melville, that journey appears as a plunge into a "whelming sea" from which the voyager may, after all, as Ishmael did in *Moby-Dick*, emerge in some kind of "victory"—the last word of the poem.

The message of ongoing journey is here far removed from questions of nationalism, social progress, or anything like Manifest Destiny. The journey structure of *Clarel* is a "profound remove" from the patterns that serve as archetypes of national myth, and the journey to which Clarel is directed is personal, not social. Nevertheless, the conclusion of the poem strikes a characteristically American note.[22] Clarel's persistence in making the journey of discovery will put him in company not only with the characteristic heroes of Melville's work but with what we have been seeing as the American penchant for journeys. Obviously Americans have had no monopoly on either the narrative form or the experience of the journey, and indeed in *Clarel* Melville draws on narrative patterns rooted in the Old Testament, Greek myth, Dante, Chaucer, and Bunyan. But he uses these established forms in his own way, shifting from pilgrimage to an amalgam of pilgrimage, return, quest, and symposium. To this amalgam of narrative pattern and to the large theme of religious faith and doubt, he adds his firm rooting in the peculiar American readiness to view life in terms of strenuous journeys. The message of persistence in the epilogue is, in part, evidence of that readiness and of what can well be viewed as an attitude of pragmatic experimentalism:

> Emerge thou mayest from the last whelming sea,
> And prove that death but routs life into victory.

(IV. xxxv. 33-34)

In short, taking the most American of philosophic attitudes, Melville concludes that his pilgrim should try it and see if it works.

NOTES

1. Walter Bezanson argues heroically that "it is not possible for bad poetry to communicate a significant, ordered world of imaginative values," but even he concedes that the verse is "often. . .endangered by ineptitudes." "Introduction" to Herman Melville, *Clarel: A Poem and Pilgrimage in the Holy Land* (New York: Hendricks House, 1960), p. L. This edition of *Clarel* is used throughout the present chapter; references to book, canto, and line number are shown parenthetically.

2. Merlin Bowen, *The Long Encounter: Self and Experience in the Writ-*

ings of Herman Melville (Chicago: The University of Chicago Press, 1960), p. 280, comments that *Clarel* is "the fruit of its author's ripest maturity."

3. Newton Arvin, *Herman Melville* (New York: William Sloane Associates, 1950), p. 270.

4. See Donald Arthur Daiker, "The Motif of the Quest in the Writings of Herman Melville," doctoral dissertation, Indiana, 1969. Abstracted in *Dissertations Abstracts International*, 30: 4979A-80A. Franklin D. Walker, in *Irreverent Pilgrims: Melville, Browne, and Mark Twain in the Holy Land* (Seattle: University of Washington Press, 1974), p. 135, offers this and several other nutshell definitions of *Clarel*, including "a sort of *Moby-Dick* in verse."

5. The sexually escapist implications of the work are argued energetically by Nina Baym in her article "The Erotic Motif in Melville's *Clarel*," *Texas Studies in Literature and Language*, 16 (1974), 315-28.

6. Various critics have commented on the circular movement of the narrative and on Clarel's failure to find any point of orientation. Vincent Kenny, for example, refers to the structural pattern as a "circle of despair." *Herman Melville's Clarel: A Spiritual Autobiography* (Hamden, Conn.: Archon Books, 1973), p. 119. Kenneth A. Requa, in his article "The Pilgrim's Problems: Melville's *Clarel*," *Ball State University Forum*, 16, no. 2 (1975), 16-20, speaks of the "unbreakable" circular patterns that imply Clarel will "but travel the circuitous route once again."

7. Walker, *Irreverent Pilgrims*, p. 135. The resemblance to Chaucer's pilgrimage is more in evidence in the overall patterns of movement and the presentation of characters than in the narrative strategy of the work.

8. Bezanson, "Introduction," p. xv.

9. Requa states that Clarel's pilgrimage "has no goal." Rather, his goal is so complex, so total, as to be virtually undefined. "The Pilgrim's Problems," p. 17.

10. All of the characters in the narrative are given one-word names, apparently in part to make their presence in the verse more manageable and in part to suggest anonymity. The device also, in most cases, underscores the masculine quality of the narrative, since it is far more common to refer to a man by last name only than to a woman. Nehemiah, however, is clearly a first name.

11. Clarel's response to Jerusalem is a restatement of Melville's own. See Herman Melville, *Journal of a Visit to Europe and the Levant, October 11, 1856-May 6, 1857*, ed. Howard C. Horsford (Princeton, N.J.: Princeton University Press, 1955), pp. 139-61.

12. Melville, *Journal*, pp. 136-37

13. Referring to the quality of dread that appears in travellers' accounts of the area, Bezanson writes that the Dead Sea was, "for the

imaginative mind. . .still a powerful symbol" and that the biblical story of Sodom and Gomorrah had "invested the area with a violent sense of evil" (p. xxiii).

14. The metaphoric equivalence of ocean and desert runs throughout *Clarel* in a variety of direct assertions and figures of speech. It is made directly in the present canto, "Of Deserts," in lines 38 through 40:

> Sands immense
> Impart the oceanic sense:
> The flying grit like scud is made.

Regarding the significance of land and sea as indicating types of journey, as well as ascending and descending motion and the relationship of travel literature to the "journey of life" theme, see Martin S. Day, "Travel Literature and the Journey Theme," *Forum* (University of Houston), 12, no. 2 (1974), 37-47.

15. Joseph G. Knapp, S.J., "Melville's *Clarel*: Dynamic Synthesis," *American Transcendental Quarterly*, 7 (1970), 67-69. Knapp's statement that the vertical motion of part one is "reenforced by the iambic line" is scarcely plausible. The iambic foot is the most common English metrical unit, used for a great variety of effects, and its occurrence here cannot bear the mimetic or affective load Knapp attempts to place on it.

16. Kenny, *Spiritual Autobiography*, p. 119; Bowen, *The Long Encounter*, p. 267; Bezanson, "Introduction," p. lviii. The parallel with the *Divine Comedy*, which plays throughout *Clarel*, is explicitly stressed as Derwent, climbing back up from what Bezanson glosses as a "mock descent into hell," jokingly cries to his companion:

> "Dear Virgil mine, you are so strong,
> But I, thy Dante, am nigh dead."

> (III.xxv.82-83)

17. Cf. Knapp, "Melville's *Clarel*," p. 71: Mar Saba is "a startling correlative of man's own condition, since it, like man, is perched between earth and heaven."

18. Henry Wells, *The American Way of Poetry* (New York: Columbia University Press, 1943), p. 85; quoted by Bezanson, p. 631.

19. Bowen, *The Long Encounter*, p. 274.

20. It is clear throughout, but especially in the concluding cantos, that Clarel is very much like Melville's Bartleby, a quietly mournful, estranged figure who does not so much possess a character as elicit

assertions of character and of meaning from others. Such a character is nevertheless an aesthetic liability in an extended narrative. However, the indeterminacy and passivity of both these figures are essential to the works in which they appear; Bartleby and Clarel must be outwardly passive if they are to suffer the full spectrum of the world's meaninglessness as a given without, from the outset, shaping that meaninglessness into a defined and therefore narrowed and distorted form.

21. It is just here, in its imagery of the street, that *Clarel* most clearly betrays the influence of Hawthorne, for whom the public street signified involvement in day-to-day life.

22. Henry Wells, one of the earliest critics to write on *Clarel*, viewed the work as "a product of the American mind" that "betrays conspicuous signs of its native growth." His comments to this effect, however, are more an effusion of patriotism than an assessment of *Clarel*. *The American Way of Poetry*, pp. 79-83.

8
Bungling Pilgrims: Faulkner and *As I Lay Dying*

Round and round we go, all of us, and ever come back thither
—Walt Whitman, "Song of Myself"

In the darkness with a great bundle of grief
the people march.
—Carl Sandburg, *The People, Yes* (107)

One of the most familiar bits of lore relating to William Faulkner is his reference to *As I Lay Dying* as a tour de force. Apparently in saying that he was referring to his burst of creative energy in writing the novel, as he said, in six weeks. Then, too, the phrase can well be applied to his brilliant elaboration, amounting almost to a reductio ad absurdum, of the modern novel's concern with narrative point of view. In this, as well as in his sheer feat of creation, Faulkner was flexing his novelistic muscles. The book can also be seen as a tour de force, a feat of skill or ingenuity, in its response to the challenges posed by the road narrative form. Indeed, Faulkner transforms the weaknesses of the road narrative into strengths.

Critics have typically regarded the fact that the novel is cast in this ancient form as a hurdle or limitation to Faulkner's art, as if he succeeded in the work in spite of it. Thornton Parsons, for instance, refers to the "crude and stark efficiency of the road-story form," the "limitations" of which Faulkner had to "overcome."[1] Andre Bleikasten notes the "episodic" quality inherent in the form.[2] It is quite true, of course, that the road narrative commits an author to a rather loose, episodic sequence of action, creating an effect of apparent looseness. As a principle of organization, it is inherently disjunctive; it provides a serial pattern of this, then that, then something else. It is this simple serial quality that causes the road narrative to be regarded as a primitive, inherently loose form.

In *As I Lay Dying*, the episodic quality of the road narrative is evident in the movement of the story from one complication to the next. After the death of Addie, the wife and mother, the Bundren family must cope with a variety of delays and problems before setting out on their burial journey. At once they face conflict over whether to stop at the nearest cemetery. Pushing on, they ford a flooded river that carries away their team of mules, threatens three of them with drowning, and causes Cash to break a leg. While waiting to get the leg set and trade for a team, they have increasing difficulties with the odor resulting from the decaying body. Jewel disappears for a time. They pause to cement Cash's leg and, though they don't know it, to let Dewey Dell try to get an abortion. At another stopover Darl sets a barn on fire as an attempted cremation, but Jewel rescues the coffin. With criminal action threatened, arrangements are made in secret to have Darl committed as insane, and keepers take him by ambush, but not until after the additional adventures of a near brush with a knife fight in the road and an encounter with a potential new wife for Anse. As this summary shows, action is plentiful, various, and only loosely connected.

Faulkner, however, rises to the challenge of this episodic quality of the road narrative form and makes it, in *As I Lay Dying*, not a limitation but an opportunity. It is precisely because of the inherent looseness of the road narrative that he is able to achieve the multiform, multidimensional quality of the work. In addition, the form takes on a thematic function for him. Besides serial sequence, it provides a sense of open possibility, of anticipation. That is, the road narrative has an inherent potential

for effects not only of variety but of surprise and discovery—
discovery, moreover, of the surprising in the course of the familiar. Clearly, Faulkner capitalizes upon this potential of his
form in *As I Lay Dying*. Further, he utilizes the loosely associative
nature of the form to accommodate his thematic concern with
order and flux.

Like Melville's *Clarel*, *As I Lay Dying* is a complex blending of
several traditional forms of journey narrative. This multifar-
iousness of formal patterns within the relatively simple linear
structure of the whole derives ultimately from the nature of the
family group making the journey. If Steinbeck's Joads, in that
other family journey novel *The Grapes of Wrath*, are among the
great memorable families of literature, Faulkner's Bundrens are
equally so. Each member of the Bundren family has the solidity
and the ultimate mystery of a real human being, yet the fullest
vitality of each lies in his relation to all the others. That is, the
Bundrens are both individualized and clanned. Accordingly, in
their remarkable, revolting journey to Jefferson, their motives
are, as critics have remarked, both individual, or various, and
clanlike, or unified. It is this melding of unity and diversity that
gives the novel its distinctive structural quality, at once simple,
integral, familiar, and, in its smaller structures, diverse, disjunct,
startling.

The Bundrens' journey is unified and given a stark integrity
by their overriding purpose of burying Addie. Thus they participate in a social ritual and a set of iconography that are deeply
ingrained in our cultural lives.[3] This familiarity, the sense that
the Bundrens are repeating an act common to humanity for
centuries and thoroughly allegorized in religious teaching, gives
their relatively short journey an exaggerated dimension, an enlarged significance. Because their journey of burial is so common
and they are so insistently brought into conflict with the natural
elements, they appear to move on the plane of myth.

Other familiar patterns of journey narrative develop within
the overall structure of the burial procession and interact in the
dynamic of the novel. In its effects of surprise and adventurous
happening, combined with the status and the peculiarities of
the family members, the novel is a picaresque tale. Each of the
keenly individuated narrators is in effect the "rogue," the picaro,

telling his own adventure as he moves through a real and diverse roadside world. The picaresque narrator is traditionally a figure removed from established society—as are the Bundrens. Though resourceful, the picaro is traditionally simple, a naif who shows up, by his simplicity, the pretenses of society—as do all of the Bundrens except Darl. The picaro's simplicity gives his narrative a disarming artlessness. What I'm telling you, he says, is no high-flown literary invention; it's just what happened to me.[4] This is the stance that becomes a ploy for Faulkner as it has for master writers of picaresque throughout the tradition. The art-lessness of the narrative is in fact a great artfulness. As a narrative strategy it is much like the straight-faced approach of the tall tale, though in this case the knowingness behind the mask is not so much that of each narrator but, behind them all, the orchestrator, Faulkner himself. The amateur status of the narrators gives their tale all the possibilities of directness and fresh discovery that it gives, similarly, to Huck Finn's simple tale, but, as Darl's sections in particular demonstrate, it also leads the reader into more than he expected.

Another narrative mode that contributes to the shaping of *As I Lay Dying* is the night journey, the harrowing journey through extraordinary and symbolic ordeals. Horrors aplenty, of course, fill the pages of this novel: fire, flood, bizarre intensities of pain, violence, and abuse. Indeed, criticism has tended more often to stress its horrific aspects than any other. The horrors of the story are, particularly in the cases of Darl, Jewel, and Cash, an effectual descent into the hell of the inner self. For Jewel, the night journey descent remains undefined, both in the reader's understanding of it and in Jewel's own. To the end, Jewel is a seething brute force, covering up in furious reticence the insights that, as occasional glimpses suggest, he does possess. For Cash, the descent is integrative; in the course of the novel he comes to awareness as he comes to expression.[5] Those who see Cash as a growing, emerging character may, in fact, view his share in the journey less as a night journey than as a moral pilgrimage, though a pilgrimage in which the chief call is not to make moral choices but to suffer, to endure. For Darl, the descent into the self is fully realized but destructive; he achieves wisdom, but of a sort that absolutely estranges him from society. His becomes the descending journey of immersion in schizophrenia.[6]

Another formal structure developed in the novel is the heroic quest. Unlike the other patterns, however, the quest appears as comic inversion. In Dewey Dell's and Anse's determination to gain their own prizes in Jefferson, abortion and false teeth, the journey becomes a parody of the quest.[7] This aspect of the novel, as well as the fact that its total form is a complex mingling of traditions, has received considerable critical attention.[8] However, yet another journey narrative pattern that is also in evidence has not been generally noted. It is in terms of this pattern, the homeward journey, that the work will be considered. Various as they are, tonally as well as formally, the journey patterns of the novel are contained, subsumed, in a homing pattern that is the primary structure of action and of meaning.

* * *

As we noted earlier, the homeward journey narrative falls naturally into two basic configurations, the return home and the search for a new home, which is itself a kind of quest. By stressing the cyclical quality of his fable, Faulkner has managed to encompass both forms at once. The novel begins with the Bundrens at home, that is, in place at their collective dwelling, and takes them away from home to a place where they are strangers. At the same time, however, in at least two distinct ways, it takes them *toward* home.

First, the Bundrens' journey takes Addie from a place where she never felt fully "at home" back to her "home" in the sense of origin. This sense of the word "home" commonly occurs in the South in the term "homecoming," used to designate local reunion gatherings that may attract people who are not native to the particular area at all but whose ancestors lived there. Jefferson was where Addie "had people."[9] Her burial journey takes her from her personal, but in her mind unreal, home to her clan home, which she chooses to regard as her real or permanent home. In so choosing, she denies the importance of her own family, placing her allegiance instead with her family of origin. She affirms her unmarried, un-"violated" identity. The choice is not only a final vengeance on the despised husband and children (though they seem not to recognize it as such), but essentially a choice of death over life. Addie quotes approvingly her father's dictum that "the reason for living is getting ready to stay dead" (p. 167). If so, the place of death, the grave, is both a more important and a more lasting "home" than the place of life.

Addie's journey to her grave in Jefferson, then, is both a return to her ancestral home and at the same time a seeking of her new and permanent home, the grave. To make the home search actually a grave search, of course, radically inverts the traditional home-seeking form, and the reader who is aware of the novel's relation to such a tradition in American letters and ultimately in biblical epic will experience an added dimension of irony beyond those other ironies and mockeries more immediately apparent in the novel. As we have seen, the home-seeking narrative re-current in American literature characteristically involves hazard-ous crossings, usually of rivers, which may well be seen as symbolic death followed by resurrection in the new life of the new home, and it also characteristically involves pregnancy or birth embodying that new life. But if Dewey Dell's pregnancy is a new-life symbol, it is so in an ironic and unwilled way, since what she hopes for is an abortion. And the symbolic deaths by water and fire are followed, not by resurrection, but by the ritual of the permanence of death, burial, the actual completion of Addie's dying.[10] In traditional Christian terminology, a quest for the true home in death is not only a journey toward the final resting place, the grave, but a departure to a world beyond. That world, commonly accorded terminology of home in hymns and folk religion, is to be reached by crossing the Jordan. Accord-ingly, Addie reaches her resting place after crossing a river, though not a peaceful one. But the novel offers no indication that she will reach any such realm as a home beyond; her home is simply, as Jewel puts it, to his father's discomfort, "a hole in the ground" (p. 218).

In very specific ways, then, the novel parodies both an Amer-ican and a biblical context of epic home seeking. At the same time, however, the Bundrens' struggles are ennobled by being arrayed against such a backdrop of collective hardship and achievement.[11]They are continuing mankind's urge to push toward a vision, albeit they continue that grand procession in a bumbling and humble manner.[12]

The echoes of migration epics, both the real ones of American history and such literary migrations as those of the Old Testament and the Aeneid, are indisputably *there* but subdued. More directly, the Bundrens make a collective home-founding journey out of their burial journey by the apparent accident of Anse's finding a new wife. Incredible though it is that the inert Anse could meet, ask, and wed her without prearrangement in so brief a stay as they make in Jefferson, it is even more incredible that he could have planned out so momentous an act. He seems merely to have fallen into it. But by doing so he transforms an end into a beginning. Thus we have this scheme of action: Addie's return to her home (blood origins) is coterminous with Addie's settling into her real home (the grave) and that action directly gives rise to, indeed overlaps, Anse's founding of a new home (the redefined family unit). The three actions occur at once, as aspects of the same action, the trip to Jefferson. To be sure, the ease with which Anse founds his new home is rather chilling. The individual, it seems, has no importance or at any rate so little that Anse's introduction of the new woman to his offspring makes no distinction between the old and the new wife: "Meet Mrs Bundren" (p. 250). What is important is that the family of Bundrens (bungling pilgrims, mankind) goes on. Perhaps that is reassuring enough, if one can take the long view. The family has proceeded from a disintegrating home—disintegrating in the sense both of Addie's dying and of their unbearable emotional stresses—to the founding of a new "home" or family unit. The cost is great: the burying not only of Addie but of whatever she meant as an individual, and in addition the expulsion of Darl. Indeed, one of the great themes of the novel is the question of whether any "home" (family, social structure) is possible without great loss to the individual. In other words, the novel asks what is the price of order.[13]

Faulkner never doubts that order is necessary, but *As I Lay Dying* is one of the strongest testaments to the fact that he was fully sensitive to its cost. The achievement of order is a function of home founding, here and in the home-seeking story or experience generally. Out of the ferment of far-reaching social changes and the chaos of ocean, the original settlers arrived on the New World shore to plant their homes and form their own social order: founding a new home meant founding a new order. The Pilgrims did so very consciously and methodically before landing, in the Mayflower Compact. In later pioneer fiction, as in the pioneering experience, the need for order during the unstable wagon train passage and the creation of a family and community system in the unstructured wilderness were important concerns. Similarly, the Bundrens proceed from a decaying order through chaotic upheavals to a new though possibly repressive order. They proceed from home to "home." Neither of the two homes is fully satisfactory, but they are at least preferable to the flux and conflict of the road.

At the opening of the novel, order is external and apparent only. The family is together—and Faulkner never challenges the rightness of family in itself as an idea—and the rituals of the death watch are being duly observed. Beneath the appearance of unity, however, order is collapsing. Addie, who is or should be the source of order in the family, is dying. Anse is already disguising his motives (by letting himself appear indifferent to the three dollars to be earned by hauling wood, a sum he wants for his false teeth) and is abdicating his responsibility of leadership (escaping the onus of the wood-hauling trip by manipulating Darl into pushing the question and Jewel into making the actual decision that he hates). The motives and feelings of all are disguised and misinterpreted, with the only accurate assessments being voiced by Mrs. Tull and by Dewey Dell. Mrs. Tull, who is almost always wrong, correctly perceives that Addie "was partial to" Jewel (p. 21), and Dewey Dell's intuitive grasp of relationships leads her to ask Darl bluntly why he is "taking Jewel" if Addie is to die soon (p. 27). It becomes evident that beneath this lack of understanding and unity within the family there lies an actual hatred emanating from Addie herself.

As Addie is in fact a force of real disruption in the family, Anse is a representation, not so much of order, but of specious order. The emptiness of his devotion to the customary or seemly is revealed in his mumbling of fatuous pieties. His commitment to habitual order is so devoid of inner substance or volition that it amounts merely to a commitment to stasis: his first words of narration are "Durn that road" (p. 34). Anse reasons that the Lord made man to stand vertically because "He aimed for them to stay put like a tree or a stand of corn," but a road keeps "folks restless and wanting to get up and go somewheres else" (p. 35).

Even the road itself, the avenue of the progression from home to "home," undergoes a change from order to chaos to order parallel to the experience of the family. At the beginning, before Addie dies, the road appears stable, functional. Vernon Tull predicts, "And with the roads like they are now, it wont take you no time to get her to town" (p. 18). But with Addie's death the elements return to chaos. It is as if she, the symbolic mother principle, had operated as a principle of order, even though she personally, in her own swirling emotions and urges, had actually been a force violating that order. At about the time of her death, Jewel and Darl are struggling with a broken wheel and a load of lumber on a dissolving yellow road "neither of earth nor water" (p. 48). Soon they will learn that the bridge, an extension of the road, has been destroyed by the turbulent flooded river in which animals, trees, and other objects are crazily tumbled together.

The dissolution of the road and the bridge is related to a larger pattern of chaos in the natural elements and the natural dimensions of space and time. Besides the dissolving of the road, which at one point seems to have "been soaked free of earth and floated upward" (p. 136), and the turbulence of the flooding river, which contributes the most protracted and probably the most memorable single incident in the book, destructive chaos is experienced in the elements of fire (the burning barn) and air (the smell of Addie's decaying body). As critics have observed in commenting upon Faulkner's creation of statuary-like or tableau-like effects, time and space seem often interchanged or effaced altogether. An example is Darl's description of the wagon's pace:

We go on, with a motion so soporific, so dreamlike as to be uninferant of progress, as though time and not space were decreasing between us and it. (p. 101)

The swollen river, explicitly a symbol of time, is not only displaced (out of its banks) and swirling, but "thick" (p. 139) and furiously destructive. It contains "the shape of the disaster" to come (p. 139) and appears to Darl an apocalypse: "as though we had reached the place where the motion of the wasted world accelerates just before the final precipice" (p. 139). In the conversation of Darl and Cash as they begin the crossing, time becomes mixed or, as Darl says of the river as time symbol, "looping":

"That pillow was longer than him," Cash says. He is leaning a little forward. "I ought to come down last week and sighted. I ought to done it."
    "That's right," I say. "Neither his feet nor his head would reach the end of it. You couldn't have known," I say. (p. 137)

The references to the pillow on which Jewel lay as a newborn and his size in relation to it are recalled from some time or various times earlier. They reappear in Darl's memory as he and Cash carry on their conversation about the crossing. Later, as Darl becomes more distraught, he imagines the relief of having life dissolve into primal chaos: "if you could just ravel out into time" (p. 198). All the while, of course, Addie is ravelling, dissolving, a process horribly manifest in the sounds that Vardaman hears within her coffin and interprets as her talking to them (p. 204). The fire set by Darl, another symbol of apocalypse, is also, like the river, the processes of decay, and the dimension of time, presented as a "dissolving" (p. 211).

    Chaos on the human plane parallels chaos in the natural elements. Upon his mother's death, the child Vardaman, confronted by absolute forces beyond his experience or comprehension, lapses into disordered evasion of reality. His overwrought mental state expresses itself in such chaotic verbal jumbles as "if he can make the train, why cant He make them all in the town because flour and sugar and coffee." Or, "And so if she is not a rabbit I couldn't breathe in the crib and Cash is going to nail it up" (p. 63). On that same night, Darl's narration, too, which has had an uncanny kind of exactness, becomes a confused reaching after the ungraspable: "He cannot empty himself for sleep because he is not what he is and he is what he is not. . . . Yet the wagon *is*, because when the wagon is *was*, Addie Bundren will not be" (p. 76).[14] After this point, Darl's eccentricity or madness becomes increasingly manifest, as does his antagonism to Jewel, whose special closeness to their mother is keenly felt by the acutely sensitive Darl. The disparity of all their motives likewise becomes clearer and their conflicts more open, until they culminate in the attack on Darl and in Anse's virtual robbing of Dewey Dell. At this point of fullest disorder in the family, Cash realizes that order and disorder are not always to be easily distinguished:

> But I aint so sho that ere a man has the right to say what is crazy and what aint. It's like there was a fellow in every man that's done a-past the sanity or the insanity, that watches the sane and the insane doings of that man with the same horror and the same astonishment. (p. 228)

Yet such a state of affairs, in which polarities of experience lose their meaning, is intolerable; one needs to be able to rely on something, not merely regard all acts or conditions with equal "horror." Therefore, a principle of seeming order is needed. However specious, it is preferable to none at all, just as Addie's symbolically ordering presence, despite its submerged destructiveness, was preferable to the chaos and conflict that ensued when she died. Hence the new Mrs. Bundren.

Faulkner thus states his conviction of the need for order and implies that an ordering principle will appear when needed. (Addie is not really dead until placed in the ground. The fullest outburst of family chaos ensues immediately upon the disappearance of this last symbol of the mother/order presence, and almost at once a new ordering principle comes to fill the void.) But he is not unaware of the cost of order, particularly of the essentially empty, though necessary, outer appearance of order. Darl, the most perceptive and verbally creative member of the family, is set upon, beaten, and turned over to outsiders. The step is necessary; Darl is not only a barn burner but a source of dissension within the family. But it is acutely regrettable, indeed tragic. In Cash's words, "It'll be better" for Darl at the mental institution, but "it was bad so" (pp. 228, 227). Darl serves as scapegoat for the Bundrens. His removal allows them to reunify and to evade the retributions that society would surely take on him. Thus, in a highly ironic departure from the happy and confident ending of the conventional homeward narrative, Darl sets out on his own homeward journey to the asylum that will apparently be his permanent refuge. Yet the irony of Darl's bitter journey to his "home" is enveloped in the conclusion of the larger homeward journey. Thus, as critics have observed in other connections, Faulkner has merged the traditional genres of epic, tragedy, and comedy. The reestablishment of the Bundren "home," in the various senses we have mentioned, has its own irony, deriving from Anse's callous haste and the defiant hardness of his "duck-shaped woman" (p. 249). But for all that, it is both a comic (ludicrous) and comedic (affirmative) ending.

* * *

Faulkner makes extended use of the journey or pilgrimage form not only in *As I Lay Dying* but in a number of his other novels as well. The journey as a pattern of action accords well with his noted statement, "Life is motion," though it would be reductive to identify that statement with the motion of travel alone. Cleanth Brooks accurately observes that "the heroic journey, as in *As I Lay Dying*" is among characteristic "Faulknerian themes and situations."[15] Particularly memorable journeys are, from *The Unvanquished*, Granny's quest for justice through mules; from *Go Down, Moses*, the journey of burial as a return home in the title story and in "The Bear" the annual horse- and mule-drawn retreat to the woods that metamorphoses into a last train trip, anticipated and balanced by Ike and Boon's train trip to Memphis to buy whiskey for the hunters; from "Old Man," the tall convict's struggle to return "home" to prison; from *Light in August*, Lena Grove's persistent search for her baby's father; from *The Reivers*, the entire riotous adventure.

Of all these, only *The Reivers* can be regarded as belonging to one particular pattern or category of journey narrative. It is pure picaresque.[16] To be sure, Thomas Sutpen's journey to Frenchman's Bend in *Absalom! Absalom!*—specifically the virtual caravan expedition that actually brings him there, but in a more general sense also his entire life-journey from the front-porch affront of his childhood through the West Indies ventures that equip him for his assault on respectability—is explicitly a home-founding journey. But Sutpen's preparation and his arrival actually comprise only a part of the vast novel, with other kinds of journeys also contributing to the complex pattern. In both *Absalom! Absalom!* and *The Sound and the Fury*, for instance, Quentin Compson's removal to Harvard is an escape.[17] The result, for *Absalom! Absalom!*, is that no one journey pattern becomes the key to the significance of the work. Here and in Faulkner's fiction in general, meanings accrue to fundamentally simple actions, simple in the sense of being lifted out of the complicating and blurring circumstances of life and being enlarged through that isolation— so richly enlarged that these actions, for all their compressed integrity and starkness, radiate multiple and multilevel meanings.

In just this way, for example, the direct and unprepossessing foot journey of Lena Grove in *Light in August* takes on a nimbus of significance ranging from woman's instinct to provide a secure, nurturing environment for childrearing to the steady westward plod of American civilization. (Lena's journey proceeds from east to west, and the novel otherwise concerns itself with the historic process in terms of the heritage and evolution of social or racial problems.) Her journey even suggests the continuity of life itself.[18] Lena's undaunted foot-progress encloses the desperate events of the novel and provides, not so much an affirmation of some qualities at the expense of others, but a redemptive absorption of those events back into the basic human process. This redemptive unification of the disparate strands of the novel is a forceful demonstration of Faulkner's ultimate allegiance to mankind, rather than to individual humans, despite his fascinated creation of the exceptional individual character. Lena's persistence in her journey of search represents less a personal victory for herself than a victory for mankind. It has none of the grim tone of the solitary hero's doing something doggedly, in spite of hardship, nor is it rewarded with successful discovery of her intended object (though she has found a better substitute, Byron Bunch). After all the misery and self-destructive rancor the race has endured, it can still produce people who go on, and indeed go on with a sense of wonderment: "My, my. A body does get around. Here we aint been coming from Alabama but two months, and now it's already Tennessee."[19]

Lena's journey is typical of Faulkner's general practice in that rich meaning is implied or evoked through a minimal basic action, rather than adumbrated as the parallel of an elaborate, dense action. In this respect, Faulkner very much resembles Hawthorne.[20] Certainly one experiences a greater density in Faulkner's novels than in Hawthorne's, deriving partly from his baroque style, so unlike Hawthorne's limpidness, partly from his multiple and diffracting narrators, and partly from the surging, larger-than-life passions of his characters and situations. Still, the two are similar in that neither is concerned with incident or social documentation (contrast, for instance, Dos Passos) so much as with atmosphere and significance. Both develop their meanings through symbolic actions that appear as carefully structured expressive gestures or, frequently, as tableaux, characters or small groups frozen in situations (more accurately yet, arrested in midaction, a cross section of an action) and then turned around, examined, elaborated upon. One vibrant tableau becomes not only the key or a major key to an entire literary structure, but an emblem resonating succeeding waves of suggestiveness.[21] For both Hawthorne and Faulkner, physical movement functions in much the same way as symbolic objects and tableaux. Minimal journeys are so structured as to bear heavy freights of meaning.

This is not the loading of "hidden" referents onto elements isolated from an artistic fabric,[22] but a total event so constructed that it recalls allusively a complex of familiar structures and their implications. Hawthorne and Faulkner achieve this ramifying effect in very different ways. Both begin with carefully chosen and deeply contemplated events or images. In *The Scarlet Letter*, for instance, the famous prison and rose bush of the opening chapter are such images. Hawthorne presents these images stripped of detail and discusses them in abstract, general terms that accommodate numerous examples or instances. Faulkner, on the other hand, generalizes, not by the lucid abstraction of Hawthorne, but by the magnifying of images through intensifying descriptive terms that make them seem not only larger than life but more violently *alive*. Two, from a myriad of examples, are, from *As I Lay Dying*: "her leg coming long from beneath her tightening dress: that lever which moves the world;

one of that caliper which measures the length and breadth of life" (pp. 97-98); a log "upright upon that surging and heaving desolation like Christ" (p. 141). Such intensity proclaims importance. The naked gesture absorbs and embraces the import of all the significant gestures that its contours recall.

One result of this tendency toward enlargement is that Faulkner's narratives can contain large elements of comedy or parody. They can maintain a serious or epic tone in combination with low, comic, or even mocking elements. Such a containment of counter-tension is evident in *As I Lay Dying*. Faulkner accords the Bundrens' journey the dignity of any ritualistic, deeply motivated, or perilous act and affirms the worth of their survival power even while he shows us a degree of foolishness, confusion, and shabbiness that would ordinarily vitiate an exalted effect. This is no mere tacking on of a "happy ending," but a vitalization of the positive aspects of the Bundrens' journey to the point that these aspects—the courage, effort, and resiliency they display—are adequate both to their trials and to the deflation of themselves as individuals. In achieving these virtues the Bundrens escape their individual limitations and participate in the important virtues of mankind.

The effect is much the same as that of Lena Grove's journey, which encloses the horrors of *Light in August* and provides assurance that life does indeed go serenely on, that it is adequate to the worst. But the implications of the journey in *As I Lay Dying* have not been so readily recognized as the implications of Lena's journey. Probably this is because, in *Light in August*, Faulkner depicts the contrary patterns in different groups of characters, while in the story of the Bundrens he makes the more stringent demand on the reader of asking him to distinguish two contrary patterns, two sets of values, within the same characters. In *The Reivers* he makes the yet more outlandish demand that we believe the old heartwarming clichés of the virtuous whore and the beneficent influence of the child. The mastery of the novel is that he makes good this demand; he creates a fictive world in which these wish-fulfilling clichés are not only true but vital enough to contain the dark threats that occur during the journey.

The common element of all three is Faulkner's use of a journey as an undercurrent to other, more spectacular, actions. Often, as in *Light in August*, he adverts to the journey near the beginning and near the end of the work, but in any event his occasional adversion to the background movement of characters creates the sense of ongoing process. V. K. Ratliff's selling trips in the Snopes trilogy have much the same effect. Ratliff may not be entirely undaunted in all his efforts against Snopesism, but he is never daunted for long. Whatever horrors are perpetrated by others, he goes confidently about his business, and his travels serve in part to knit his geographically diffuse society together.

The regular significance of such journeys in Faulkner, whatever may be their other implications, is persistence. It is a quality much admired by Faulkner, perhaps even the cardinal virtue. The journey, particularly as travelled by such slow and dogged means as walking or mule and wagon, is admirably suited to suggest the quality of persistence. It involves steady pace and long duration, and its naturally episodic nature becomes a significant factor as the traveller is able to continue, to persist in his road, despite mishaps along the way. In this respect, then, it becomes clear that Faulkner characteristically uses the journey in much the same way that Steinbeck uses his Joads' trek or the stubborn land turtle in *Grapes of Wrath*. But he uses it more subtly and with richer nuances. Both Steinbeck and Faulkner, for all the horrors that once prompted readers to call them depressing or sordid, are finally optimistic. People, they imply, are able to take it and keep going, and this quality of persistence usually sustains them in finding a "home," a place of balance.

NOTES

1. Thornton H. Parsons, "Doing the Best They Can," *Georgia Review*, 23 (1969), 292-93.

2. Andre Bleikasten, *Faulkner's As I Lay Dying*, trans. Roger Little, rev. and enl. ed. (Bloomington and London: Indiana University Press, 1973), p. 45.

3. See Samuel Chew, *The Pilgrimage of Life* (New Haven: Yale University Press, 1962).

4. Robert Scholes and Robert Kellogg, *The Nature of Narrative* (New York: Oxford University Press), p. 73, comment that the traveller's tale is "the amateur's answer to the professional rhapsodist."

5. A debated critical issue. I see him less as changing than as coming

to expression, his traits becoming more clearly evident but not altering. Cf. Robert Reed Sanderlin, "*As I Lay Dying*: Christian Symbols and Thematic Implications," *Southern Quarterly*, 7 (1969), 163: "Cash becomes more and more communicative." It is plausible even to argue that the apparent change in Cash or at least in his speaking consciousness is only the reader's increased willingness to listen to him as the disruptive Darl is driven to the background. Such an argument implies a view of the novel as a dramatic interchange between reader and narrating voices, with the reader's responses serving as an essential part of the work, complementing that which is presented in print on paper.

6. Cf. Joseph Campbell, *Myths to Live By* (New York: Viking Press, 1972), p. 202: "the imagery of schizophrenic fantasy perfectly matches that of the mythological hero journey."

7. See Elizabeth M. Kerr, "*As I Lay Dying* as Ironic Quest," *Wisconsin Studies in Contemporary Literature*, 3 (1962), 5-19. It is characteristic of Faulkner, however, that his parodic irony is not a rejection of these characters, merely a humorous realism that is finally tolerant, even affectionate.

8. Bleikasten points out the variety in journey structures present in the novel and comments that it is as though Faulkner "sought to bring into play the different forms that travelers' tales have taken over the centuries, or at least to make echoes of them reverberate throughout." *Faulkner's As I Lay Dying*, pp. 6-7. The plurisignificance of the Bundrens' journey is demonstrated in the critical response to the novel, which has been seen as being grotesque, crude, heroic, mock-heroic, comic, and even, chiefly in earlier times, sociologically descriptive. A useful summary of critical assessments is given by Bleikasten, pp. 138-48 and 168-75.

9. William Faulkner, *As I Lay Dying* (1930; rpt. New York: Random House, 1964), p. 163.

10. Peter Swiggart suggests this meaning of the title in *The Art of Faulkner's Novels* (Austin: University of Texas Press, 1962), p. 121.

11. Bleikasten, in *Faulkner's As I Lay Dying*, stresses the novel's "unmistakable affinities with the epic" and applies to it the epical terms "odyssey" and "exodus," but rightly concludes that one cannot "force" the novel into "the genres of traditional poetics" because it is an epic, a tragedy, and a comedy "all three at once" (pp. 5-6).

12. The odd last name Bundren is an amalgam, *a la* Lewis Carroll, of "bungle" and "burden," a combination which neatly reflects the elements of both pilgrimage and comedy in the work. Cf. Michael Millgate, *The Achievement of William Faulkner* (New York: Barnes and

Noble, 1965), p. 110, on allusions to *Pilgrim's Progress* through the bur-den/Bundren echo.

13. More generally, Thornton H. Parsons comments in "Doing the Best They Can" that one of the "strongest themes in this novel is the awesome disparity between what things are worth and what people must pay for them" (p. 304).

14. Robert Hemenway interprets the passage in which these sentences occur, Darl's nighttime soliloquy, as a "struggle with the abstract idea of human existence." "Enigmas of Being in *As I Lay Dying*," *Modern Fiction Studies*, 16 (1970), p. 136. His article gives a useful summary of critical responses to this passage.

15. Cleanth Brooks, *William Faulkner: The Yoknapatawpha Country* (New Haven and London: Yale University Press, 1963), p. 350.

16. Brooks, in *The Yoknapatawpha Country*, labels Ned "the picaresque hero" and "the wily Odysseus," pp. 354, 356.

17. Quentin's escape is, of course, futile. Panthea Reid Broughton comments in *William Faulkner: The Abstract and the Actual*, p. 163, that for Faulkner "there is no escape."

18. Millgate, *The Achievement of William Faulkner*, pp. 124-26, comments that Lena Grove's "pursuing her tranquil way steadily across the face of Mississippi . . . provides a steady imperturbable groundnote, an onward linear progression that offers a constant contrast to the desperate contortions—moral, emotional, and physical—of the other characters."

19. William Faulkner, *Light in August* (1932; rpt. New York: Random House/Vintage Books, 1972), p. 480.

20. For example Faulkner's title *The Marble Faun*, borrowed from Hawthorne, "signalizes much more than a coincidence; for the outlook of the poet-novelist, like that of Hawthorne's prototype, has developed in the dark." Harry Levin, *The Power of Blackness* (New York: Knopf, 1958), p. 233. Specifically, Addie Bundren has been likened to Hester Prynne. See Richard Bridgman, "As Hester Prynne Lay Dying," *English Language Notes*, 2 (1965), 294-96. Also, Harold J. Douglas and Robert Daniel, "Faulkner and the Puritanism of the South," *Tennessee Studies in Literature*, 2 (1957), 1-14.

21. For both, the most accurate artistic affinity is with statuary. Numerous critics have commented on this quality of Faulkner's work. See, for instance, Karl E. Zink, "Flux and the Frozen Moment: The Imagery of Stasis in Faulkner's Prose," *PMLA*, 71 (1956), 285-301. Citing Zink, Andre Bleikasten, pp. 101-4.

22. Kenneth Burke comments on this kind of symbolic reading with devastating incisiveness in *The Philosophy of Literary Form*, 3d ed. rev. (Berkeley: University of California Press, 1973), pp. 8-9.

9
Poets' Journeys: Hart Crane and Wallace Stevens

> I was the world in which I walked, and what I saw
> Or heard or felt came not but from myself;
> And there I found myself more truly and more strange.
> —Wallace Stevens, "Tea at the Palaz of Hoon"

Modern fiction has often appropriated the techniques and the lyricism of poetry, with the result that its journeys have tended to become emblematic motifs or images rather than continuous narrative lines. In poetry, the traditional generic lines between narrative and lyric have also tended to become blurred. Short or fragmented narrative sequences and action images occur in meditative poetry far more insistently than they did in earlier periods, and the long narrative poem tends to be markedly lyrical or meditative, and hence relatively halting or turgid in its movement.[1] This blending of narrative and lyrical qualities is evident, in varying ways, in the works of the two poets considered here—Hart Crane (1899-1932) and Wallace Stevens (1879-1955). It derives largely from the recurrent presence of journey motifs that, for both, gain much of their power from the creative intersection of a contemporary idiom with a tradition having its own well-established and very powerful set of associations.

Hart Crane

It is a familiar but nonetheless valid point of critical departure when discussing Hart Crane to note that his aspiration was to produce a great epic of America. Whether he achieved that aim in *The Bridge* is open to debate. The consensus—and it is a valid one—seems to be that Crane produced, not epic, but lyric poetry with an epical quality. This epic dimension, which might better be termed a mythical dimension, emerges primarily through Crane's frequent use of journey motifs with connotations of heroic endeavor within a context of historical allusion.[2]

Crane's journeys are of three main kinds: the journeys of the historic past, contemporary journeys of withdrawal or escape, and the symbolic journey of the poet's development. The first, the American historic journey, occurs chiefly in *The Bridge*, where Crane retells both specific and representative journeys of American history in order to establish a background of epical scope, to indicate the heroic possibilities of American life and the poet's life, and to establish a past standard against which to measure contemporary society. Measurement against the past leads to the second kind of journey, the escape, which expresses the perceptive individual's disavowal of a repressive and materialistic society and his reorientation toward private experience and values. This journey appears in compressed or incipient ways in "The Wine Menagerie" and "For the Marriage of Faustus and Helen" and is most fully developed in "Voyages." The seeming conflict between Crane's use of the journey as an analogue for withdrawal into the self and private values, on the one hand, and his interest in the public, historic journeys, on the other, is only superficial. Not only does he use the heroic journeys of the past as a rationale for satire and protest, as many writers have done; more distinctively and powerfully, he formulates a great "Nevertheless," a positive assertion, like the "And yet" which opens "Voyages II," that the public dimension has value despite its very real shortcomings, just as the private journey of withdrawal has its own validity. Because it is possible for people to experience the awakening of vision within the public context and because private vision of an absolute ideal is lifeless without immersion in process and in common experience, Crane insists, they should "praise the years" ("For the Marriage of Faustus and Helen," p. 33)[3]—embrace the fleeting moments and with them the quotidian world. The poet's embrace of this everyday public dimension, like the historic hero's embrace, is, for Crane, redemptive. Crane's ultimate journey is the poet's journey of enablement, a natural extension of the journey toward private meanings as it impinges upon the historic journey. The poet's is the most radical withdrawal from social to private values, but he reaches his goal of a redemptive, prophetic art only if his withdrawal is combined with encounter, only if in his private journey he comes to perceive and value the historic journeys.

It is important to realize and to remember the significance of these public and historic concerns for Crane if one is to reach an understanding of his difference from the other poet to be considered here. He is much more deeply involved with American history than Stevens. True, every aspect of Crane's biography suggests the arch-romantic, the arch-rebel, the emphatically private poet. The peculiarities of his poetic idiom support this view; with its snarled syntax, its compressions and abrupt shifts, its reliance on metaphor and ecstatic exclamatory tone, his is scarcely a language for public utterance. Indeed, this yoking of public and even historical concern to extreme privacy of both sensibility and language is at the root of the critical uneasiness that has generally surrounded Crane's work.[4] Nevertheless, Crane maintained a hold, however tenuous, on both sides of the public/private duality, and the critic disregards either of the two at his peril.

Crane's association of journeys and in particular sea voyages with heroism and the heroic temper (a very traditional association) is conveyed with great clarity in his poem "At Melville's Tomb." The title itself suggests this sense of moral grandeur and heroic endeavor, both because of Melville's own seafaring and his heroic refusal to submit artistically and because of the figure of the defiant Ahab that looms inescapably behind the author himself. The poet's choice of the sea (Melville's "tomb") for his visit and veneration, then, tells us a good deal about his own values and aspirations. Directing his imaginative vision toward the sea, he perceives the redemptive glory that is shown forth by the world's heroes even in defeat: their "frosted eyes" lift altars[5] of, in the Nietzschean phrase, transvalued values that are vindicated or substantiated ("answered") by the wordless stars, the preverbal and therefore prehuman universe, the order of reality itself as it exists outside man's notions. Melville, Crane says, reached the farthest possible reaches of moral daring: "compass, quadrant and sextant contrive/No farther tides." The instruments of discovery are, of course, aids to mental voyaging by which Melville reached "azure steeps" beyond the call of "Monody," commemorative verse or by extension any memorial tomb, except the sea itself, the medium and symbol of limit-lessness for mortals: "This fabulous shadow only the sea keeps."

The heroic connotations of voyaging asserted in "At Melville's Tomb" recur throughout Crane's work. The hero will dream of "new thresholds, new anatomies" ("The Wine Menagerie," p. 24) until, determined to leave the shabby world and all shab-biness of spirit, he will

> Rise from the dates and crumbs. And walk away,
> Stepping over Holofernes' shins.
>
> (p. 24)

The matter-of-factness of the phrasing does not obscure the moral decisiveness of the act, which is, in Lewis's words, the start of a "journey toward fuller vision" (p. 198). Similarly, in "For the Marriage of Faustus and Helen," Crane envisions personal tran-scendence (moral, emotional, or spiritual) as a departure on different ways, whether long journeys or a mere "fall down-stairs" (p. 30).[6] He is tantalized by thought of escape to another, better dimension:

> And yet, suppose some evening I forgot
> The fare and transfer, yet got by that way
> Without recall,—lost yet poised in traffic.
> Then I might find your eyes across an aisle. . .
>
> (p. 28)

The "you" here is an ordinary woman transformed by poetic vision into Helen, the symbol of ideal beauty beyond the world's shabbiness, to which he would cling "endlessly" if his hands were not "too alternate/ With steel and soil" (p. 28). The symbolic Helen is not the ideal itself, but is associated with it and brings him intimations of that transcendent realm; she will help him "scud past shores" (p. 30) of spiritual timidity in order to reach it with her. Though the ideal destination of the voyage is not clearly defined, the poet envisions a state of being in which the most solitary values are the real values and a kind of purity (whiteness) latent in the real world is realized within the self:

> White, through white cities passed on to assume
> That world which comes to each of us alone.
>
> (p. 29)

It is this journey toward realization of the inmost man, "each of us alone," that is Crane's concern in the sequence "Voyages." The voyage metaphor signifies qualities of discovery, enlightenment, openness to experience, and commitment to process; these are the means to real understanding. However, these values are not discovered through the dramatic device of a single narrated voyage, but rather through a series of emotional clashes and meditations in which images of sea journeys provide the chief vehicle for abstract meaning.

Critical readings of "Voyages" have varied considerably, from Lewis's "almost mythic" journey "into love" in which the sea represents "experience generally," to Monroe Spears's "harbor of resurrection and fulfillment" or Maurice Kramer's achievement of a "serene" transcendentalism. Evelyn J. Hinz regards it as a poem in which "communication" through emotional impact without discursive argumentation is "the central concern."[7] But we are closer to the real life of the poem, which readers find compelling even when they cannot formulate its import, when we remain nearer the voyage metaphor and the ideal heroic openness to experience, however destructive, and in particular to love. "Voyages" achieves a heroic resonance similar to that of the traditional epic voyage in that it shows that a full commitment to the solitary voyage of discovery, with no clinging to safeguards, is a daring and eternally valid act. The poem does this by moving dramatically from an initial reluctance to venture out, through a series of voyages into experience, to a defeat, which is in turn succeeded and redeemed by a heroic renewal of the commitment to launch forth.[8]

"Voyages I," originally titled "Poster," anticipates the journey in its beach setting with children at play and its translation of the children's bodies into figurative ships ("spry cordage of your bodies"). The children may embark, but at this point they keep to the shore even though they are not fully conscious of the dangers that would await them at sea. Their immaturity gives them no means of grasping the message that the poet would deliver if he could: "The bottom of the sea is cruel." Against this warning is poised the "And yet" which opens section two, a splendid debate between stasis (or transcendence) and process. The postulated sea voyage is under way. The poet and his lover ("my Prodigal") dare the dangers of the sea, knowing it is "cruel," because it gives them intimations of eternity (it is "this great wink of eternity") and therefore of lasting love. At this time, however, the poet believes that lovers have some exemption from the sea's terrors; they perceive the splendors of its "samite sheeted and processioned" surface, not its "cruel" floor, and conceive themselves to be above the sentences it passes on those who are in time, because they themselves belong to eternity. Yet the poet perceives his love voyage in terms of earthly beauties in time: the voyage takes them past specific places (San Salvador appears as an example) and brings a luxuriance of sense impressions—the sounds of bells, crocus-blue night skies with crocus-yellow stars, and tides fragrant and beautiful as flowers appropriate to the tropical location (tides like "poinsettia meadows"). All of these sensed details of the living world, a world subject to time and death, draw the lovers back to an awareness of their involvement in time and its processes, even as they are involved in the eternal value of love. The "adagios of islands," the kinesthetic sense of voyaging past these tropic islands, "complete the dark confessions her veins spell," complete, to the lovers, the message buried in the veins of the sea, that it is at once a glimpse of eternity and a power in the enforcement of time, as its "turning shoulders wind the hours."

The lover's realization intensifies their love. Therefore, because time and process make life more precious even while they bring death, the poet prays to the "Seasons clear" (not only clear weather but the seasons clearly distinct from one another) that they "bind" himself and his lover "in time" and in "awe," in the fullest wondering perception of all that time brings. Further, he prays that they may continue to voyage into the dangers of experience until they die and thereby provide an answer, an exemplum, for the mortal creature's time-bound wish for the eternal, "the seal's wide," that is, wide-eyed, "sprindrift gaze toward paradise."

The idea that the lovers' condition corresponds to the sea is developed in section three. The sea bears an "infinite consanguinity" to them and shares their urge to raise up their discoveries and sacred emblems of truth, to lift "reliquary hands." The relics are of course the beauty and intensity of time-bound, sensual experience because that, temporal as it is, is the only eternally valid plane of being. The profane is thus transmuted into the sacred. Therefore, if life lived to its (erotic) fullest in each moment is an eternizing redemption of temporality and therefore of mortality, then death—even passage through the sea's "black swollen gates," or drowning—becomes no longer a "carnage" but a completion of the aesthetic/amorous experience. It becomes, not a savage rending, but a "silken skilled transmemberment," a taking apart of the body's life, "of song"—that is, worthy of song or poetry, like that idealized in poetry, and a part of the poetic act. Death becomes a part of the intensity of living. Perceiving all this, that his voyage will mean death but that death is to be trusted as a part of the life of daring and creativity, the poet expresses his entire willingness to undertake the full journey: "Permit me voyage, love, into your hands. . ."

The fourth poem is dramatically climactic, as the fullness of love is consummated in a kind of shattering of the lovers' selves, a *liebestod*. The verse is undeniably turgid and frenetic here, but that failure is the inherent failure of imitative form, which is in a way a success. The clashing images and fractured syntax enact very powerfully the dramatic action of the poem. Although the total statement may not be clear, specific images and phrases, such as "singing, this mortality alone/ Through clay aflow immortally to you," convey very poignantly the total surrender and the joyous grieving of the love experience and continue the earlier concern with joining a full acceptance of mortality to a full devotion to eternal values. The poet's surrender to the "widening noon" of the lover's breast "gathering" all the "bright insinuations" of his "years" (a surrender of his full selfhood) is the exact moment of erotic climax, after which the poem closes more quietly with the sharing of "the secret oar and petals of all love"—a figurative expression of the genital realities that are the basis of the love ideal. The voyage metaphor is dispersed into fleeting figures (gulf, palms, albatross, port, tides, harbor) that support the poet's belief that his lover's presence will indeed lead him to ultimate reaches, "islands," of discovery.

In section five, the destruction that the poet dared to court as he ventured out has indeed come upon him; he and his lover break off their relationship. The poet's feelings of defeat and hopelessness create a sense of stasis; the journey is suspended. The note of despair carries over to section six where, despite the poet's wish to continue his journey, he finds his visionary faith thwarted, his "eyes pressed black against the prow." Yet in the very act of expressing that despair he finds the promise and vindication of further voyages of discovery. Dynamic images retrieved from the voyage—the enlivening of still earth by viewing it from a moving perspective ("like a cliff swinging") and the glad surrender to inspiration and its forward urge ("or a sail/ Flung")—convey to him "Creation's blithe and petalled word" and offer him again the vision of a far off "Belle Isle." The poet's heroic persistence here is like the heroism of a voyager who resolves to shove off again despite first-hand experience of the sea's cruelty.

Crane draws on the journey to more perfect effect in "Voyages" than in any other poem. However, his reliance on the journey for explicit subject matter, imagery, and form is more fully evident in *The Bridge*, which also develops the vision of tragic defeat followed by renewal of vision that we have seen in "Voyages."

The Bridge is one of those magnificent failures that litter, or perhaps adorn, the path of romantic literature. Crane fails to integrate into a persuasive whole the three basic dimensions of the poem: the heroic past of history (which he hopes to bridge to the present), the spaces of twentieth-century America (which he hopes to bridge together and to bridge as a whole to a re-deemed America worthy of its history), and the poet's search for a vision (which he hopes to reach by means of the bridge of the poem). As a result, the work succeeds rather as a series of pieces than as a structural whole.[10] Lacking even the degree of wholeness we expect of the loose-limbed epic, let alone its as-sured authorial presence and its sense of cultural integration, the work is not an epic. Even so, for all its unevenness, its incohesiveness, and its lapses of poetic tact, *The Bridge* does have certain epic dimensions. It offers a large perspective, a vast sweep both temporally and spatially; it is concerned, at least in part, with large cultural movement and a sense of social density; it is varied; it attempts to link the private actions to the growth and quality of a culture; and it is colored, at least sporadically, by a sense of heroism. However imperfectly developed, these qual-ities are undeniably *there*, and they are qualities proper to the epic.

The intermittent atmosphere of heroic endeavor derives chiefly from the heroic journeys that recur throughout the work. Al-together, at their most abstract, these journeys represent the poet's quest for vision, for "Cathay"; they form, as Lewis puts it, "sallies of Crane's poetic soul toward new visions of truth."[11] The hero-poet is specifically a "traveller" ("Atlantis," p. 115), and the bridge itself, as well as the poetic "Bridge," is named as "Vision-of-the-Voyage" (p. 115). But the journeys are also, in a less abstract sense, a panorama of various kinds of journeys by various Americans and their historic predecessors. Their dis-tribution through the work is:

Proem. "To Brooklyn Bridge." The movement of New Yorkers around the city; the bridge itself, seen as an invitation to farther journeying.
1.   "Ave Maria." The return voyage of Columbus.
2.   "Powhatan's Daughter." The poet's awakening and prepara-tion for his visionary journey; Rip van Winkle's return to town and his subway ride; a train ride west on the 20th Century Limited; the flow of the Mississippi River into the Gulf of Mex-ico; the poet's visionary approach to the spirit of the continent; a frontier woman's recollections of her pioneering journey and her son's departure to make his fortune.

3.   "Cutty Sark." Voyages recalled by a derelict sailor; the poet's vision of Yankee clippers.
4.   "Cape Hatteras." Glimpses of the world of mechanized flight, the Wright brothers' flight, and Walt Whitman's Open Road.
5.   "Three Songs." The poet's attempts to locate an ideal female, a Pocahontas, in the debased present.
6.   "Quaker Hill." Only the movements of the poet's consciousness, searching through modern America for a cause for hope.
7.   "The Tunnel." The poet's subway ride from Manhattan to Brooklyn.
8.   "Atlantis." References to heroic voyagers of the past; reassertion of the bridge's invitation to greater journeys.

As we see from this overview, journeys of varying magnitude occur in all eight major divisions except section six, where movement is virtually suspended in a state of disillusionment. The occurrence and scope of journeys are parallel to the contours of emotional pitch and to the poet's approach to a socially signifying and poetically enabling vision. Thus "Ave Maria" and "Powhatan's Daughter," ecstatic visions of the early glories of American history and the American continent, are the most fully devoted to journeys. "Cutty Sark," "Cape Hatteras," and "Three Songs," weighted by the deterioration of contemporary America from its past glories, have progressively less and less journey movement. In "Quaker Hill," where the poet's hopes for recovery of America's glory and his own achievement of poetic vision are swamped by deterioration, shabbiness, and death, he can project no lateral journeys but only a downward motion from high ideals to a destructive earth. In "The Tunnel," the poet moves lower still, to a symbolic hell, but because this confrontation in the depths is an essential preliminary to the recovery of vision and heroic endeavor, just as it is to the heroes of traditional myth, it is the beginning of an emotional rise. Therefore, the journey is renewed, though in cramped, underground ways, and when the poet bursts out in an ecstatic reassertion of confidence, in "Atlantis," he summons up a cluster of images of journeying, all of them expansive, all centering on the great bridge.

As many critics have observed, Brooklyn Bridge serves Crane as a unifying symbol of the act of mediation. In the proem, the bridge seems to be offering New Yorkers only a passage from one living death to another; and indeed the bridge serves as a passageway to actual death in the "bedlamite's" suicide leap of the fifth stanza. Yet all the while it offers the promise of real mediation between the living death and the life of the spirit, or between debased society and redeemed society. The bridge is addressed in deifying capitals as "Thee, across the harbor" (p. 45). It offers, though Crane does not say how, "reprieve and pardon"; it is a "harp and altar," and its cables are not merely structural necessities but "choiring strings" of beauty. The bridge, then, is two different entities at once: the utilitarian roadway of the unimaginative daily life and a promise of redemption that can "breathe the North Atlantic still," that is, participate in a larger life despite the failure of New Yorkers to recognize its promise. In rare moments "we," we who have glimpses of the redemptive vision to which the poet aspires, have seen it "condense eternity," bridge the way from the moment to the eternal, and, Pieta-like, gather up the dark world in its beautifully sustaining arms: "we have seen night lifted in thine arms" (p. 46). In moments like these we see the promise of the symbolic bridge. It offers mediation between the Old and the New World, the widely separated reaches of the continent, and between everyday life and exalted life. Accordingly, on our behalf, the poet invokes the bridge as deity, the "Sleepless" one:

> Vaulting the sea, the prairies' dreaming sod,
> Unto us lowliest sometime sweep, descend
> And of the curveship lend a myth to God.

> (p. 46)

In this prefacing view of the bridge's dual nature, Crane communicates the great theme that runs through the multidimensional, loosely connected reaches of the work as a whole: that the Ideal, the redeemed life, can be achieved within ordinary, debased life; the means are there if awakened vision can perceive them. Further, unyielding determination to achieve vision despite the reverses of the real world is genuine heroism.

The first major section of the poem, "Ave Maria," presents Columbus's voyage and prayer as an analogue of this heroic act.

Columbus himself in part represents the poet, who, if he manages to persevere and if he is granted Divine (aesthetic) favor, makes wondrous discoveries, which he brings back to a society in need of inspiration and redemption. Columbus returns from his discovery bringing back "Cathay!" (p. 48), news of the far realm that he has taken to be the Orient. At the end of the poem, Crane, completing his own "voyage" of discovery, will ask, "Is it Cathay?" (p. 117)—has he too discovered new territory and brought us, the readers, the report of it? The heroism of Columbus is both physical and moral; he dares to persevere despite the adversities of stormy seas and of discouragement. Within his trials, he is able to achieve not only his physical triumph, the discovery of "Cathay," but also his confident outreach to transcendence, conveyed in the exalted language of the concluding four-stanza section, that will be echoed at the end of "The Tunnel," as Crane's own ecstasy of vision flashes out from his disillusionment. Columbus's relative ease of access to the sacred, a readiness of sensibility prepared by his immersion in a religion-centered society, is unavailable to Crane, a man of the secular twentieth century who must create his own visionary awareness. But the two visions are equally transcendent and equally valid. They are verbally linked by images that reach backward to the Proem and forward to the entire work.

In section two, "Powhatan's Daughter," the poet begins his journey westward into America and his simultaneous journey into the past. The many journeys of the poems in this section are attempts to mediate between the American past of myth and folklore and the America of the twentieth century and ventures of the poetic imagination into the spatial and temporal reaches of America in search of a vision. The opening poem, "The Harbor Dawn," redirects the poetic journey from the beckoning "shore beyond desire!/ The sea's green crying towers a-sway, Beyond" at the end of "Ave Maria" to a beckoning "distant hill" (p. 56) in the west. The poet lies between sleep and waking, on the Brooklyn side of the bridge, hearing the sounds of the city below, the seafront and a figurative "tide of voices." Submerged allusions to Ulysses' voyages (through a punning on "sirens" and towers that are "Cyclopean") continue the association between imaginative discovery and the heroic quest.[12] The poet's actual movement west and into the past is heralded by Rip van Winkle, whom Crane designated in personal correspondence as "the 'guardian angel' of the journey into the past."[13] The poem "Van Winkle" opens with what Richard Sugg calls a synecdoche of the bridge itself, "Macadam, gun-grey" (p. 58), a highway, spanning the continent as in the Proem the bridge had vaulted "the prairies' dreaming sod." Van Winkle is a folklore avatar of the poet himself; references in the poem slide between them, and the two are merged in the rush to catch a subway train. This is the first stage, as it develops, of the journey into the continent, although more directly it is the poet's everyday departure for work in Manhattan. Appropriately for a character who slept twenty years and became confused about his place in time, Rip's (the poet's) departure is marked by anxiety about time. The poet urges Rip not to miss the train—"it's getting late!"—and asks, "Have you got your 'Times'—?" (p. 61). The reference is to the newspaper, of course, but it also translates into the question, Have you got your times straight? are you oriented in time? The imaginative goal, however, is not so much to separate times (though getting them straight, understanding them, is desirable) as to draw them together. For that purpose, Rip is a good bridging figure.

Aboard the 20th Century Limited, the poet hero leaves New York (in the imagination; physically he remains at work until he starts for home late in the poem) in search of the elusive "spirit of the land," embodied as Pocahontas.[14] In a fast-paced narrative language of jazz cadence, the train roars past signboards advertising a digest of twentieth-century material trappings. The brassy linguistic pastiche, the equivalent of the train's rush, culminates in the second stanza in a challenge to say whether we approve of this spiritually deprived state:

> . . .an EXpress makes time like
> SCIENCE—COMMERCE and the HOLYGHOST
> RADIO ROARS IN EVERY HOME WE HAVE THE NORTHPOLE
> WALLSTREET AND VIRGINBIRTH WITHOUT STONES OR
> WIRES OR EVEN RUNning brooks connecting ears
> and no more sermons windows flashing roar

breathtaking—as you like it. . .eh?

(p. 62)

The point of view, tracing the poet's disaffection from the machine-like rush of his century, then shifts from that of a passenger on the 20th Century Limited to that of someone standing by the tracks, who, along with three hoboes, watches it pass and disappear "neatly out of sight" (p. 62). These hoboes, precisely because they are outsiders who can ride the train in their own way, are another set of avatars of the poet. They "count/ . . .The river's minute by the far brook's year" (p. 64). Their concepts of time and relationships are not dominated by the clock's minutes but are interpreted by their instinctual sense of larger natural rhythms; they have an intuitive knowledge of Pocahontas, the land-spirit, knowing her "body under the wide rain" (p. 66). The word "far" in "far brook's year" also signals these hoboes' role as modern pioneers, travellers whose goal is far across the land. Like the early pioneers, they are homeless men who go

        . . .ruminating through
        Ohio, Indiana—blind baggage—
        To Cheyenne tagging. . .Maybe Kalamazoo.

(p. 64)

Being homeless, they are free to find America for themselves, but Crane gives no assurance that they will indeed perform the pioneers' symbolic act of home founding; he shows merely that they have the potential.[15] All of these men, as well as the travellers who are cut off from the land because they remain on the train (the "Pullman breakfasters," the "Sheriff, Brakeman and Authority") can have fleeting intuitions of the land-spirit; they can "lean from the window" and feel that they have "touched hands with some ancient clown" (p. 68). And even if they do not fully understand, they participate in the river of process, here the Mississippi, as it flows irresistibly along toward the "Gulf," which is death but also rebirth. The river, then, in its own continent-long journey, is another mediator or bridge of past to present. It is for this reason that the emptying into the Gulf is accompanied by "hosannas" (p. 69): the flowing of the past into the present, even though it involves death, produces continuity and the sense of living myth.[16]

It is only the poet, however, not all those who live and die on the time-river's flow and thereby "feed" it, who perceives the infusion of the mythic past. Once he has participated in this journey—again, a journey both spatial (westward) and temporal (into the past and then recapitulating its flow into the present)— he is able to complete his quest for the essence of the continent, Pocahontas. The last leg of this journey is made not by train or riverboat but by canoe, the vehicle of the primitive, therefore mythic, past. The poet performs the symbolic and archetypically American act of retreating from society to nature: he "left the village for dogwood" (p. 70).[17] This final journey to his consummation with the Idea of the continent follows the conventional pattern of the night journey: it is pursued under "one star" and through an undefined landscape ("Over how many bluffs, tarns, streams I sped!"); the journeyer has a sense of involvement in larger forces ("I could not stop"); and the outward journey projects an inner discovery ("I. . .knew myself within some boding shade"). At the end, the poet witnesses the ecstatic dance of the Indian sachem Maquoqueeta and becomes himself identified with the dancer: "I, too, was liege/To rainbows currying each pulsant bone" (p. 73); "we danced, O Brave, we danced" (p. 75).

Through this experience, the outward climax of *The Bridge*, the poet becomes himself the carrier of myth, and therefore the bridge of consciousness. Yet he is not ready to convey his vision until he has completed journeys into reality complementing the journey into myth. Part of that second journey movement is an additional view of the great West, this time focusing on the pioneer experience, which occupies a position somewhere between myth and reality. This view is given in the final poem of "Powhatan's Daughter," "Indiana," in which an aging pioneer woman tells her experience. Dramatically, the poem is a mistake; it vitiates the culminating effect of Maquoqueeta's dance and thus blurs the purpose of "Powhatan's Daughter" as a whole. Logically, however, it provides transition from the elevation of myth to sobering reality, as it moves from the past and the storied journeys of pioneers to the present and the ordinary departure of the woman's son to make his fortune. Also, it follows the familiar contours of America's historic journeys, re-capitulating the westward search for gold, the disheartened jour-neys of easterly back trailers, the Indian's dispossession, and the poor boy's venture out into the world.

In sections two through seven, journeys appear chiefly as either allusion or short movements within narrowed spatial lim-its and within the poet's present time. He now pursues his "journey-quest in the modern world," but it is a fragmented quest.[18] In section three, "Cutty Sark," the poet starts "walking home across the Bridge" (p. 84), an act interposed between two passages related to sea voyages. First he meets a derelict sailor, who ushers in a series of glimpses of degeneration; later, pausing in his return crossing of the bridge, he views in his imagination the great sailing ships of the past. What he envisions is a hardy and joyous life of

> Pennants, parabolas—
> clipper dreams indelible and ranging,
> baronial white on lucky blue!

He calls the ships by name and asks "where can you be?" (p. 85). But the past is lost, the present a deterioration from it, and stories of past wonders like the clipper ships do not form a viable myth unless the creative imagination brings them to life in the present.

In section four, "Cape Hatteras," the poet begins to find a model for his own creative imagination, the great visionary of the Open Road, Whitman. The journeys of the present viewed here are flights, first of the Wright brothers, then of fighter pilots. We live in an age of flight—"the eagle dominates our days" (p. 89)—but instead of the glorious quest it could offer, the "rule/ Of wings imperious" is "strident." Instead of realizing Whit-man's dream of freedom to reach toward "infinity," the poet fears this "rule" imprisons the great "Saunterer on free ways" (p. 89), making him a grounded Columbus, a "Great Navigato[r] without ship" (p. 89). Whitman had the vision of a voyaging hero—"Sea eyes and tidal, undenying, bright with myth!" (p. 89). Yet the poet fears that Whitman's vision will be inadequate in the "new universe" of unrestrained power that he sees epitomized in the airplane that has "splintered space" (p. 91). He sees the age, like a fighter plane, crashing "down gravitation's/ vortex" (p. 92). In truth, what he fears is that he himself, as the poet-seer struggling to bring mythic utterance to his own age, will be inadequate to bring forward his inheritance from the great "Saunterer." Whitman "held the heights more sure" even than pilots in their machines; he reached "there and beyond!" (p. 93). Therefore, he can serve Crane as an inspiriting prede-cessor, even more compellingly because more intimately than Columbus. Whitman first "set breath in steel," as Crane now attempts to make the poem of "that great Bridge, our Myth" (p. 94). Therefore, he provides Crane a model and alter ego: "As-censions of thee hover in me now" (p. 93). Inspirited by Whit-man, he dares to assert that "thy vision is reclaimed" even in this age of the machine. He can now resume his journey of confrontation of the modern world, confident that he is the inheritor of Whitman's mission:

> yes, Walt,
>
> Afoot again, and onward without halt,—
> Not soon, nor suddenly,—no, never to let go
> My hand
> in yours,
> Walt Whitman—
>
> so—
>
> (p. 95)

The poet's appropriation of the spirit of Whitman does not mean he has already succeeded in his quest, but only that he is enabled to continue the effort. In the "Three Songs" of section five, he wanders his urban world searching for living avatars of Pocahontas. It is a debased world that offers him no clues. He is left with only his nostalgia for an absent "Cathedral Mary," a reminder of Pocahontas, whose guidance he needs. After searching all the city's faces, he confronts only the spoilage of what was once "the Promised Land." His literal journey can go no farther; he must resign the "hawk's far stemming view" in favor of a descent to the depths of fear. Like the leaves, with his poet's year apparently near its end, he must "descend—/ descend—"(p. 106).

In section seven, "The Tunnel," he foregoes return by way of the bridge to go down the "scuttle yawn" of the subway, which "yawns the quickest promise home" (p. 108). As Lewis writes, this is "the most desperate" of his journeys, because it is a giving up, a return by the same way he set out, in the guise of Rip van Winkle, with no vision achieved. But the subway ride this time is at night, the appropriate time for what Lewis recognizes as a "plunge . . . down into the land of the dead . . . corresponding to the visit to the underworld in the eleventh book of *The Odyssey*, the sixth book of the *Aeneid* and the *Inferno*."[19] After an emphatic downward movement in the opening stanzas, arrival in the subway is signalled by hellish "rattling" of "gongs" (p. 109). On the train he overhears random fragments of empty talk that amount to "phonographs of hades" (p. 110). In the distraught state of mind to which this plunge has brought him, he sees a vision of the poet's plight in society: the head of Edgar Allan Poe "swinging from the swollen strap," his "eyes like agate lanterns" (p. 110). Poe's sufferings are applicable to his own: "Death. . ./Probing through you—toward me, O evermore!" (p. 110). Searching for some reassurance that the symbolic castration of the poet's imagination is not the final word, he cries out to the apparition of the great romantic,

> And when they dragged your retching flesh,
> Your trembling hands that night through Baltimore—
> That last night on the ballot rounds, did you
> Shaking, did you deny the ticket, Poe?
>
> (p. 110)

If so, if Poe was able to resist and "deny the ticket," the poet may likewise be able to deny the constrictions and cheapness of his time in order to release his creative imagination. After a stop where people shuffle off or on, "each eye attending its shoe" like the downcast crowds of Eliot's *Waste Land*, and after the "dive/ Under the river" (p. 111), he notices a "Wop washerwoman" also riding home on the Daemon, the subway. A far-removed approximation of Pocahontas, she gives him hope by providing a glimmer of maternal love in the hellish world. With this awakening of hope—minimal enough, but precisely the kind of hope he has most needed—the poet feels the subway rise toward his stop on the Brooklyn side, a rise that corresponds to his return from imaginative death. He, "like Lazarus," reawakens to life. Having reached the Brooklyn side, he finds himself again, as in the Proem, at the foot of the bridge. Now, however, he has completed his journey and is able to speak on his own behalf the prayer of Columbus:

> Kiss of our agony Thou gatherest,
> > O Hand of Fire
> gatherest—
>
> (p. 112)

He is now ready to write his summary of what he hopes is a myth for modern America, which is coextensive with a description of and hymn to the image of that myth, the bridge.

The conclusion, "Atlantis," may be, as critics have generally been agreed to call it, extravagant, but if one has accepted Crane's premises, its extravagance is justified. He is writing in praise of no less than the symbol at once of a redeemed history and a redeemed aesthetic vision. This is not to say that the language of the poem necessarily *works* merely because the poetic motive justifies exhilaration, though it may, but simply that the tone of the finale has been prepared for by what has gone before.

"Atlantis" opens with a three-stanza description of the bridge, emphasizing its ascending cable lines that produce in the viewer a sense of exultance or inspiration. Yet it is not only a real but a symbolic bridge that is celebrated, an image for mediation and thereby mystical unity; it is an "arc synoptic" unifying all of history both spatially (the westward movement of history) and temporally ("tomorrows into yesteryear" p. 115). Crane senses in the bridge as symbol—and, I think, in his own *Bridge*—"hails, farewells" to the storied past, specifically (and his choice of a typifying figure here signifies his emphasis) "you, aloft there—Jason!" What is important in the past is its instances of heroism and willingness to launch out on voyages, visionary enterprises. In greeting Jason, Crane shows that his own society speaks to, communicates with, that age of heroism; he establishes the link of communication, the bridge between them. Similarly, both bridge and *Bridge* (for the reference of the phrases, "Vision-of-the-Voyage" and "Choir" is purposely unspecified) speak in the present the vibrant word of past heroism like Columbus's voyage toward Cathay. They are

> . . .translating time
> Into what multitudinous Verb the suns
> And synergy of waters ever fuse, recast
> In myriad syllables,—Psalm of Cathay!

(p. 115)

The bridge is an "intrinsic Myth" (p. 116), an image-story unifying its own mechanistic and dispersed society and, because it is a culmination, unifying the present society with the past and with myths of the past. It is Crane himself who, by writing this revelation of the significance of the bridge, becomes a bridge between myth and the reality within which he finds his new vision and myth.

At any rate, that is his aspiration. In sober fact, Brooklyn Bridge has not been the aesthetic redemption of our history, however much Crane or its designer, John Augustus Roebling, may have wanted to see it as such. The central pointed arches of Roebling's towers may "proclaim themselves. . .as monumental passageways," but they have long since been overtopped by surrounding skyscrapers so that visually the bridge is not an aesthetic center, and both in the history of its construction and in subsequent events such as the fatal stampede on its opening day it has proven to be more a part of its crass context than a redemption of it.[20] Crane says that nevertheless it can be seen as an emblem of redemption *within* the crass context if one has the will to see it as such. But in his own *Bridge*, unless the reader is predisposed to acquiesce in the undemonstrated, Crane can only assert, he cannot establish the argument. Crane's bridge, finally, is tenuous. Moreover, his purposed wedding of public matter to private experience with a resulting birth of new life in both spheres is also more claimed than achieved. Again, his bridge is stretched too thin, between too disparate bodies of material, and as a result it is only in occasional stretches, not in the entire span, that he can build his mediating structure in the responses of the reader who demands to be convinced.

Wallace Stevens

Wallace Stevens's poetry is generally neither dramatic nor narrative. In this respect, though not in its exuberant diction and startling imagery, "The Comedian as the Letter C" is an uncharacteristic work. It is his one truly narrative poem and needs to be approached as such, whatever else one finds in it. However, relatively few critics—Helen Vendler, notably, and K. E. Marre are two—have cared to examine its narrative techniques. Most have preferred to ignore or, at any rate, disregard the surface in their eagerness to consider symbolism or abstract implications. This is a mistake. Crispin may be a comic version of the American Adam, as critics have said,[21] and his story may project an account, in some ways autobiographical, graphical, of the growth of the poetic sensibility or even the unfolding of poetic history.[22] Stevens refers to his poem as an anecdote—that is, a little story with a somewhat allegorical point. But it is first a story.[23]

Like any other story, "Comedian" has a main character, a setting, a narrator, and a plot (or at any rate action). Crispin, the protagonist if not hero, is a fully individuated character, unlike the shadowy symbolic personages that populate many of Stevens's poems. Nor is he a composite, an Everyman representing the totality of American immigration. He is a defined character with a stated occupation, valet, and other interests peculiar to himself, notably botany and poetry. Setting too is fully, vividly present and is recognizable as the real world. Crispin's quest is felt by the reader as real motion through a series of clearly differentiated places. True, the various settings of the poem and Crispin's interactions with them serve the themes or extended meanings of the poem, but they are not mere allegorical somewheres or nowheres.

Narrative tactic is also managed as in a capably told story. The narrative voice is clearly distinguished from Crispin, but it is not, as Marre suggests in his generally salutary article on the subject, consistently or rigidly separated from him, making ironic, knowing comments from outside his story.[24] Like a variable omniscient narrator in a novel, varying the pace of the story through such basic techniques as indirect discourse, the narrator of "Comedian" is sometimes detached and knowing but sometimes involved in the story; he can, at various times, pronounce judgment on Crispin and his confusions from above or become virtually his spokesman.

The story line of the poem can be briefly summarized. In fact, much of its comic tone is created by the disparity between the slight story line, with its paucity of incidents despite its wide spatial and temporal scope, and the elaborate language in which it is told. Crispin, a native of France, a valet by trade and a dabbler in both botany and poetry, leaves his rather tame homeland and sails to the New World. He lands first in southern Mexico and then in North America, apparently North Carolina, where he settles down to an agricultural life, marries, and fathers four daughters. His life becomes finally rather tame, as it had been in France, but his travels have awakened Crispin to various new ways of thinking, so that even if he does seem to come full circle his adventures do not end in futility. He has gained an acquaintance with a fairly sizable slice of the world, he extracts whatever understanding he can from experience, he enjoys his family, and his interest in the imaginative process continues. It is a happy ending.[25]

It is evident that the shape of Crispin's journey reflects at least three of the journey patterns that we have discussed in earlier chapters: the exploration, the quest, and the home-seeking journey. Crispin leaves a stultifying Old World and voyages to the New. Like Columbus, he lands in lush tropic regions, more or less of Central America. Like the visionary founding fathers, he goes to North America with intentions of founding a reformed society. Like them, in their more hopeful moments at any rate, he exults in the promise of the New World:

> A still new continent in which to dwell.
> What was the purpose of his pilgrimage,
> Whatever shape it took in Crispin's mind,
> If not, when all is said, to drive away

The shadow of his fellows from the skies,
And, from their stale intelligence released,
To make a new intelligence prevail?

(IV, 9-15)

It is clear that a parallel with the hopeful historic patterns of founding and immigration is intended. The tone in which it is intended, however, is not so clear. In specific passages the tone is ambiguous, and it varies from one passage to another. In addition, more abstract aesthetic and philosophical questions are playing through the poem at the same time, so that even if "Comedian" is not so obviously difficult a poem as some of Stevens's other long works, since it offers the advantage of a simple narrative line to carry the reader along, it is nevertheless close-grained and subtle.

It is very quickly apparent that whatever Stevens may do with American history here, he is not rewriting the national epic. His opening trumpet of theory, which is actually Crispin's opening philosophical premise,"Man is the intelligence of his soil,/ The sovereign ghost," is quickly undercut by the traditional comic technique of the sudden drop. The philosopher who thinks this big thought is only a "Socrates of snails," a rather small-scale thinker and teacher. When he goes to sea, the theorizer finds that he goes from small influence to none at all; he cannot be a "preceptor to the sea" (I,6) because he has come to a reality that defies human intellection. Having left the world he knew, a world of "simple salad-beds" and "honest quilts" that revealed human shaping and was receptive to human imagination, he has confronted the "inscrutable" (I,15). He is therefore bemused, "at sea" mentally as well as physically. In the face of this raw and shapeless reality, Crispin quickly loses his conception of himself as a shaping intelligence even on so small a scale as "lutanist of fleas" and "botanist" of "mute/ And maidenly green-horns" (I, 22, 25-27; the greenhorns, as Sukenick suggests, are simple young plants). He had been to himself, when he indulged this "mythology of self," the "imperative haw/ Of hum," the organizing assertion in a humming world.[26] He is now forced to see himself as merely a "skinny sailor" (I,28). The narrator's comment is even more unflattering: Crispin is "this short-shanks" in a world of force, "all that brunt" (I,31). The initial impact of his voyage, then, is overwhelming. Crispin is "washed away by magnitude" with his whole vision of life reduced for the moment to the "slap and sigh" of the reality-chaos, the sea.

He has been given a lesson in radical humility. His sense of identity is washed away as if it were one of the old myths that projected anthropomorphic forms upon the natural world. Triton, for instance, is reduced to the mere natural motions that led men to imagine him in the first place.[27] "Just so" the former self-conceived Crispin is "dissolved" (I,52); that is, the idea of the godlike man, like that of the manlike god, disappears in the face of reality. What remains to Crispin is a self denuded of preconceptions and therefore so unfamiliar that it scarcely seems the self at all. The narrator offers an analogy to clarify this state of puzzlement produced when experience does not follow the patterns of past experience and preconceptions:

> . . .nothing of himself
> Remained, except some starker, barer self
> In a starker, barer world, in which the sun
> Was not the sun because it never shone
> With bland complaisance on pale parasols,
> Beetled, in chapels, on the chaste bouquets.
>
> (I,60-65)

Crispin had proposed for himself a "simple jaunt" to Yucatan, Havana, and then Carolina. Now, feeling his more grandiloquent assumptions challenged by the raw universe, he finds things more complicated. He becomes an "introspective voyager" (I,68). At this point, the voyage becomes multidimensional, a journeying between diverse inner states. "The sea," reality, "severs not only lands but also selves" (I,77-78). If the old Crispin was dissolved, he was enabled to become a new Crispin, or, as he makes a series of only partially satisfying attempts to come to terms with reality, a series of new Crispins. Therefore, the violent forces of the ocean and the sea wind are not only a "swift destruction" but at the same time "something given to make whole" (I,86-88). At the end of the first section, "The World without Imagination," then, Crispin is shaken, but his situation is hopeful.

Arrived in Yucatan, Crispin finds that even here men's imaginations cling to outworn conventions: they "made their plea," presumably in poems, to nightingales as if their own spectacularly real birds were "barbarous," not suited to art. The emphasis given to this passage about the "Maya sonneteers" by its position, the first six lines of the canto, is one of the more indisputable reasons why critics treat the narrative as an allegory for poetic theorizing. Certainly that dimension is established here, if not sooner. However, it is important to recognize that poetry serves Stevens as a metaphor for the engagement of men's imaginations with the real world, whether that engagement actually occurs in poetry or in any other art form or simply in their alert responses and cogitations.

Crispin, having been "made new" (I,80) by his experience of deconstruction and clarification at sea ("luminous traversing," II,10), will not accede in the sonneteers' decadence. He immerses himself in the lush reality of the place, its "savage color" (II,14). The narrator is here speaking omnisciently, analytically; his assessment of the change in Crispin is his own. Crispin's former mentality he sums up as a habit of viewing nature within a tamed and humanized sphere and through the haze of the traditionally correct artistic sensibility. Now Crispin is more open to experience unfiltered by tame, falsifying preconceptions:

> How greatly had he grown in his demesne,
> This auditor of insects! He that saw
> The stride of vanishing autumn in a park
> By way of decorous melancholy; he
> That wrote his couplet yearly to the spring,
> As dissertation of profound delight,
> Stopping, on voyage, in a land of snakes,
> Found his vicissitudes had much enlarged
> His apprehension. . .
>
> (II,15-23)

Now open to this plurality of experience and determined to render it honestly in his poetry, he produces verse of "an aesthetic tough, diverse, untamed,/ Incredible to prudes, the mint of dirt" (II,34-35). His new effacement before reality allows the "green barbarism" of the place to become a "paradigm," the determining pattern for what he creates.

Stevens's narrative tone here is nicely balanced between sympathy and ridicule. To the extent that Crispin has been undeceived of stale relics of sensibility, he has improved; the poetic diction of the passage does not undercut his real gain. Further, Stevens, in his modesty, and therefore the reader as well, can sympathetically identify with a character who feels himself dwarfed by the universe and who gropes his way through experience. Still, however recognizably one of us, Crispin is ludicrous in his self-conceits. His efforts are never very grand; as an observer of the universe he is about on the level of counting up bugs ("auditor of insects," II,16), and his poetic output is virtually a "couplet yearly." But he goes on humanly magnifying his importance and the scope of his understandings even when he has received lessons in his insignificance. For instance, no sooner has he turned humbly to the transcription of what is— itself a pretentious enterprise, though he does not yet know it— than he again begins to hope for a grandiose aesthetic.

> Crispin foresaw a curious promenade
> Or, nobler, sensed an elemental fate,
> And elemental potencies and pangs,
> And beautiful barenesses as yet unseen. . .
>
> (II,37-40)

The narrator, of course, knows better, and it is the disparity between his understanding and Crispin's that colors the passage with irony.

To show us what comes of this new aesthetic hope, which is what the narrator knew would come of it, he assumes Crispin's consciousness, though reporting it to us indirectly.

> The fabulous and its intrinsic verse
> Came like two spirits parleying, adorned
> In radiance from the Atlantic coign,
> For Crispin and his quill to catechize.
>
> (II,44-47)

The excitement of the language is Crispin's; to the extent that the reader feels it to be overdone, it conveys the narrator's foreknowledge of failure. In this foreknowledge, he builds to a linguistic crescendo in the "juicily opulent" lines about the excesses of tropical experience (II,48-57), preparing for a comic drop: "So much for that." Crispin, the "affectionate emigrant" (affectionate in that he is subject to his affections, his immediate impulses) finds that unfiltered reality brings not only a "jostling festival" of sense impressions but also harsh disturbances, "parrot-squawks" (II,59). He wants to ignore the squawks, to "let that trifle pass"—a phrase that conveys both Crispin's own voice and the narrator's irony. The squawk becomes a seeming "gasconade of drums" (II,65), then a "tempestuous clarion" (II,70): the thunderstorm of Yucatan referred to in the canto title. A nice structural parallel to the storm at sea, this thunderstorm convinces Crispin that he cannot be an "annotator" of reality, a dilletantish poetaster converting the better bits of reality into verse. Sometimes the world comes at one with such force that it is time to stop taking notes and hide, as Crispin "took flight" into a convenient cathedral.

What he feels in the storm is energy, the "quintessential fact" of a universe that is not, after all, mere raw material. In a fine climax to the canto, Stevens offers us a Crispin once again chastened but aspiring. Feeling himself possessed by a force beyond himself, the reality of energy lying behind the surface presences of color and form, he is "elate, intent" (II,89)—and ready for more.[28]

The third canto, "Approaching Carolina," presents a third distinct setting to which Crispin must react. He pursues his "pilgrimage" north and, omitting his intended visit to Cuba, seeks out a place he expects to be strikingly different. What he seeks, however, is a Carolina of preconception that does not tally with reality. Eager as he is to move onward and upward in his pursuit of truth, he has fallen back into his old habit of mistaking the imagined for the real. He expected a "polar, polar-purple, chilled/ And lank" North America of "boreal mistiness" and "morose chiaroscuro, gauntly drawn" (III,14-27). But the cold moonlight of the land is actually the "legendary moonlight" (III, 10) of imagining; it is dispelled by the sun-like reality that greets him. He approaches Carolina in self-conscious austerity, thinking he wants the "fecund minimum" (III,71) of wintriness (fecund because it is this cold nothingness that gives rise to the confusing multiplicity he is now avoiding). Instead, he finds springtime and a welter of crudely vital sensations:

> A river bore
> The vessel inward. Tilting up his nose,
> He inhaled the rancid rosin, burly smells
> Of dampened lumber, emanations blown
> From warehouse doors, the gustiness of ropes,
> Decays of sacks, and all the arrant stinks
> That helped him round his rude aesthetic out.
>
> (III,76-82)

That is, in what might be called his process of Americanization, Crispin continues to pursue an aesthetic that responds to reality, an aesthetic "tough, diverse, untamed" (II,34), as before, but now responding, as Sukenick puts it, to a "prosaic reality, as opposed to the exotica of Yucatan" (pp. 53-54). Undaunted, Crispin takes this new surprise as another revelation. "He savored rankness like a sensualist" (III,83). The "rankness" that he savors is a crudeness reminiscent of Dickens's *Martin Chuzzlewit* and other fictional satires on the raw American society.[29] It is a matter of "the crawling railroad spur, the rotten fence" (III,85). This immersion in plain American reality is, the narrator comments, "curriculum for the marvelous sophomore" (III,86). It is a tricky line, tonally. Crispin is marvelous both in being full of wonderment and in being marvellously adaptable, and he is indeed sophomoric in his undaunted eagerness to think he has found final answers every time experience shakes up his beliefs. This crude rankness he somewhat amusingly accepts as a revelation: "It purified." But one recalls that in the first canto he had been "made new," and in the second he had launched a new aesthetic, given it up, and felt "elate, intent, profound" upon finding another. The narrator quietly conveys the amusing optimism of Crispin, "the marvelous sophomore." However, in lines that immediately follow he displays neither amusement nor irony, but seems instead to make his own straightforward pronouncement:

It purified. It made him see how much
Of what he saw he never saw at all.
He gripped more closely the essential prose
As being, in a world so falsified,
The one integrity for him, the one
Discovery still possible to make,
To which all poems were incident, unless
That prose should wear a poem's guise at last.

(III,87-94)

This is the point of farthest departure for Crispin, both geographically and theoretically. He has completely abandoned his early notions that man's imagination is free to control reality. The remainder of the poem chronicles his efforts to apply his devotion to prosaic reality and then his relaxation into a measure of compromise.

The opening of the fourth canto, "Nota: his soil is man's intelligence," demonstrates the extent of Crispin's reversal. It is not Stevens's pronouncement in his own person, however, any more than was the first, that man was the intelligence of his soil, though as several critics have remarked, it is in fact a dictum very near Stevens's artistic beliefs. Even so, the breezy following line makes it clear that the narrative voice here is adopting Crispin's satisfied view of his progress: "That's better. That's worth crossing seas to find." The narrator's vantage point then moves somewhat further off as he refers to Crispin directly in the third person and summarizes his present housecleaning mentality in the kind of grandiose language with comic drops that he regularly utilizes to show up foolishness:

Crispin in one laconic phrase laid bare
His cloudy drift and planned a colony.
Exit the mental moonlight, exit lex,
Rex and principium, exit the whole
Shebang. Exeunt omnes.

(IV,3-7)

Again Stevens's narrative stance is an elusive blend of ridicule and sympathetic approval. However, he quickly moves away from this comic verbiage to a statement of Crispin's purpose that is not overtly satiric at all.

> What was the purpose of his pilgrimage,
> Whatever shape it took in Crispin's mind,
> If not, when all is said, to drive away
> The shadow of his fellows from the skies,
> And, from their stale intelligence released,
> To make a new intelligence prevail?
>
> (IV,10-15)

It is a clear and direct statement of Americanness in intellectual aspiration and probably the best single justification for connecting Stevens with the Emersonian strain in American literature.[30] However, Stevens knows better than did his transcendental forebears the real limitations on the noble aspiration for newness of thought. No one, and especially not Crispin, is capable of bootstrap levitation. Every attempt to apply his theories, whether in his own verse or in the founding of a colony, leads him into absurdity. These attempts are another kind of "voyage" (IV,25), but it goes nowhere. The ludicrousness of Crispin's schemes for a colony based on the principle of a direct efflux of local reality into culture is that its oddities reveal at work the very imagination he thinks he has foresworn.[31] Fortunately, Crispin has the sense to realize that he has wandered into a blind alley as constricting as the stale European scene he escaped. This realization irks him "beyond his patience" (IV,88). In effect, in a mood of despair, he renounces journeying altogether, physical or mental. Though he remains "an aspiring clown" (IV,91; note the combination of approval and ridicule in the phrase), he dreams reluctantly, "in a gingerly way" (IV,97). He will indulge in no more runaway theories, no more botched efforts to find the truth, but will submit himself solely to the discipline of the unglossed "text" of life:

> All dreams are vexing. Let them be expunged.
> But let the rabbit run, the cock declaim.
> Trinket pasticcio, flaunting skyey sheets,
> With Crispin as the tiptoe cozener?

No, no: veracious page on page, exact.

(IV,98-102)

At this point, Crispin's life becomes rather stagnant; he is no longer a voyager. Readers have generally been agreed that the final two or three cantos are a drop, poetically, from the first. The decline, such as there is, results from the relative absence of movement, which has been so in evidence in cantos I through III and which provides an inherent dynamic quality. Crispin's major discoveries, like his travels, have ended before the final two cantos begin, and these two cantos therefore have the quality of a prolonged denouement. Nevertheless, the mental and emotional modulations in Crispin that occur in these final cantos, are indispensable to the comedy of the poem if it is to be a comedy of the happy ending as well as a comedy of the ludicrous. In fact, the two comic modes are neatly blended. The canto titles, "A Nice Shady Home" and "And Daughters with Curls," laugh at Crispin's comeuppance and the conventionality of his later life, but at the same time the poem laughs *with* his pinioning by ordinary human happiness. His defeat, as Sukenick says, "is turned into rout" in a kind of situation comedy ending.

Simply enough, Crispin finds it hard to be a discontented visionary when life as it is is so pleasant. He is

> . . .alert
> To the difficulty of rebellious thought
> When the sky is blue. The blue infected will.

(V,13-15)

The reader who complains of dullness in this resolution would apparently prefer to see Crispin throw himself into futile tragedy. Actually, he is bemused by his own "haphazard denouement" (V,22) but finds contentment preferable to useless and melodramatic protest. Realist that he is, he in effect shrugs:

> Was he to company vastest things defunct
> With a blubber of tom-toms harrowing the sky?
> Scowl a tragedian's testament? Prolong
> His active force in an inactive dirge,
> Which, let the tall musicians call and call,

> Should merely call him dead? Pronounce amen
> Through choirs infolded to the outmost clouds?
> Because he built a cabin who once planned
> Loquacious columns by the ructive sea?
> Because he turned to salad-beds again?
> Jovial Crispin, in calamitous crape?

(V,38-48)

These rhetorical questions—and more that follow—obviously invite an answer of "No." If there is a note of defiance in the insistence with which Crispin, speaking through the narrator here, piles up his questions, he is nevertheless unable to find a happier solution. The narrator observes that Crispin "lies quilted to his poll in his despite" and offers us a little skit of his matrimonial good night. He finds himself with a "prismy blonde" on his hands (V,60) and goes off to a "congenial sleep." He may be reduced to being "magister of a single room," his urge to walk a "prickly" round of philosophical inquiry "sap[ped]" by the demoralizing "quotidian" (V,79; puns surely intended), but that single room contains happy "cabin ribaldries" in which he happily "poured out upon the lips of her/That lay beside him" "saps like the sun" (V,70-93). The narrator extracts from this happy reduction of his character's ambitions a little moral observation on life:

> For all it takes it gives a humped return
> Exchequering from piebald fiscs unkeyed.

(V,94-95)

From its piebald (varied) fiscs (treasuries), life draws returns that are "humped" in àt least three ways: misshapen, i.e. having unexpected configurations; heaped-up, or more than one expects; and basically sexual, even if one had not asked for that favor.[32]

The final canto is a high-spirited celebration of Crispin's final state, surrounded by the children who prove that, after all, reality and imagination are inseparable:

> . . .four blithe instruments
> Of differing struts, four voices several

In couch, four more personae, intimate
As buffo, yet divers, four mirrors blue
That should be silver, four accustomed seeds
Hinting incredible hues, four selfsame lights
That spread chromatics in hilarious dark,
Four questioners and four sure answerers.

(VI,56-63)

From his hilarious "rout" by biology, Crispin "concocted doctrine" (VI,64); that is, he is still formulating theories, still trying to verbalize judgments about the nature of things. Thus, whether he writes poems or merely creates other live, imaginative beings, daughters, he is still a poet: an intelligence confronting the raw material of reality and operating on it through the imagination. His "doctrine" is a discovery about journeying: even though he "carried overseas" his world, his being, and sowed it into the strange soil of America, it still came up the same purple turnip. That is, however far one goes on voyages of discovery, whether geographic or mental, life comes back essentially the same.

The narrator's concluding comment on this "doctrine" is that his story of Crispin is to be "scored," set to music or completed aesthetically, in the music (poetry) of physical life itself, the voices of the daughters. That is, the only conclusion to the "anecdote" is life itself; Crispin the realist has simply swallowed the pill of experience (VI,71). The story may, especially to readers with a deep thirst for the completion of intellectual quests or the vindication of ideals, seem to have no satisfactory ending at all, but merely to prove that "what he proves/Is nothing" (VI, 94-95). To such a reader, Stevens says,

. . .what can all this matter since
The relation comes, benignly, to its end?

(VI,95-96)

The story *does* end, whether it has a satisfactory message or not; furthermore it ends happily, and that's what matters. His additional comment is more general: "So may the relation of each man be clipped." That is, it is possible that every person's story may end so inconclusively; and indeed let it be so, if it is a happy ending like Crispin's.

In addition to the explicit narrative comment, the poem has a more conclusive and more general answer to the question of whether Crispin's search has been futile. Stevens has wisely chosen to let this answer remain implicit in the entire shape of the narrative. Even though he has not found what he wanted, and thus his quest is frustrated, Crispin has gained sufficient experience and self-knowledge to discard what was false in his beliefs and thus to confront reality in greater maturity and good cheer than before. Therefore, it was worth his while to set out on his voyage, and the form of the mental voyage or quest is after all fulfilled and vindicated, though in a minor key.

The Americanness of Stevens's quest narrative is a matter of more than vocabulary and place, though these elements are important in establishing its brash American tone. Beyond these localizing touches, its concern with the tensions between art and a pragmatic sort of reality is a particularly American kind of concern. Even more fundamental, of course, is the fact that in its general shape it follows the patterns of American history.

Stevens's use of history is greatly different from Crane's use of history in *The Bridge*. Unlike Crane, he makes no direct references to historic personages or events; as a result, the surface texture of the poem lacks Crane's frequent nodules of specific reference and association. Since Stevens leaves his historical frame implicit and in the background, he simply presents a less crowded canvas than Crane. His tone, too, is considerably different. While Crane is adulatory, bitter, and the like, Stevens holds heroism lightly and regards both past glories and subsequent decay with skepticism. Furthermore, for Stevens history has a less direct relevance to the poet's role in society than it does for Crane; he does not regard himself, the poet, as having a prophetic voice, communicating the meaning of history to the present world and shaping the future. History enters his work chiefly as a shaper of aesthetic purpose; in "Comedian," it provides a structure of comparison for Crispin's evolution of aesthetic theory and his personal adjustment to reality as he perceives it, that is, for his achieving new modes of perception. It is not there in its own right. Plainly, if the course of American history is recapitulated in the story of Crispin, with all his oddities, the underlying conception of that history must be very idiosyncratic indeed.

Finally, then, we can see that Crane is in a sense a far more public poet than Stevens. He is more interested in public, historical material, and his interest is of a less specialized, hence more public, nature than Stevens's. Nevertheless, Crane applies history to his personal situation and enters into his poetry in a more directly personal way than does Stevens, who preserves a certain decorum of poetic presence. However specialized and idiosyncratically stylized Stevens's treatment of historic materials, he is finally less personal in his poetry than Crane, even while he is less public. His poetic journey, then, is a peculiarly shaped metaphor but is nevertheless a metaphor for subjects of discourse more than for matters of private revelation.

NOTES

1. An exception, worth noting here simply because it is so unduly neglected, is C. Day Lewis's wonderfully cogent and fast-paced narrative poem "Flight to Australia."

2. Monroe K. Spears, who is always both judicious and decisive, writes in his University of Minnesota pamphlet on Crane, "*The Bridge* is not the Great American Epic, or any kind of epic." (1965; rpt. in *Six American Poets*, ed. Allen Tate, Minneapolis: University of Minnesota Press, 1969), p. 221. However, see R.W.B. Lewis, *The Poetry of Hart Crane: A Critical Study* (Princeton, N.J.: Princeton University Press, 1967), especially pages 219-45. Lewis refers to the work as an epic, but hedges the term about with qualifications and states that "nothing could. . .be more misleading" than to compare *The Bridge* to the *Aeneid* (p. 222). Alan Trachtenberg, in *Brooklyn Bridge: Fact and Symbol* (New York: Oxford University Press, 1965), pp. 147-48, argues that the "mode" of *The Bridge* is actually that of "myth." It is a "sophisticated and well-wrought version of the archaic myth of return" elucidated by Mircea Eliade in *Cosmos and History: The Myth of the Eternal Return*. Thomas Vogler warns against approaching the work out of a "precommitment to Crane's own statements" of intention. Vogler reads *The Bridge* not as the "symbolic expression" of an epic vision, as Crane hoped, but as "a search or quest for a mythic vision." See *Preludes to Vision: The Epic Venture in Blake, Wordsworth, Keats, and Hart Crane* (Berkeley: University of California Press, 1971), p.146.

3. All references are to *The Complete Poems and Selected Letters and Prose of Hart Crane*, ed. Brom Weber (1933; reprint ed. Garden City, N.Y.: Doubleday Anchor Books, 1966).

4. R. P. Blackmur refers to a "confusion of tools and purpose" in the work. *Form and Value in Modern Poetry* (Garden City, N.Y.: Doubleday, 1952), pp. 273-74.

5. Lewis says of this line, "This. . .is what he believed Herman Melville to have done, and what he wanted his poetry to do: to postulate, to bring into view by the exercise of vision and language, a divine being, a godhead that might exist at least inside and for the duration of the poem." *The Poetry of Hart Crane*, p. 209.

6. Lewis, *The Poetry of Hart Crane*, reads the "fall downstairs" as "an invitation to sin with grace." Sinning, deviance from a public moral norm, is also a way of departing on separate ways.

7. Lewis, *The Poetry of Hart Crane*, pp. 171, 152-53; Spears, *Six American Poets*, p. 219; Maurice Kramer, "Six Voyages of a Derelict Seer," *Sewanee Review*, 73 (1965), 410-23; Evelyn J. Hinz, "Hart Crane's 'Voyages Reconsidered,'" *Contemporary Literature*, 13 (1972), 315-33.

8. L. S. Dembo, *Hart Crane's Sanskrit Charge: A Study of The Bridge* (Ithaca: Cornell University Press, 1960), comments that the vision of "Voyages" is rooted in tragedy. See especially pp. 3-22.

9. The "dark confessions her veins spell" have been troublesome to critics, and readings of the line vary considerably. Spears, *Six American Poets*, interprets the "dark confessions" as a correspondence: the sea's "veins are like his veins," the poet's (p. 217). This is true to the text, but the reference is more specific. Robert A. Day, in an essay devoted entirely to "Voyages II," reads the "dark confessions" as "the evidences of shipwrecked mariners, carried along undersea by the currents," suggesting that the lovers' search "must end in death." Day, "Image and Idea in 'Voyages II'," *Criticism*, 7 (1965), 230. But this puts us right back to the "cruel" end of I; the voyage might as well not have occurred.

10. But see John Unterecker, *Voyager: A Life of Hart Crane* (New York: Farrar, Straus and Giroux, 1969), pp. 623-24, arguing the "tight structure" and "extraordinary coherence" of the work.

11. Lewis, *The Poetry of Hart Crane*, p. 246.

12. Richard P. Sugg, *Hart Crane's The Bridge: A Description of Its Life* (Birmingham: University of Alabama Press, 1976), pp. 41-43.

13. *The Letters of Hart Crane*, ed. Brom Weber (New York: Hermitage House, 1952), p. 306.

14. Trachtenberg, *Brooklyn Bridge*, p. 150. As Dembo points out, however, the more extended meaning of Pocahontas is "simply the Platonic Ideal"; *Hart Crane's Sanskrit Charge*, p. 10.

15. These hoboes, like the tramp at the end of John Dos Passos's *U. S. A.*, indicate both the rottenness of twentieth-century American life and the possibility for finding new "homes," new definitions of America.

16. Sherman Paul, whose reading of *The Bridge* follows its journey structure with an emphasis on Crane's need to locate an acceptable mother within his memories, views the emptying of the river as an altogether defeating end. See *Hart's Bridge* (Urbana: University of Illinois Press, 1972), pp. 214-15.

17. This retreat is "the symbolic act of leaving the known for the unknown." Sugg, *Hart Crane's The Bridge*, p. 56.

18. Paul, *Hart's Bridge*, p. 225.

19. Lewis, *The Poetry of Hart Crane*, p. 354. Sherman Paul, *Hart's Bridge*, compares the night journey here to Aeneas' (p. 263). Critics often comment that the entire poem is one day, but actually it is one day containing other one-day cycles.

20. Trachtenberg, *Brooklyn Bridge*, p. 84 and *passim*.

21. See, for instance, Edward Guereschi, " 'The Comedian as the Letter C': Wallace Stevens' Anti-Mythological Poem," *The Centennial Review of Arts and Science*, 8 (1964), 465-77, and A. Poulin, Jr., "Crispin as Everyman as Adam: 'The Comedian as the Letter C'," *Concerning Poetry*, 5 (1972), 5-23.

22. Virtually every critical commentary on "Comedian" has dealt with it as a piece of poetic theory. The pioneering study setting this tone was Hi Simons's article " 'The Comedian as the Letter C': Its Sense and Its Significance," *The Southern Review*, 5 (1940), 453-68. Daniel Fuchs treats the poem as Stevens's "spiritual autobiography" in *The Comic Spirit of Wallace Stevens* (Durham, N.C.: Duke University Press, 1963). Ronald Sukenick corrects some of their excesses in *Wallace Stevens: Musing the Obscure* (New York: New York University Press, 1967).

23. *The Collected Poems of Wallace Stevens* (New York: Alfred A. Knopf, 1954), p. 45. Canto and line numbers are given parenthetically.

24. See K. E. Marre, "Narrative Comedy in Wallace Stevens' 'The Comedian as the Letter C'," *University of Dayton Review*, 12, no. 3 (summer 1976), 133-50. Marre ignores the instances of the narrator's submerging himself in Crispin, thereby enabling himself to insist that Crispin never appears directly and that in fact the reader's attention is directed "away from Crispin and toward the godlike narrator himself" (p. 137). This particular kind of argument is not at all uncommon in modern criticism, but here it is a piece of ingenuity that distorts the poem. Helen Vendler is perhaps less searching but certainly less rigid in her assessment of the narrative strategy of the poem as a "third voice which modulates into both of the voices of Crispin, high and low." *On Extended Wings: Wallace Stevens' Longer Poems* (Cambridge, Mass.: Harvard University Press, 1969), p. 41. I am uncertain how she can cleanly separate two distinct voices of Crispin, and her statement that "Crispin in fact is dead" is open to question.

25. The ending is sometimes seen as tragic, despite the outlines of the story and Stevens's own narrative pronouncements. See, for example, Poulin, "Crispin as Everyman as Adam," suggesting that Stevens's "vision" in "Comedian" is "perhaps. . .pessimistic" and that Crispin's "quest was futile" and has "tragic implications." Guereschi, " 'The Comedian as the Letter C'," calls the ending "sardonic" at one point in his article (p. 468) and "a benediction" at another (p. 477). It is an ambiguous ending but not, I believe, incoherent.

26. One is reminded of William James's phrase for natural reality, a "booming, buzzing confusion."

27. It is over-reading to stretch these lines to a statement of modern conflict between religion and science.

28. Of Crispin's determination, Fuchs comments that he is "a clown not only because he falls on his face once every so often, but because he subjects himself to special ridicule by the violence of his quest for reality." Even though the quest ultimately fails in its object, the "energy" with which he pursues it "makes him a gay clown rather than a sad one" (*The Comic Spirit*, p. 52).

29. John Enck points out in *Wallace Stevens: Images and Judgments* (Carbondale: Southern Illinois University Press, 1964), p. 88, that "Carolina stands not just for the United States itself but a new twentieth century."

30. For such an interpretation, see Harold Bloom, *Wallace Stevens: The Poems of Our Climate* (Ithaca: Cornell University Press, 1977).

31. It is a close and perhaps a directly satirical parallel to the resurgence of sentimentality in the American local color school, supposedly given to direct transcription of bits of local reality.

32. Sukenick, *Wallace Stevens*, pp. 58-59, cleverly and I think rightly glosses "a humped return" as having "a sly sexual reference" to Crispin and his blonde's "rumpling bottomness," which he glosses as their rumpling "their sheets with their bottoms." For all the admirable qualities of Fuchs's reading in *The Comic Spirit*, he goes astray, I think, in his reading here: "Crispin meditates here on the diabolical slyness of the conditions of quotidian existence. For all that it requires of us, its return is grotesquely less than we expect. So it is that the quotidian taxes motley (in the sense of common) personal treasuries with a disregard that amounts to lawlessness" (p. 58).

10
Back and Back: Bellow's *Henderson the Rain King*

Back out of all this now too much for us. . .
—Robert Frost, "Directive"

Saul Bellow's *Henderson the Rain King* is one of the few examples in modern literature of a complete quest narrative. Eugene Henderson, Bellow's eccentric bear-like hero, renounces the life he has led and sets out on a journey of search for personal wholeness. He has been a drunkard and a troublemaker, quarrelsome, slovenly, confused in his loves and his affairs, impulsive, tormented. In summary, he has been much like the general run of modern antiheroes. His difference is in the totality of his self-judgment and his successful struggle to change. Henderson not only yearns for regeneration, rebirth, but achieves it.[1] In imagining the completion of a quest in the modern world—a world which the novel fully realizes and never evades—and, even more fundamentally, in his spirited insistence that people can escape the "knitting machine" universe of determinism.[2] Bellow has produced an excitingly affirmative novel.

Henderson is presented at the outset in a state of personal as well as philosophical despair. "All is grief" for him and the world a "mighty. . .oppressor."³ He feels estranged from his own past, chiefly from his father, whose spirit he has been trying to reach and appease by playing his father's violin. He is in continual conflict with everyone he knows and most of all with himself. Indeed, he sees himself as a "bum" or some gross animal (specifically, a pig) and so despises "my habits, my money, my music lessons, my drunkenness, my prejudices, my brutality, my teeth, my face, my soul" (p. 3) that he twice threatens suicide. His life is a burden, a set of self-destructive compulsions beyond his control that he believes have distorted and blighted his physical appearance as well as his character. Yet he is powerless to form new patterns of behavior to replace those he finds so shameful. The ultimate source of his anxieties is an obsession with death. He feels the "last little room of dirt. . .waiting" (p. 40) and longs to reach a sense of secure "Being" to counteract his sense of onrushing process leading toward death. The opening four chapters, a kind of prologue explaining why Henderson decides to make his journey, clearly establish that what he must search for is regeneration from the destructive life he has led and his obsession with death.

The four-chapter prologue establishes with remarkable clarity and force the real singularity of Henderson as a character. Indeed, it is Bellow's revelling in the eccentric personality, or more specifically the eccentric narrating voice, that is the most immediately striking quality of the novel. Eugene Henderson is one of the quirkiest, liveliest, most fully realized, in the reader's sense of his physical and emotional presence, of all characters in modern fiction. The reader apprehends him only through his voice, what he says and how he says it; the reader knows him as voice. To the extent that one hears this startling, energetic voice and believes its authenticity, he accepts or posits the fully individuated, fully rounded character of Henderson as person.⁴

The character apprehended through Henderson's narrative voice is both comical and odd—odd to the point of anomaly. He is large of frame and massively overweight, with a face, as he says, like Grand Central Station, a big nose, and little piglike eyes. At home he likes to dress in a red velvet bathrobe and a hunting cap. He has fits of violent, yelling rage or of maudlin self-pity, and is given to waggishness. On sudden whims he takes up such diverse endeavors as pig farming and the study of the violin. He has a dental bridge that gives him trouble, and he stores a spare bridge in the trunk of his car. His life is oddly tied in with animals of various kinds. The list of individuating characteristics could go on. The point is that a great number of oddities in appearance, behavior, and belief individuate Henderson almost to the point of a monstrosity.

Two factors, however, operate to make Henderson, odd as he is, sympathetically human, one of us, and his story not only intelligible but admonitory. First, his emotions are essentially universal, however singular his mode of expressing them: fear of death, need to love and be loved, desire for a sense of purpose and meaning in life. Second, the shape of his journey is familiar, even archetypal. At first it appears to be a function of his eccentricity; few people try to solve their problems by going to Africa, and fewer still strike out on foot, without plan, into uncharted regions. Yet the reader does not finally perceive the journey as a one-of-a-kind oddity, but as an occurrence of the familiar pattern of the religious quest. Like the heroes of religious myth, Henderson must depart on his own way, endure hardship and deprivation, encounter fearful truths, and return transformed, both within himself and in his social function. Because of its universal form and an extensive fabric of incidental allusion, primarily biblical, the journey, for all its oddity, conveys a broad significance.

Henderson's quest is preceded by another journey that evokes another familiar pattern. Included in the first structural division of the novel, the four-chapter prologue, is a brief narrative of a journey to Europe made some years before the crisis that sends Henderson to Africa. Spiritually ailing but not yet awakened to the full dimensions of his need for regeneration, he had undertaken a "tour of cathedral towns" merely as a sightseeing jaunt. The tour is not presented as a pilgrimage. But as we have seen, the journey to Europe in American fiction has traditionally appropriated that meaning and has conveyed the values of a homecoming to venerated shrines. Bellow is careful to evoke that tradition as the backdrop to Henderson's tour by invoking as precedent the more weightily interpreted tour of cathedrals in *The Education of Henry Adams* (1918). (The seeds of the parallel with Adams's *Education* are planted some ten pages before, when Henderson points out that his father was a friend of William James and Henry Adams.) The evocation is ironic, however, its emphasis on contrast. Henderson's tour is a failed pilgrimage, ending in a vision of shapeless, meaningless death, mere obliteration, as, laden with anxiety, Henderson confronts an octopus in an aquarium tank. The octopus speaks to him, he says, of "cosmic coldness"; it is "Death. . .giving me notice" (p. 19).

In *The Education*, Henry Adams found in the cathedrals of Europe a vision of history and of America's modern brittleness. For him, as for the pilgrims of Henry James and others, both fictional and real, art and in general a highly evolved culture provided the kind of awakening traditionally associated with religious relics and sites. But Henderson's visit to the cathedrals, because of his unconventional and even at times flippant attitude and manner, is drained of the spiritual import of the traditional pilgrimage.

Both works, *The Education* and *Henderson*, develop through interesting combinations of the pilgrimage and the quest forms. Henry Adams's tour of European cathedrals and his visit to the industrial exhibition where he sees the dynamo ("The Dynamo and the Virgin") have a dual nature related to the distinction between pilgrimage (a journey toward a foreknown goal) and quest (a journey of search for an envisioned but not clearly known or located goal). Adams finds both the actual sights he had intended to see and a vision of historic process. He originally undertook his pilgrimage to the monuments of a past culture, a spiritually centripetal culture, as a part of his "education." But in a materialistic, spiritually diffuse culture, for Adams at any rate, this educational process is the only possible spiritual awakening. The sole spiritual enlightenment available to him is the full realization of why he cannot achieve spiritual enlightenment. The process by which Adams achieves this unforeseen state of awareness or education is in part projected narratively in his pilgrimage to Europe, which thus, because its scope becomes broadened beyond its originally foreseen and defined object, becomes a quest. In contrast, Henderson's discoveries leading to regeneration are not reached in the course of his pilgrimage but as a result of the failure of the pilgrimage. Ad-

ams's journey, then, is a pilgrimage that takes on the dimensions
of a quest; Henderson's, a quest that initially has the appearance
of a pilgrimage.

After the death vision (the sight of the octopus) that ends his
trip to Europe, Henderson returns to America to a life of continuing and even deepening disorder. When his second marriage
falls into greater and greater disharmony, his drinking gets more
and more out of hand, and his outbursts of temper become so
violent that an elderly neighbor helping out as housekeeper
actually dies of heart failure from fear of him, Henderson de-
termines to go to Africa on a desperate search for renewal.

He is driven to the search, finally, by a voice within that
repeats "I want, I want." Since the voice has persisted despite
a variety of alterations in his outward self and manner of life,
it is clear that the voice of dissatisfaction represents Henderson's
"real" self, as opposed to both his external appearance and the
behavioral marks he adopts as ways of dealing with outer pressures. Therefore, the answer to the question of what the voice
wants will involve not only a change of place, with all its social
encumbrances, but a stripping away of false selves in order to
reach the true self within. The journey out mirrors a journey in.
Also, since the real self involves memories and impulses from
childhood, overlaid by confusions and anxieties, just as the authentic social relationships of the past have become overlaid by
a smothering accumulation of modern artificialities, the inner
journey will involve a journey backward in time. Simultaneously, the outward journey in effect moves backward in time,
from mechanized twentieth-century civilization to a primitive
culture. The region through which Henderson travels to reach
the first of the two villages he visits, the Arnewi, is "like the
original place. . .older than the city of Ur," and gives him the
feeling of "entering the past—the real past, no history or junk
like that" (pp. 46-47). Indeed, he wonders if he didn't "penetrate
beyond geography" (p. 55). As he penetrates deeper into unknown territory, he sloughs off superficialities and reaches es-
sentials, both of himself and of human history.

Henderson's visits to the two tribes, making up the two central
sections of the novel, are made in an atmosphere dense with
biblical echoes, a pattern of allusiveness initiated in the prologue

section. Before he decided to make his trip, while he was still lost in the welter of his confusions, Henderson had found in one of his father's old books an aphoristic sentence, vaguely biblical in language and import, promising regeneration: "The forgiveness of sins is perpetual and righteousness first is not required" (p. 3). His response to this discovery and to other unexpected boons is also vaguely biblical: "Blessed be God for the mercies he continually sends me!"(p.15) Because Henderson has not yet undergone the ordeal of the quest for purgation and rebirth, he cannot appropriate the aphoristic message for use within his life; accordingly, he loses the slip of paper on which it was written. But the discovery is a turning point for him, and its promise of forgiveness will recur in his consciousness throughout the journey. His transforming encounters with animals at both African villages are also anticipated in the prologue. Expressing misgivings about his pig farming, he quotes Daniel 4:25, "They shall drive thee from among men, and thy dwelling shall be with the beasts of the field" (p. 21), a passage that will be explicitly cited at two later points in the novel. He comes to feel himself driven from among men to a shameful involvement with animals, and in the Wariri section he will reenact the story of Daniel in the lions' den. The incorporation of these biblical echoes into the prologue helps to establish our expectation that the solution of Henderson's problems will have a religious dimension. This expectation is fulfilled both in a series of pointed biblical parallels and in the completion of the quest for rebirth.

In the second structural division of the novel, the chapters relating Henderson's visit to the Arnewi (five through nine), his journey is quickly placed within the tradition of the withdrawal to the desert for spiritual purgation. We recall the stories of the Israelites' wandering in the desert, John the Baptist's retreat into the desert for repentance and purification, and Jesus' forty days— all of them variations of the biblical archetype of the desert experience, which is one of the basic patterns of Judeo-Christian myth.[5] Henderson and his guide, Romilayu, travel by foot through a dry, elevated plateau region, "hot, clear, and arid" with "no human footprints," where Henderson has "a great time out. . .among the stones" and asserts hopefully that in this "simplified and splendid" place he has "got *clean* away from everything" (pp. 45-46, emphasis added). The spiritual function of the landscape becomes clear when he arrives at the Arnewi village and is greeted with tears and lamentation. Unaware that the natives are grieving for their starving cattle, he takes their behavior as a judgment on himself and offers to go back into the wilderness:

'Shall I run back into the desert,' I thought, 'and stay there until the devil has passed out of me and I am fit to meet human kind again without driving it to despair at the first look? I haven't had enough desert yet. Let me throw away my gun and my helmet and the lighter and all this stuff and maybe I can get rid of my fierceness too and live out there on worms. On locusts. Until all the bad is burned out of me.' (p. 49)

Although he feels a "great change" in himself from his days of walking over the desert, he needs more purgation in order to be made "ready for society" (p. 49).

The Arnewi village is the point of origin for a process in which Henderson finds himself by reenacting the evolution of the Judeo-Christian tradition.[6] His first impression of the village links it with Ur, the place at which the history of the Israelites begins, in Genesis 11:20, with the story of Abraham (p. 47). His next biblical stopping-place is the story of Moses. He reenacts, but in parody, the episodes of the burning bush (p. 48; Exodus 3:2) and the plague of frogs (pp. 59 ff.; Exodus 8: 1-14). In both instances, the result is failure: the bush merely falls to the ground in embers, impressing no one, and when he attempts to rid the village of the plague of frogs he blows up its cistern, the only water supply. In projecting himself into a starring role in the biblical drama, he has revealed his inadequacies for the part. He has not yet realized the difficult discipline required for renewal. However, he has gained an important preliminary lesson, a message spoken by the queen of the Arnewi tribe: "Grun-tu-molani," "man want to live" (p.85). However despondent he may be at subsequent stages of his quest, he will continue to recall this lesson in persistence and devotion to life.

If the gentle Arnewi are children of light, the next tribe, the Wariri, are in Romilayu's words "chillen dahkness." Henderson completes the allusion: "wiser in their generation and all the rest" (p. 115). The Wariri are indeed wiser in the sense that they provide, though it may be unwittingly, the experiences through which Henderson gains renewal of life. It is in the long central section giving an account of his stay among the Wariri (chapters eleven through twenty-one) that Henderson experiences the night portion of his journey, his descent into hell, and his reemergence as a transformed hero, ready for his triumphant and socially redemptive return from the quest.

As Henderson and Romilayu approach the Wariri village, they first encounter a "herdsman. . .in a leather apron" (p. 115) who is presented through biblical analogy as an oracular-warning of the trials ahead. Henderson explicitly notes the parallel:

Something about his figure struck me as Biblical, and in particular he made me think of the man whom Joseph met when he went to look for his brothers, and who directed him along toward Dothan. My belief is that this man in the Bible must have been an angel and certainly knew the brothers were going to throw Joseph into the pit. But he sent him on nevertheless. (p. 116)

Both of these monitory figures lead the heroes, Joseph and Henderson, into traps. Yet in both cases the traps will prove redemptive rather than ultimately destructive. Joseph is, of course, an early "type," or analogue, of the Suffering Servant figure, a role to which Henderson himself is increasingly related in the latter portions of the novel, for instance when he is stripped and beaten in order to cleanse the water supply of the Wariri in his capacity as Rain King. To be sure, Henderson is a comic analogue of the Suffering Servant, the Christ figure. But his suffering is stressed throughout the novel, and at the end his intention is to become a physician, a medical servant of mankind. Through his use of the allusion to Joseph and his captivity in this relatively minor incident of Henderson's encounter with the "leathery" herdsman, Bellow directs attention to the Suffering Servant aspect of Henderson's character and foreshadows both his trials among the Wariri and his eventual redemptive return.

Like Joseph's captivity ordeal, Henderson's trials include a symbolic descent into hell, in this case the deep cellar which serves as the lair of the lioness Atti. Here he undergoes the ordeal of approaching and touching the animal, despite his great terror, and an arduous therapy directed by the Wariri king Dahfu which consists of symbolically becoming a beast by acting out an imitation of the lion's posture, motions, and roaring. Dahfu's idea is that Henderson will rid himself of his anxieties and assume lionlike traits of insouciance and courage. Instead, he plumbs the depths of his fears and, by roaring out what he feels to be cries of religious supplication, brings to consciousness his spiritual needs.

For a while Henderson's lion therapy appears only to make him more miserable. Instead of becoming leonine, he becomes bestial; he becomes increasingly slovenly (piggish, he feels) in appearance and even develops a habitual snuffling, grunting sound. This temporary worsening, however, reflects the working to the surface of the bestial traits of which he is ridding himself by a process of purgation from within. With these traits purged, he can reach the valid animal nature at the center of his being, a lionesslike capacity for fierce acts of devotion and a kinship, which he now recognizes for the first time, to a comical, long-suffering bear with which, long ago, he had performed a roller-coaster stunt in a carnival.

Henderson emerges transformed from his journey of descent and recapitulation and his ordeals of self-examination and encounter. He has gained a new self-assurance and is ready to take whatever actions are necessary in order to return home and fulfill his long ambition to become a doctor. In contrast to the outward journey, characterized by confused wandering and descent, the journey of return from the Wariri village to an outpost of civilization and then back to America is presented in terms of persistent goal-directed march and finally ascent (flight). These motifs unmistakably reflect the shape of the traditional myth of the completed quest. In addition, they reflect formally the affirming vision at the center of the novel.

Henderson is by no means a tract for philosophical optimism. Its protagonist's exuberance is never generalized to a depiction of a best of all possible worlds. He finds in Africa a world of famine, death, and treachery, within which his spiritual exemplars (his guide Romilayu, Itelo and Willatale among the Arnewi,

Dahfu among the Wariri) exist as they can or succumb. The society he has left behind is grasping, vicious, and repressive. Those closest to him are beset by neurosis and depression, and his second wife, Lily, seems scarcely better able than his first to understand or even to tolerate him. Nothing in Henderson's experience alters these conditions or gives him reason to modify his view of them. Nor does Bellow offer any suggestion that the world may be improving or that mankind can either make or discover any satisfying reason for the way things are. Both the natural and the social world are forces antagonistic to the individual soul. In its depiction of outward conditions, *Henderson* might better be regarded as a pessimistic than an optimistic work.

Nevertheless, Bellow has imposed on this negative picture of things a structure of affirmation both comic in its incidental textures and fully comedic in its outcome.[7] Henderson manages to survive and to complete his journey triumphantly, accepting some features of the world against which he had previously rebelled to no purpose and escaping the destructive logic of cosmic determinism. It is this escape from determinism that is the foundation for Bellow's comic vision[8] and the motive force behind his celebration of individual personality, eccentricity. In what may seem a paradox, though in fact it is not, that celebration is conveyed structurally through Bellow's use and adaptation of one of the most traditional of story patterns. The completed quest, including an endurance of the descent into the hell of the self and a socially redemptive return, is the form of the great religious myths celebrating the transcendent individual soul. Two such heroes from the religious mythic tradition, Moses and John the Baptist, serve as measures of Henderson's transformation.[9]

Moses is one of the major biblical prototypes for Henderson. The story of Moses first appears in connection with a foundling infant brought home by Henderson's daughter Ricey. In this episode Henderson is cast as the Pharaoh, the blocking figure of the story: when he first looked at the baby he "felt like the Pharaoh at the sight of little Moses" (p. 36). The situations are similar: Moses in the ark, the foundling in a valise; Moses crying, the baby a "child of sorrow" (p. 36); the racial identity of both

(Moses "one of the Hebrews' children" and Ricey's foundling the "colored child") quickly noted. The point is that the one change Henderson makes in referring to the story is to show as the discoverer of the baby, not the active reliever of its misery as in the Bible, but the authority figure against whom Moses later must struggle (using, we recall, plagues involving animals). Later, when he is among the Arnewi, Henderson attempts to cast himself as Moses in the episodes of the burning bush and the plague of frogs. But in both attempts he appears merely foolish. Yet at the end, when he succors the lone orphan child on the flight to America, we see Henderson as the nurturing figure in the story. This time he does not thrust himself into a dramatized role, but unself-consciously shifts from the blocking figure to the nurturer.

Henderson's relationship to the story of John the Baptist likewise undergoes dramatic change between his arrival in Africa and his departure. As in the early occurrences of the Moses story, in the early references to John the Baptist, Henderson is self-conscious and self-dramatizing. Approaching the Arnewi village he offers to go live "on locusts" (p. 49). He does this in thought only; we do not believe that he will act on the impulse, but merely enjoy indulging it. When his conquest of the frogs ends in disaster for the villagers, he melodramatically offers to go on alone and "eat locusts" if Romilayu wants to turn back (p. 113). In both cases, he self-consciously thrusts himself into the role of the holy seeker. The biblical parallels of situation, such as the archetypal image of the desert, indicate the potential value of his quest, but he has not yet achieved redemption and his eager entrance into the role of John reveals only his unfitness for it.

But at the end of the African adventure, in the escape sequence, Henderson is a parallel to John the Baptist, rather than a parody of him. He finds himself in the role and lives it, his care no longer for self-image but for service. He endures hardships without making melodramatic gestures, he accepts and uses "the given" as Dahfu had urged him to do, and, in what we may see as a parallel to the Baptist's service to Jesus, the Lion of Judah, he cares for the lion cub that he is taking back with him. Echoing Matthew 3:4, he says, "So at last I'm living on locusts, like Saint John" (p. 326). No longer does he wish to be some exalted character; by the logic of typology, he *is* the Baptist. In the final chapter, Henderson is bound for Newfoundland (a new-found life), and sings, not for the first time, Handel's "And who shall survive the day of his coming." Here the implication is that Henderson himself, having been renewed and redefined as a religious hero of a modern myth, is now able to survive judgment in those terms.

It is characteristic of Bellow's work that his hero must withdraw from the complex superficialities of twentieth-century American life to an experience in a simplified or "primitive" cultural milieu in order to achieve personal wholeness. In similar fashion, Augie March goes to Mexico and Herzog, a less flamboyant personage in Bellow's gallery of odd characters, goes to the country and paints his child's piano green. Tommy Wilhelm, of *Seize the Day*, who is trapped and unable to withdraw from New York, can only daydream about what appears to the reader a very pathetic version of the primitive life, a backyard in suburban Roxbury. All of these rustications are, of course, escapes from social pressures. More accurately, they are retreats, in the religious sense of temporary withdrawals for purposes of spiritual encounter and renewal.

Henderson is one of the few heroes of modern fiction to complete the circle of withdrawal, renewal, and return, and thus become a full questing hero. He is therefore in a sense the fullest version of Bellow's own characteristic hero—the confused and alienated man who is, however, aware of his state and prepared to alter it. His story is a parable of America's need for renewal and Bellow's vision of how American society can in fact achieve such renewal by recourse to the past and rediscovery of itself.

NOTES

1. Cf. Donald W. Markos, "Life Against Death in *Henderson the Rain King*," *Modern Fiction Studies*, 17 (1971), 195: Henderson is "profoundly excited by images of rebirth." Portions of the present chapter are adapted from my articles "The Possibility of Affirmation in *Heart of Darkness* and *Henderson the Rain King*," *Philological Quarterly*, 57 (1978), 115-31, and "Biblical Allusion in *Henderson the Rain King*," *South Central Bulletin*, 40 (1980), 165-67.

2. Joseph Conrad's phrase, in personal letters, for the universe viewed deterministically.

3. Saul Bellow, *Henderson the Rain King* (New York: Viking Press, 1958), p. 3. Additional citations indicated parenthetically in the text.

4. The concept of "mimetic voice" is discussed by Stephen M. Ross in his article " 'Voice' in Narrative Texts: The Example of *As I Lay Dying*," *PMLA*, 94 (1979), 300-310.

5. For an extended discussion of the biblical emblematic landscapes, see George H. Williams, *Wilderness and Paradise in Christian Thought* (New York: Harper and Brothers, 1962).

6. The idea that Henderson is indeed recapitulating for himself the Judeo-Christian religious history is conveyed in the sequence of his prayers during the cleansing of the Wariri water supply, which reflect the evolution from propitiation of a wrathful Jahweh to the full emergence of the suffering servant concept:

And with all my heart I yelled, 'Mercy, have mercy!' And after that I yelled, 'No, justice!' And after that I changed my mind and cried, 'No, no, truth, truth!' And then, 'Thy will be done! Not my will, but thy will!' (p. 199)

7. An excellent discussion of the complex allegiance of Bellow's comic vision to the adverse realities is found in Robert Shulman's article "The Style of Bellow's Comedy," *PMLA*, 83 (1968), 109-17.

8. See Marcus Klein, *After Alienation* (Cleveland: The World Publishing Company, 1964), pp. 56-59. Cf. David D. Galloway, "The Absurd Man as Picaro: The Novels of Saul Bellow," *Texas Studies in Literature and Language*, 6 (1964), 253: "Henderson achieves a vision which permits him to take hold of his own fate."

9. The importance of these two biblical forebears makes it clear that the biblical allusions that occur in what sometimes appears a random order throughout the novel are not a mere collection of verbal ornaments but a fully organic thematic pattern.

11
The Great American Novel and the Great American Novel

But where is what I started for so long ago?
And why is it yet unfound?
—Walt Whitman, "Facing West from
California's Shores"

. . .this game that I loved with all my heart, not simply for the
fun of playing it. . .but for the mythic and aesthetic dimension
that it gave to an American boy's life.
—Philip Roth, "My Baseball Years"

American fiction in the postmodern period has maintained its traditional involvement with the symbolic action of the journey. However, novelists have tended to draw away from the clearly defined, elaborately structured, and intellectually weighted forms of the high modernists, with all of their implications of the capacity of art to order life and to create truth, finding these forms no longer expressive of their sense of reality and of the nature of literature. Instead, they have turned insistently to the old and in a sense primitive mode of the picaresque, with its relative looseness of structure and its openness to the unconventional hero, the hero as outsider or "rogue." Novels such as Bellow's

Adventures of Augie March, Kerouac's *On the Road*, Heller's *Catch-22*, and Kesey's *One Flew Over the Cuckoo's Nest*, in all of which unconventional heroes signal their defection from society and assert their freedom by taking to the open road, have set the pattern of development for American fiction at mid-century.

It is tempting to see this development as an indication of a waning sense of national character and mission, a growing uncertainty about values and goals. The truths that can be apprehended either directly or in fiction, it is clearly recognized, are not only multiple but acutely limited, modest, and tentative. Accordingly, the fictional forms through which they are apprehended have become less symmetrical, less consciously shaped. Fictional journeys less often appropriate the highly patterned linear quest or pilgrimage or the return home or even the escape, to the extent that the escape was often treated in the past as an end-stopped form, and more often take on looping, less clearly directional patterns of movement. Certainly this tendency in fictional form entails a loss of aesthetic focus and coherence, a loss of the sense of high art. But it entails, at the same time, a heightened sense of imaginative verve, an explosive and liberating vitality. The liberation is not only from pattern but from probability. In a parallel development to the tendency away from traditionally defined forms of journey narrative, we have also seen a turning away from the narration of real-life or pretended real-life journeys, which in travel literature and in other biographical and autobiographical materials have often been treated as neat linear segments, destination-centered sequences with clear demarcations at either end. Instead, we are seeing improbable and improbably footloose journeys with indefinite limits and uncertain ties to the real world. The typical fictional journey has become a creative wandering, an abandonment to the chance, unchosen road—the road of the picaresque tale.

As we saw in chapter six, these loosely structured, circling journeys are often empty and depressing, conveying a sense of having lost all centering forces and organizing symbols. That emotional sense is, indeed, inherent in the phrase used here to designate such journeys, "lost and wandering." But it is clear that such journeys as these, which we have examined chiefly in the novels of modern Texas by Larry McMurtry, often have a sizable capacity for the comic and the zestfully odd, qualities that signal real affinities with the picaresque. It is a matter of emphasis. If the patternless journey as it appears in tales of endless wandering is a form of emptiness, it is also a form of open possibility. The uncertain, unplanned road allows for surprise, for chance happenings and fortuitous discoveries. As one scholar has commented in summarizing his study of the contemporary resurgence of the picaresque, many American writers have turned to its "form and ethic" in an attempt to "cope with a society which they see as becoming ever less hopeful and ever more complex."[1] Resort to the picaresque mode is a strategy for maintaining the openness and affirmation of comedy despite a vision of the modern world as a society inimical to individuality and freedom. The drifting hero, outside the rewards of a highly structured society but also outside its demands, is less subject to repressive control than his, or her, more clearly defined and purposive brother and is therefore more at liberty to shape her, or his, own reality.

It is within this context that one of the more eccentric novels of recent years, Philip Roth's baseball pseudoepic *The Great American Novel*, becomes pertinent to the study of American journey narrative.[2] Professional baseball offers a subject matter peculiarly suited to treatment in a loosely picaresque form, since circuitous travel is an essential aspect of league play. The baseball novel as a type, a minor but lively fictional tradition with which Roth has allied himself in choosing his subject, demonstrates this suitability. In Ring Lardner's *You Know Me, Al*, in Mark Harris's *The Southpaw* and *Bang the Drum Slowly*, in Bernard Malamud's *The Natural*—as in Roth's novel—road trips are a prominent and stressed motif. Robert Coover's *The Universal Baseball Association, Inc.* is a somewhat different matter, since the baseball action of the book occurs entirely in the mind of the character who imagines the fantasy Association, and in *The Natural* the baseball journey is shaped as a quest rather than simply an endlessly looping circuit. But in all of these a footloose kind of travelling is basic. The baseball novel as a form affords Roth a set of conventions—the team road trips, the player as rogue—that place his novel with the resurgence of the picaresque in mainstream American fiction.

Further, baseball is, after all, "the national pastime," and for that reason is an inherently appropriate metaphor for America itself. Roth builds on this inherent potential for symbolism by stressing the traditionally American qualities of his fictitious team's journeys and by developing a theme of imperilled freedom, as well as by other means that we will discuss. Never one to be excessively subtle, he calls attention to the figurativeness of his baseball story at several points in the novel. He tells us, for instance, that "when baseball goes, you can kiss America goodbye" (pp. 263-64).[3] Word Smith, the outlandish narrator and sometime character in the novel, accuses Bowie Kuhn of trying to "bury the truth about the history of this game—*of this country*" (p. 18). In writing a myth of baseball, then, Roth can also write a myth of America and, more specifically, of American letters.

At its most literal level, the novel follows the latter-day career of a once mighty baseball team, the Ruppert Mundys of the now defunct Patriot League, a fictional third league that once operated in parallel with the National and the American and competed against them in some unexplained triangular sort of World Series. The Mundys are doomed to spend the World War II years as a homeless team, playing all their games on the road, when their home park is converted to a military embarkation camp. The strain is too much for them, and the team collapses into ruin. The tale of their glorious past history, as well as the successive stages of their decline and demise, is told by their lone surviving fan, an aged sportswriter named Word Smith, or Smitty for short. Every year Smitty shows up at Cooperstown and casts his Hall of Fame vote for the Mundys' greatest player, Luke Gofannon. But Smitty is a voice crying in a wilderness of denial and scoffing. No one will even admit that the Mundys ever existed. So dismal was their wartime record, when the players were a group of military rejects and cripples, and so thoroughly were they disgraced by the Communist double agent Gil Gamesh, a vengeful outcast from baseball who returned in fake penitence promising to ferret out Communist spies, that all records of the team's and indeed the league's and even its home cities' existence have been expunged. Smitty finds no hearing in America and at last appeals to Chairman Mao Tse Tung in the hope of gaining an impartial ear.

Even this most literal level, however, is a pastiche of jokes, fantasy, and figurative representation. Roth himself says that the "imaginary world" of the novel is only "loosely connected to the actual."[4] Everything in the book runs to improbable extremes. The oft-noted amorality and profanity of the baseball world—generally presented as part of its folk appeal, for instance, in Roger Kahn's *The Boys of Summer*—becomes a litany of scatology, a parade of exhibitionism, and a riot of debauchery (such as the "banana league" custom of using the dugout for between-inning copulation). The American male's supposed hunger for a Mom becomes resort to houses of ill repute that sell maternal care complete with bottles and diapering. A pitcher has such perfect control that he can deliberately throw a ball "low by the hair off a little girl's slit" (p. 66). And so on. The distinction between reality and fantasy is questioned as the narrator announces that baseball players' memories would "rival the tales out of ancient mythology" (p. 14). And indeed the players on Roth's fictional team are drawn from world mythology. At any rate, their names hint at mythic stature in a comic vein.[5]

The lineup of the 1943 Mundys is dotted with familiar and less familiar names out of mythology and names that at least sound mythological though they are apparently fictitious. The applicability of these names to characterization or plot is tenuous. Frenchy Astarte is neither Phoenician, like his namesake, nor particularly associated with fertility. John Baal is indeed a rip-roaring, heathenish sort, as a Baal should be, but the main function of his deific name is to allow Roth a comic excursion to John's ancestors, grandfather Base Baal and father Spit. The "legendary" Base (and, one supposes, the lowercase baseball as well) appears as a kind of nature spirit or emanation; he "played on just about every cornfield and meadow in America before the first leagues were organized" (p. 104). Spit Baal represented a kind of fall from his father's primal innocence. Not only did he establish the spitter, but he was so uninhibited in his application of foreign substances that he once even threw a pissball, for which he was banished from the game. From the gods of Memphis we encounter Hothead Ptah, but he is not the creative force his name indicates. From Hinduism, Joe Garuda, who is not particularly swift; Roland Agni, who does turn out to have two faces (virtuous hero and cheat) and is so superior a performer that he might well have seven arms and an extra leg; and Mike Rama, who, like his namesake the unwitting reincarnation of Vishnu, does not understand his mixture of mortal and divine, but continually goes running full tilt into the outfield wall without regard to his mortality. From the Greeks, neither Deacon Demeter nor Howie Pollux emulates his namesake. Nor is Specs Skirnir a messenger, like Skirnir in Norse mythology, nor Red Kronos a father-figure, destructive or otherwise, to the team. Applejack Terminus does fill in as catcher, however, and thus represents the ending of the circuit of bases as well as its beginning.

More consistently significant though ambiguous is Gil Gamesh, the only Babylonian ever to play in the majors. Gamesh, a remarkable pitcher for the Tri-City Greenbacks in 1933, claims from the outset to be "an immortal" (pp. 62 and 67). Ousted from the game for his intentional beaning of umpire Mike Masterson, he plunges into a night journey of obscure wanderings that finally takes him, if we are to believe his own account, to the very depth of disloyalty, enrollment in "the International Lenin School for Subversion, Hatred, Infiltration, and Terror, known popularly as SHIT" (p. 327). But apparently he does pluck the watercress of immortality. Long rumored dead, Gil Gamesh returns from Moscow like a man reborn. Unfortunately, he does not provide regeneration for mankind; indeed, as manager of the Mundys, though he restores the team to winning, he destroys them morally and brings down the league in a series of trumped-up revelations of Communist infiltration, thereby accomplishing the ultimate infiltration himself.

In a lengthy opening prologue to all these fantastic doings, Word Smith gives a wordsmith's tribute to his medium and his subject (or, depending on one's view of what the book is really about, his medium and subject). It is a dark story of fall from an Eden, an uncorrupted pastoral world centering on the green baseball diamond. Smitty's preview ends with a spectacle of universal destruction. The survivors of the final universal wreck, if there are any, will find themselves "dispossessed" of their planet, just as the Mundys were dispossessed of their field in

Port Ruppert, and will have to go in search of another. So, Smitty ends windily,

> Farewell, fugitives! Pleasant journey, pilgrims! *Auf Wiedersehen*, evac-
> uees! *A demain*, d.p.s! *Adios*, drifters! So long, scapegoats! *Hasta Mañana*,
> émigrés! *Pax vobiscum*, pariahs! Happy landing, hobos! *Aloha*, outcasts!
> *Shalom, shalom*, shelterless, shipwrecked, shucked, shunted, and shut-
> tled humankind! Or, as we say so succinctly in America, to the unfit,
> the failed, the floundering and forgotten, HIT THE ROAD, YA BUMS!
> (p. 45)

With the phrase "hit the road" the novel moves into its major action and its major theme, the journey of the outcast team.

The Ruppert Mundys are defined by their status as a homeless team, a team perpetually on the road. They are also peculiarly and comically inept, of course, but ineptness is a quality they share with the other teams of the World War II years, decimated as they are by military demands. Only the Mundys are always the visiting team, "the homeless team of baseball" (p. 49). As individuals, both literally and through the symbolism of their mythological names, the players have come to Port Ruppert from all over the globe. As John Baal points out, "we ain't none of us from that there town to begin with" (p. 138). Frenchy Astarte, for example, a French Canadian who has been traded around the world to places where he cannot even understand the language, is surprised to arrive in Port Ruppert, having thought his Japanese owners were trading him to Calcutta. Instead, "like Columbus before him," he discovers the New World: "It was not India he had reached, but America" (p. 98). The New World that he finds is, of course, Astarte's own Old World, the hemisphere of his Canadian childhood. But that irony itself echoes one of the recurrent overtones of the New World myth: the fresh new world discovered in the West is the lost Eden of mankind's past and the lost Eden of childhood. What is playing around the edges here is a parable (to be sure, not a very coherently ordered parable) of the American myth in its broadest outlines: discovery, represented by Astarte's arrival; settlement of an East Coast home, represented by the establishment of the team in Port Ruppert; then dispersion into further wandering, as the homeless team travels even to the frontier town of Terra Incognita, the farthest western stop on the circuit.

The Mundys are driven from their home by complex outside forces that impinge on the pastoral world, first war, then greed and corruption.[6] The owners of the Mundys, the sons of Glorious Mundy, who had treated baseball like "the national religion" (p. 82), are men whose only motivation is money. Viewing baseball as "a business" and realizing that the Patriot League is faltering, they first sell their father's star players, then lease the park to the army for a high price. The move springs from no "overflow of patriotic emotion" (p. 81), however much it may be gilded in rhetoric; indeed, the local political boss of Port Ruppert, Boss Stuvwxyz, would not object to "consigning the ball club to Hell, so long as his pockets had been lined with gold!" (p. 51). The motif of greed and betrayal operating in the ouster of the Mundys continues through the novel in the cheap publicity stunts of Frank Mazuma, crass owner of the Kakoola Reapers, and the rigged gambling of Isaac Ellis, son of the Tri-City Greenbacks owner Abe Ellis.[7]

Against so corrupt a world, the fragile innocence of the baseball Eden cannot long remain unsullied. Corrupt, materialistic owners operate within the baseball world as well as outside it, and the players themselves are not in fact either innocent children or heroes of mythic status but men, with all the ordinary liabilities to depravity, greed, and violence. So long as the rules of the game are maintained, these qualities are kept in check. For all his ludicrous bombast about the sacred rules of the game— "if the distance between the bases were to be shortened by as little as one inch, you might just as well change the name of the game"(p. 52)—General Oakhart, the president of the Patriot League, is right about that. But the decision to send the Mundys perpetually on the road violates the fundamental tenets of league play:

By sanctioning an arrangement wherein twenty-three major league teams played at least half of their games at home, while the Mundys alone played all one hundred and fifty-four games on the road, Organized Baseball had compromised the very principles of Fair Play in which the sport was grounded; they had consented to tamper with the Rules and Regulations. (pp. 51-52)

With this tampering, the Fall has occurred.

The manager of the Mundys, however, Ulysses S. Fairsmith, insists upon regarding the Fall as Fortunate. More precisely, he views his team's period of homeless wandering as a socially redemptive sacrificial act after the pattern of the Children of Israel in the Wilderness. It is "the will of the Lord," he believes, to "send forth the Mundys into the wilderness until the conflagration is ended." There, through "trial and tribulation" and through "suffering," they will find "their purpose and their strength" (pp. 90-91). By interpreting the Mundys' experience typologically, in terms of the biblical wanderings of the Israelites, Fairsmith is following in a long line of ministerial interpreters of American experience. Indeed, he is using the very same biblical pattern that was the Puritan divines' favorite interpretive "type." But Fairsmith's typology distorts the truth and prevents him from seeing events clearly. General Oakhart, more nearly a realist despite his moralistic bombast, rightly sees that the Mundys' exile is "more like an endless road trip" that can only make a bad team worse (p. 90). But Fairsmith is intoxicated by the prospect of leading the "chosen," and in Moses-like terms he calls upon the General to "let my players go" (p. 93).

The General's realistic prediction, of course, proves correct. However eloquently Fairsmith preaches to his team the "moral and spiritual benefits that can accrue from wretchedness," what they learn "in the Wilderness" is only "how it is to have your home away from home instead of having it *at* home like everybody else" (p. 133). They find themselves squarely in the American tradition of being the permanently displaced. No amount of tawdry rhetoric or parades in festooned garbage trucks will obscure the insecurity and the unfairness of their situation. Homeless wandering produces not only an all-time losing record but a state of demoralization leading to behavioral aberrations such as John Baal and Nickname Damur's regression to childhood in the care of the illicit "moms," one-armed Bud Parusha's willingness to have his deformity shabbily exploited in order to be traded to a better team, and Roland Agni's great (and classically nocturnal) temptation to win unfairly. The Mundys so lose their grip on reality that they rejoice when they are able to win an exhibition game from a group of patients in a mental hospital. In this crazy world it becomes hard to tell who is more irrational, those who are locked up or those who are "sane."

In their endless journeying, the Mundys epitomize, in parody, an unstable society gripped by crass commercialism. The founding of a team "home" in Port Ruppert has eventuated in a misconceived quest for greatness that degenerates into mere wandering. Utterly disoriented, the team falls apart in an apocalyptic breakup of the Patriot League, or of patriotism itself. The truth tellers of the tradition, represented by Word Smith, must appeal beyond the parameters of that tradition, in this case to Chairman Mao. The American ideal thus once again reaches across an ocean to another shore, on a voyage to more than India, but it is left uncertain whether the ideal of untrammeled truth telling will be endorsed or squelched by this rising new society in the East.

What is at issue, finally, is the question of freedom. For the Mundys as a team, protracted wandering in the wilderness, though it offers the possibility of liberation from the corrupt powers controlling professional baseball, brings destruction. Roth's comically inept heroes are pitted against entrenched power structures in a struggle they can never win, within an atmosphere of continual plotting and deviousness. As Sanford Pinsker writes in his essay on Roth, there is in the novel a "sinking feeling. . .that someone, or something, is controlling our lives. An omnipotent, but ill-defined, *they* emerge as the major force that moves contemporary society chaotically along."[8] The government involves the nation in war and manipulates its people to serve the war goals. The Mundy brothers not only trade players in the usual kind of quasi-slavery of professional sports but conspire to uproot the entire team and play upon the sentiments of the fans by invoking patriotism. Isaac Ellis plots to manipulate the results of games by means of magic Wheaties that Roland Agni feeds to his teammates without their knowledge. Unspecified gambling interests use the game for their own purposes. The Communists in Russia plot against America *via* the Patriot League, and Senator McCarthy undermines freedom by playing on fear of communism. Gil Gamesh plays on both for the furtherance of his own vengeful ends. He insinuates himself into the managership of the Mundys by capitalizing on the popular eagerness to find a hero in the fight against communism, and once in that position, he destroys the spirit of the American game by turning the players into cynics and hate mongers. In the apocalyptic conclusion, Gamesh pits the one repressive force against the other, McCarthyism against communism. As undercover superpatriot he "exposes" Russian agents in baseball, and as Russian agent he brings down the Patriot League.

At the center of this swirling corruption, the Mundys occupy a fragile pastoral world of innocence—not innocence in the sense of childlike virtue, for they are indeed a raunchy set, but innocence in its radical sense of childlike unawareness—that represents the potential for freedom. Outsiders by virtue of their deformities and ineptness, the qualities that occasion so much of the physical comedy of the book, and their status as outsiders sealed by their lack of a home field, the Mundys stay on the road. Thus they possess, to a peculiar degree, the property most firmly associated with freedom, mobility. Like the ebullient beats of Jack Kerouac's *On the Road*, the Mundys signify through constant motion their escape, or at least their hope for escape, from a fixed social structure. So long as they keep moving, they can appear to elude the complex powers ranged to ensnare them.

Actually, of course, their liberty is not only doomed but from the outset illusory. Roger Kahn, who travelled with the 1952 and 1953 Brooklyn Dodgers as a newspaper writer, recalls the illusoriness of the baseball player's sense of freedom in *The Boys of Summer*:

The road with the Dodgers was a lonely, thrilling chaos, at once seductive, free, and wild. There were no telephone bills to pay, no relatives to meet, no office to visit and no planning to suffer when you were on the road. Your life was prearranged. . . .You had only to be: *be* in Chicago for the start of a three-game series Tuesday; *be* at Wrigley Field by noon; *be* outside the Players Gate at 5:15 Thursday, chartered bus leaves for Union Station. Being and writing. The road asked nothing more. But with time—very little time—the sense of freedom ebbed.

Like the Dodgers and their reporter in the real baseball world, the Mundys of Roth's fantasy league do not in fact move freely, however footloose their homeless journey may appear. They follow a rigidly limited circuit, travelling between the cities of the Patriot League, in the order mandated by the schedule of games. The players come to realize that they are trapped in a repetitive cycle of frustration. In the bizarre concluding sequence, even their illusory freedom is destroyed as the corrupt outer world intrudes upon the pastoral and imposes its own mechanistic values of suspicion, profit, and winning at all cost.

The journey of homeless wandering, then, is not finally an expression of freedom but of powerlessness and despair. However, there is a more potent assertion of individual freedom within the oppressive outer world of the novel: the colorful, earthy speech of the players, asserting their irrepressibility. This aspect of the novel, like the endless travel, is based on the real baseball world. Indeed, the peculiar mingling of innocence and profanity in baseball talk is one of the reasons baseball serves so well for Roth's tale of freedom and repression in modern America. Roth himself, in the acknowledgments to the novel, cites as a "source of inspiration" the tape-recordings of players' recollections housed at the Hall of Fame in Cooperstown, New York, and states that "some of the most appealing locutions of these old-time players have been absorbed into the dialogue." The Mundys' speech offers such richly aberrant phrasing as:

But as I am facin' two hundred pounds of gristle wavin' a stick what wants to drive the ball back down my gullet, why then, I will use the wax out of my ears, if I has to. (p. 107)

This here is just about all that I am fit to do now, and, as you see, I ain't fit for it. (p. 116)

You don't find that kind of consideration every day, you know, especially from the other team, which is usually tryin to hair-ass you, one way or another. (p. 117)

Woulda don't count, Charles—it's dudda what counts, and I dud it! (p. 173)

Their dialogue expresses the players' state of raunchy amorality combined with the innocence of idyl. Through their ungrammatical, unconventional speech, they elude established codes and establishment demands.

Similarly, the narrative style of Word Smith, or of Roth as controlling narrator, bears the stamp of personality, even of idiosyncrasy, and thus the stamp of personal freedom.[10] Smith himself is known to us only through his own words, what he tells us about himself and how he gives account of other matters. Though narrative control is inadequate for assurance on this point, Smith is apparently, in his intentions at any rate, the voice of truth in a corrupt society. Unfortunately, his vehemence in declaiming truth, as well as his other eccentricities, cause him to be generally considered insane and disregarded. Smitty's narrative style is the appropriate prose realization of such a personality. It is as eccentric as Smith himself, or as the Smith the reader postulates behind the voice, marked by frequent exclamations and exaggerations and a devotion to repetition and verbal excess, simple long-windedness, for its own sake. Smith's adjectives and figures of speech are often energetically far-fetched, bringing in surprising and improbable allusions. He shifts abruptly between elevated or even pompous diction and the slang of a pop culture or unexpected street expressions. Most remarkable is his peculiar devotion to alliteration, an ornament present simply for its own sake and often extended to comical lengths. (The prologue offers page on page of alliteration of various letters of the alphabet.) His speech is contagious. Explaining that he must give up alliteration for health reasons, a physician urges that it is "simply too much of a stimulant and a strain for an eighty-seven-year-old man, and you are going to have either to control yourself, or take the consequences" (p. 10). Smitty himself realizes that his style may be too uninhibited to please a staid world:

. . .alert to the danger of appearing just another crank to the savvy secretaries of the great, I employ in my correspondence a style as dignified as any an investment banker or a funeral director might use on a prospective client: I am respectful, I am thoughtful, I am restrained. I wrestle insistence into submission; I smother upper case howls in the crib; exclamation points, those bloody daggers, I drive back into my own innards; and I don't alliterate (if I can help it). (p. 379)

The physical energy of the metaphors in the disavowal indicates how unlikely it is that this spirited personality will be bridled.

So long as Word Smith has his voice and can go on asserting his resistance, the forces of repression will not have utterly won out. And the last words of the novel are, indeed, his continuing plea for the hearing that he does not seem likely to get. Only the most eccentric voice goes on, just as only the most grotesquely malformed of the players stubbornly, "arrogantly" maintains his independence before the McCarthy Committee. In a world where the spirit of McCarthy prevails, there remain only a surly dwarf and a possibly crazed old writer—scarcely a reassuring force to resist the array of oppressors.

Despite its overt comedy, then, the ending of the novel is dark, with the prospects for the continuance of truth and individuality dim indeed. The baseball idyl has been destroyed in an apocalypse that pits the superpatriots against the Patriots. Yet the novel as a whole offers an affirmation of the solitary human voice and, after a fashion, of art. It offers an affirmation, too, of the fun along the way, however dismal the destination. If this is a pattern for the Great American Novel, as the title indicates, Roth is telling us that American fiction of greatness must be subversive, given to resistance rather than reinforcement of the established order. And indeed, that is what our greatest novels have generally been, with their resistance characteristically expressed in motifs of free movement, journeys.

Roth is keenly aware of his literary predecessors. However eccentric it may be in some ways, *The Great American Novel* is not finally a sport but a novel seriously engaged in the testing of its tradition. The title itself places the book within the context of American literary tradition and is indeed, in a very special way, the key to the novel. It should be taken in at least three senses: first and most obviously as a claim for the book; second, as a joking denial of the whole idea of a "great American novel," since what issues is a piece of slapstick; and, most important, as an indication that the book is *about* the Great American novel, in the sense that it provides a definition or exemplum of what such a thing must be.[11] Roth provides a tip to these applications of his title by using as epigraph a quotation from Frank Norris,

The Responsibilities of the Novelist: "The Great American Novel is not extinct like the Dodo but mythical like the Hippogriff." Like the title, the epigraph applies in several ways. If the G. A. N. is not extinct, like the Dodo, then it may appear once again in our time, and Roth has as good a claim to try it as anyone else. If, like the mythical hippogriff, it never in fact existed and never will, then the concept is not only crippling to the novelist's imagination but really preposterous, a good target for laughter. And by laughing at this chauvinistic idea that has haunted the American literary and critical mind for so many years, Roth performs a liberating act. But creatures like the hippogriff, though they may never have existed in actuality, do have a life on the plane of the imagination. "Mythical" may mean nonexistent, "made up," or it may mean existing in the realm of myth, the realm of heroic and resonant tales that sum up and reshape mere actuality. Clearly, one of the primary qualities of any fiction entitled to lay claim to the status of Great American Novel is that it be mythic in this latter sense. The Great American Novel must be in some way a myth of America.

Roth trims his myth to manageable dimensions by approaching it obliquely. He writes, instead, a myth of the national game. The mythological names and other verbal play are means of asserting that this rambling, comic tale is indeed a myth, a heroic tale that sums up and orders a great realm of experience. But the novel is duplicitous; Roth parodies even as he praises. America may, as its earliest interpreters claimed, provide heroic matter for a new myth synthesizing the old. Roth's mythological trappings suggest that he is saying it does. But his comic tone in presenting the mythological matter implies that he is making fun of that glorious old idea—and perhaps, too, poking fun at the American habit of regarding sports stars as great heroes.

Besides verbalizing an American myth, the Great American Novel must also recapitulate and fulfill the literary past. Accordingly, *The Great American Novel* plays continually with literary allusions and parallels, most of them to American literature, most of them offered at least partly in jest. Through his allusions and direct comments on their sources, such as the comments made by "Hem," Hemingway, in the prologue, Roth both deprecates the tradition in which he is claiming a place and exposes the crass mentality that would pit works of art against each other like contenders in some peculiar sporting event. Still, it is clear that Roth does assert his claim to a place within the recognized American literary tradition. In his essay about *The Great American Novel*, he comments that Smitty is "correct in aligning himself with Melville and Hawthorne," who were also "in search of some encapsulating fiction or legend." Like those "illustrious forebears," Smitty "attempts to imagine a myth of an ailing America."[12]

The opening words of the prologue, "Call me Smitty," stake a claim to membership in the same club as *Moby-Dick*. From this beginning, Word Smith, claiming kinship with William Shakespeare through shared initials,[13] goes on to imagine himself young again, "four score and seven years ago" (p. 9), and to echo Chaucer in his introduction of the annual American pilgrimage to the Baseball Hall of Fame:

And specially, from every shires ende
Of AMERICA to COOPERSTOWN they wende
The holy BASEBALL HEROES for to seke,
That hem hath holpen whan that they were SIX.

(p. 14)

He returns in memory to a day in his glory years, the mid-1930s, when he was out fishing with Ernest Hemingway and some nameless Vassar girl, brought along for amusement, discussing the Great American Novel. After the girl proposes a long list of candidates for that honor, titles from the standard American canon, Hem rejects them all and boasts that he himself will write the G. A. N. "Whereupon a large fierce gull swooped down. . .to cry. . .'Nevermore!' " (p. 30). Devastated, Hem laments *a la* Ahab to Starbuck, "It is a mild, mild wind, and a mild-looking sky. On such a day. . ." (p.31). He ends by threatening suicide, still in Ahab's style. But the last word belongs to the "Vassar slit": "Wouldn't it be pretty to think so?" (p. 32).

Smitty takes his literary precursors seriously enough to give serious consideration to the three leading contenders for the title of the Great American Novel, *The Scarlet Letter*, *Moby-Dick*, and *Huckleberry Finn*, all of which he links to his own tale. Like

Hawthorne, he starts with a "windy autobiographical intro" (p. 37), and like Hester Prynne the Mundys wear a scarlet letter on their chests. Like Twain, Smitty writes in a colorful vernacular style. In fact, "the strategy they talk on the mound—same kind they talk on a raft!" (p. 39). Like *Huckleberry Finn*, *The Great American Novel* follows an essentially picaresque pattern; Smitty's tale is "prefigured" in the "wanderings of Huckleberry Finn and Nigger Jim, and the adventures in ostracism of Hester Prynne, the Puritans' pariah" (p. 41). Roth thus establishes the two chief qualities of the picaro, his wandering and his status as outsider, and spotlights their importance in the tradition. But the kinship is closest, Smitty says, to *Moby-Dick*. Melville's epic is to whaling as the Hall of Fame should have been to baseball; the parallel extends to their wealth of lore, their heroes, and even their doom, the sinking of the *Pequod* and of the Patriot League. The book that follows this prologue will be Smitty's corrective of the failure of the Hall of Fame to perform that leviathan function. He celebrates in detail the "methods and implements" of his chosen fictional milieu, as Melville does the profession of whaling, and even proposes a chapter on "The Tightness of the Stitching." The "crazed and vengeful" Ahab of baseball is Gil Gamesh, and its Ishmael is of course Smitty.

After the allusive prologue, the novel goes on to echo a variety of great literary precursors: Conrad's *Heart of Darkness*, Shelley's "unacknowledged legislator" dictum, Donne's "No man is an island," and Shakespeare's "undiscovered country from which no traveler returns." But most of the allusions are American. African natives being taught baseball chant inexplicably *"Omoo!"* and *"Typee!"* According to manager Fairsmith, the scarlet letter R on the Mundys' uniforms, which had "once stood for Ruppert" (as well as for Rootless, Ridiculous, and Refugee, p. 38, and Ruthless and Revenge, p. 352), will "henceforth be considered to stand for nothing less than this great Republic" (p. 310). The wanderings of Gil Gamesh took him, he says, to "Winesburg, Ohio. . .Black Hawk, Nebraska; Zenith, Minnesota; up in Michigan; Jefferson, Mississippi; Lycurgus, New York; Walden, Massachusetts"—the venerable place names of American literature. Roland Agni debates his moral quandary in terms from

Thomas Wolfe: "What am I to do? Go home again? No, no. . .you *can't* go home again" (p. 357). Agni is killed in a "shot heard round the league" (p. 356) that approximates in certain details the assassination of John F. Kennedy. At the end, with the league destroyed and its heroes discredited, Smitty once again appears as Ishmael to speak the epilogue: "The drama's done. Why then here does one step forth?—Because one did survive the wreck of the Patriot League" (p. 377).

For the most part, these sly and not-so-sly allusions are nothing more than hijinks. But lack of pertinence is typical of the novel's loosely structured comic strategy, which exhausts one comic pattern and moves on to another by means of only the most tenuous connections. The concluding rush of satiric events, for instance, grows out of the early chapters by no very compelling logic. As Ben Siegel very acutely remarks, in the later chapters "team and league—as well as plot and novel—slide downward."[14]

Reviewers and critics have almost universally agreed that *The Great American Novel* is not, after all, what its title seems to claim. It is overdone, structurally uncontrolled, and often vulgar.[15] Despite Roth's tantalizing play with literary history and the earthy yet pastoral world of baseball in the early chapters, the novel becomes tedious. And despite its engagement with some of the major forms and themes of the American tradition, it is not finally coherent. It is not, for instance, so much a journey narrative as a hodgepodge of fictional motives.

Still, after we concede all that Roth's baseball extravaganza is not, what it *is* makes it both pertinent and illuminating to a consideration of the American journey narrative. Its rapid-fire allusions as well as its approximation of familiar motifs (the decayed pastoral, the hero's night-time ordeal of temptation, the picaresque journey, the quest) and its direct concern with language bring the novel into engagement not only with mainstream literary tradition but with the question of the role and vitality of the contemporary novel. Ever a crafty and timely writer, Roth operates very consciously at the point of intersection of several important traditions, and however uncertain his product, he does clarify those traditions and cast light on their probable issue. He states that his primary purpose is comedy for its own sake. Yet the sporadic but insistent motif of the journey and, closely related to it, the idea of imperilled freedom establish a serious engagement with major themes of American literature. The numerous allusions assert a claim to be considered within that context.

Whatever else the Great American Novel may be, it has been, throughout its history, a fiction zestfully committed to motion and to the free, transcendent individual. Its context has not characteristically been the complex realities of an enclosed, highly structured society, but abundant, beckoning space. In an eagerness to explore and a need for self-definition, American fictional heroes have gone out into unsettled and unsettling space. When their effort of self-definition has meant definition of the self in relation to society, that effort has typically been made against the backdrop and in the awareness of an open road continually offering the possibility of escape and renewed journeying.

The distinctive power of American literature has in large part been a matter of the impact of motion, the journey, as at once a real event in time and a timeless symbolic action. For no other literature have the two dimensions of the journey so closely coalesced. As traditional patterns of the journey narrative, both historic and archetypal, have been drained of credible significance, the resurgence of a loose picaresque mode of the sort we see in Roth's *Great American Novel* has continued to declare that the American mind finds its deepest sense of vitality in ongoing movement. The fragmentation of traditional closed patterns, emulating the fragmented techniques of modern poetry, have opened to contemporary novelists the renewed resources of idiosyncrasy. Though goals and patterns may become ambiguous or diffuse and a prevailing scepticism may make it difficult to conceive of completed ventures and final arrivals, the picaresque, with its emphasis on the opening road and the unpredictability of experience along the way, conveys the American novel's persistent zest for process, for journeying itself. What the picaresque has to offer postmidcentury novelists is a means by which fiction can come to grips with a society in which the death of the novel has been forecast or has even been prematurely announced.

NOTES

1. Donald Dean Elgin, "The Rogue Reappears: A Study of the Development of the Picaresque in Modern American Fiction," doctoral dissertation, Vanderbilt University, 1973; *Dissertations Abstracts International*. 34: 4256A-4257A.

2. All parenthetical references are to the first edition, Philip Roth, *The Great American Novel* (New York: Holt, Rinehart and Winston, 1973).

3. To be accurate, we, the readers, are not told this directly; Roland Agni is told by a character named Angela Whittling Trust in a peroration on the Communist peril so extreme as to suggest insanity. Yet, in the end, the League is indeed undermined, just as she had warned, by a Communist agent, even if she was mistaken about his identity. Even aside from the question of Angela Whittling Trust's credibility and the even larger question of the plausibility of the concluding "Communist plot" chapters, the book as a whole tends to support the claim of the sentence identifying baseball with America. Point of view is problematic throughout the novel, since the trustworthiness of Word Smith is never well established. Part of the problem, as David Monaghan notes in "*The Great American Novel* and *My Life as a Man*: an Assessment of Philip Roth's Achievement," *International Fiction Review*, 2 (1975), 117, is that Roth "failed to solve the problem of establishing a point of view that works through clichés yet transcends them."

4. Roth, *Reading Myself and Others* (New York: Farrar, Straus and Giroux, 1975), p. 75. Robert F. Wilson, Jr., terms the book an allegory in his article "An Indisputable Source for the Spirited Account of a Baseball Contest Between the Port Ruppert Mundys and the Asylum Lunatics in *The Great American Novel* by Mr. Philip Roth," *Notes on Contemporary Literature*, 5 (1975), 12-14. However, the term "allegory" can be applied only in the sense of a very loose equivalence.

5. Bernard F. Rodgers, Jr., in his *Philip Roth* (Boston: Twayne, 1978), p. 112, identifies the element of exaggeration in the novel with the typical mode of southwestern humor and points out that in such material exaggeration was often used for "hyperbolic treatment" of heroes "shrouded in an aura of myth and legend."

6. Ben Siegel points out that the "basic ambience" of the baseball world is the "pastoral," but it is a pastoral threatened by dissolution. See "The Myths of Summer: Philip Roth's *The Great American Novel*," *Contemporary Literature*, 17 (1976), 171-90. The sense of pastoral threatened by time and corruption is very strong in Roger Kahn's *The Boys of Summer*, from which Siegel takes the title of his article. Kahn's title, of course, comes from Dylan Thomas, "I see the boys of summer in their ruin."

7. The ethnic joking that surrounds the Jewish Ellises is the low point of taste in the novel, or it shares the low point with the ethnic joking surrounding blacks. In both cases, Roth's humor embraces all the standard stereotypes, including grossly distorted speech. To be sure, Roth's ethnic caricatures are so exaggerated as to be implausible; perhaps they are there to ridicule the habit of stereotyping. However, the position of the book regarding race or racism is not clear, and the fact that Roland Agni, the one player presented consistently as a hero, is prejudiced tends to undermine the notion that Roth is satirizing prejudice.

8. Sanford Pinsker, *The Comedy That "Hoits": An Essay on the Fiction of Philip Roth* (Columbia, Mo.: University of Missouri Press, 1975), p. 88.

9. Roger Kahn, *The Boys of Summer* (New York: Harper and Row, 1971), p. 125.

10. Like Ishmael in *Moby-Dick* (specifically mentioned in the prologue as a model for the book), "Word Smith" sometimes emerges as a specific, fully realized presence standing between Roth and the reader and sometimes dissolves into a more generalized, though still distinctively voiced, narrator indistinguishable from Roth himself.

11. Richard Gilman points out this sense of the title in his review "Ball Five," *Partisan Review*, 40 (1973), 468: the novel "is satirically 'about' what the G. A. N. ought to be about and ought to look like. It ought, for one thing, to have a large subject, amenable to mythmaking on its own; hence baseball, for whaling's been taken." Gilman captures Roth's comical logic very well; however, the exemplum offered by Roth is not altogether "satiric," but provides a potentially valid definition.

12. Roth, *Reading Myself and Others*, p. 92.

13. Smitty's baseball idol, Luke Gofannon, similarly shares initials with Lou Gehrig.

14. Siegel, "The Myths of Summer," p. 185.

15. Besides being gratuitously coarse with reference to bodily functions, the book is vulgar, as Irving Howe says of *Portnoy's Complaint*, in that it submits "the rich substance of human experience, sentiment, value, and aspiration to a radically reductive leveling or simplification." Reading *The Great American Novel*, Howe adds, did not cause him to revise his opinion. Irving Howe, "Philip Roth Reconsidered," in *The Critical Point: On Literature and Culture* (New York: Horizon Press, 1973), pp. 155-56.

More succinctly summing up the general assessment, Gregory S. Sojka judges that Roth's book "failed to live up to its ambitious title" and that Roth in fact " 'struck out' in his valiant attempt at literary immortality." Sojka, "From Roth to Gaedel to Reiser: Factual Analogues for Fictional Characters," *Notes on Contemporary Literature*, 7 (1977), 3. More sympathetically but very accurately, John Leonard reviewed the novel as a "hugely inventive, often brilliant, very funny book that collapses into giggles and splinters two-thirds of the way through." Leonard, "Cheever to Roth to Malamud," *Atlantic Monthly*, 231, no. 6 (June 1973), 114. Bernard Rodgers, however, regards the novel as Roth's "funniest, most purely comic novel" (*Philip Roth*, p. 109).

Appendix: Chronological List of Selected Pertinent Texts

1616	Captain John Smith, *A Description of New England*
1630	John Cotton, "Gods Promise to His Plantations"
1651	William Bradford, *The History of Plymouth Plantation* (last year in which Bradford's journal was kept)
1702	Cotton Mather, *Magnalia Christi Americana*
1784	John Filson, "The Adventures of Col. Daniel Boon," Appendix to *The Discovery, Settlement and Present State of Kentucke*
1799	Charles Brockden Brown, *Arthur Mervyn*
	Charles Brockden Brown, *Edgar Huntly*
1809	Meriwether Lewis, *The Journals of Lewis and Clark*
1818	James Kirke Paulding, *The Backwoodsman*
1823	James Fenimore Cooper, *The Pioneers*
1826	James Fenimore Cooper, *The Last of the Mohicans*
1827	James Fenimore Cooper, *The Prairie*
1830	Catherine Sedgwick, *Clarence*
1832	Nathaniel Hawthorne, "My Kinsman, Major Molineux"
	James Kirke Paulding, *Westward Ho!*
1835	Nathaniel Hawthorne, "Young Goodman Brown"
	Washington Irving, *A Tour of the Prairies*
1837	Robert Montgomery Bird, *Nick of the Woods*
1838	James Fenimore Cooper, *Home As Found*
	James Fenimore Cooper, *Homeward Bound*
	Edgar Allan Poe, *The Narrative of Arthur Gordon Pym*
1839	Caroline Kirkland, *A New Home—Who'll Follow?*

1840	Edgar Allan Poe, *The Journal of Julius Rodman*
1841	James Fenimore Cooper, *The Deerslayer*
1844	George Lippard, *The Quaker City*
1845	James Fenimore Cooper, *The Chainbearer*
	James Fenimore Cooper, *Satanstoe*
	John C. Fremont, *Report of the Exploring Expedition to the Rocky Mountains*
1849	Herman Melville, *Mardi*
	Herman Melville, *Redburn*
1850	Nathaniel Hawthorne, *The Scarlet Letter*
	Herman Melville, *White-Jacket*
1851	Nathaniel Hawthorne, *The House of the Seven Gables*
	Herman Melville, *Moby-Dick*
1852	Nathaniel Hawthorne, *The Blithedale Romance*
1853	Herman Melville, "Bartleby the Scrivener"
1854	Herman Melville, "The Encantadas"
1855	Herman Melville, *Israel Potter; His Fifty Years of Exile*
	Walt Whitman, the first *Leaves of Grass* (Many of the important poems were added in 1856, 1860 and later.)
1857	Herman Melville, *The Confidence Man*
1860	Nathaniel Hawthorne, *The Marble Faun*
1862	Henry David Thoreau, "Walking"
1869	Mark Twain, *The Innocents Abroad*
1871	Walt Whitman, "Passage to India"
1872	Charles Dudley Warner, *Saunterings*
1876	Herman Melville, *Clarel*
1877	Henry James, *The American*
1881	Henry James, *The Portrait of a Lady*
1882	Walt Whitman, *Specimen Days*
1885	Mark Twain, *The Adventures of Huckleberry Finn*
1889	William Dean Howells, *A Hazard of New Fortunes*
1891	Hamlin Garland, *Main-Travelled Roads*
	Herman Melville, *Billy Budd* (completed)
1896	Harold Frederic, *The Damnation of Theron Ware*
1898	Stephen Crane, "The Blue Hotel"
	Stephen Crane, "The Bride Comes to Yellow Sky"
1900	Theodore Dreiser, *Sister Carrie*
1903	Henry James, *The Ambassadors*
1904	Henry James, *The Golden Bowl*
1905	Nathaniel Pitt Langford, *The Discovery of Yellowstone Park*
	Edith Wharton, *The House of Mirth*
1911	Edith Wharton, *Ethan Frome*

1918	Henry Adams, *The Education of Henry Adams*
1919	Sherwood Anderson, *Winesburg, Ohio*
1922	Emerson Hough, *The Covered Wagon*
1923	Wallace Stevens, "The Comedian as the Letter C"
1925	Willa Cather, *The Professor's House*
	John Dos Passos, *Manhattan Transfer*
	F. Scott Fitzgerald, *The Great Gatsby*
	Ernest Hemingway, "Big Two-Hearted River"
	Dorothy Scarborough, *The Wind*
1926	Hart Crane, *White Buildings*
	Ernest Hemingway, *The Sun Also Rises*
1927	O. E. Rolvaag, *Giants in the Earth*
1928	Glenway Wescott, *Good-bye, Wisconsin*
1929	William Faulkner, *The Sound and the Fury*
	Sinclair Lewis, *Dodsworth*
1930	Hart Crane, *The Bridge*
	William Faulkner, *As I Lay Dying*
1933	Nathanael West, *The Day of the Locust*
1934	F. Scott Fitzgerald, *Tender Is the Night*
1935	Edwin Lanham, *The Wind Blew West*
	John O'Hara, *Butterfield 8*
	Laura Ingalls Wilder, *Little House on the Prairie*
1936	William Faulkner, *Absalom, Absalom!*
	Paul Horgan, *Main Line West*
1937	Conrad Richter, *The Sea of Grass*
1938	William Faulkner, *The Unvanquished*
	Paul Horgan, *Far from Cibola*
	John Steinbeck, "The Leader of the People" in *The Long Valley*
	Thomas Wolfe, *You Can't Go Home Again*
1939	William Faulkner, *The Wild Palms*
	John Steinbeck, *The Grapes of Wrath*
	Eudora Welty, "The Hitch-Hikers"
1941	Eudora Welty, "Why I Live at the P.O."
1942	William Faulkner, *Go Down, Moses*
	Paul Horgan, *The Common Heart*
1943	Eudora Welty, "Death of a Travelling Salesman" in *A Curtain of Green*
	Laura Ingalls Wilder, *These Happy Golden Years*
1944	Richard Wright, "The Man Who Lived Underground"
1945	Katherine Anne Porter, *Ship of Fools*
1947	Conrad Aiken, *The Kid*

	A. B. Guthrie, *The Big Sky*
1949	Robert Frost, "Directive"
	A. B. Guthrie, *The Way West*
	Jack Schaefer, *Shane*
1950	William Goyen, *The House of Breath*
1951	J. D. Salinger, *The Catcher in the Rye*
1952	Ralph Ellison, *Invisible Man*
	Bernard Malamud, *The Natural*
1953	Mark Harris, *The Southpaw*
	Saul Bellow, *The Adventures of Augie March*
1954	Alan LeMay, *The Searchers*
1955	Joseph Heller, *Catch-22*
	Jack Kerouac, *On the Road*
1956	James Baldwin, *Giovanni's Room*
1958	Saul Bellow, *Henderson the Rain King*
1960	Mark Harris, *Bang the Drum Slowly*
	William Styron, *Set This House on Fire*
	John Updike, *Rabbit, Run*
1961	Larry McMurtry, *Horseman, Pass By*
	John Steinbeck, *Travels with Charlie*
1962	William Faulkner, *The Reivers*
	Ken Kesey, *One Flew Over the Cuckoo's Nest*
1963	Larry McMurtry, *Leaving Cheyenne*
1964	William Humphrey, *The Ordways*
1965	Alison Lurie, *The Nowhere City*
	Norman Mailer, *An American Dream*
	Louis Simpson, "Lines Written Near San Francisco" in *Selected Poems*
1966	Larry McMurtry, *The Last Picture Show*
	Theodore Roethke, *Collected Poems*
1969	Alison Lurie, *Real People*
1970	James Dickey, *Deliverance*
	Joan Didion, *Play It As It Lays*
	Larry McMurtry, *Moving On*
	Eudora Welty, *Losing Battles*
1971	Wallace Stegner, *Angle of Repose*
1972	Larry McMurtry, *All My Friends Are Going to Be Strangers*
1973	Philip Roth, *The Great American Novel*
1974	Richard Brautigan, *The Hawkline Monster*
1975	Edward Abbey, *The Monkey Wrench Gang*
	Larry McMurtry, *Terms of Endearment*
1978	John Irving, *The World According to Garp*
	Larry McMurtry, *Somebody's Darling*

Bibliography

A. Selected Primary Works

Abbey, Edward. *The Monkey Wrench Gang*. Philadelphia: J. B. Lippincott, 1975.

Adams, Henry. *The Education of Henry Adams*. Boston: Houghton Mifflin, 1918.

Aiken, Conrad. *The Kid*. 1947; rpt. ed. New York: Oxford University Press, 1970.

Bellow, Saul. *Henderson the Rain King*. New York: Viking Press, 1958.

Cather, Willa. *The Professor's House*. New York: Knopf, 1925.

Cooper, James Fenimore. *Works of J. Fenimore Cooper*. 10 vols. New York: P. F. Collier, 1892.

Crane, Hart. *The Complete Poems and Selected Letters and Prose of Hart Crane*. Ed. Brom Weber. 1933; rpt. ed. Garden City, N.Y.: Doubleday Anchor Books, 1966.

Crane, Stephen. *The Monster and Other Stories*. London and New York: Harper and Brothers, 1901.

———. *The Open Boat and Other Stories*. London: William Heinemann, 1898.

Didion, Joan. *Play It As It Lays*. New York: Farrar, Straus and Giroux, 1970.

Dos Passos, John. *Manhattan Transfer*. Boston: Houghton Mifflin, 1953.

Faulkner, William. *As I Lay Dying*. New York: Random House, 1964.

————. *Go Down, Moses*. New York: Random House/Vintage Books, 1973.

————. *Light in August*. New York: Random House, 1972.

Fitzgerald, F. Scott. *Tender Is the Night*. New York: Charles Scribner's Sons, 1951.

Guthrie, A. B. *The Big Sky*. New York: William Sloane, 1947.

————. *The Way West*. New York: W. Sloane Associates, 1949.

Hawthorne, Nathaniel. *The Centenary Edition of the Works of Nathaniel Hawthorne*. 14 vols. Columbus: Ohio State University Press, 1968.

Heller, Joseph. *Catch-22*. New York: Simon & Schuster, 1955.

Hemingway, Ernest. *The Sun Also Rises*. New York: Scribner, 1926.

Horgan, Paul. *Mountain Standard Time*. New York: Farrar, Straus and Cudahy, 1962. Includes *The Common Heart* (1942), *Far from Cibola* (1938), and *Main Line West* (1936).

Howells, William Dean. *A Hazard of New Fortunes*. Ed. Tony Tanner. Oxford: Oxford University Press, 1965.

James, Henry. *The Novels and Tales of Henry James*. The New York Edition. New York: C. Scribner's Sons, 1922.

Kahn, Roger. *The Boys of Summer*. New York: Harper and Row, 1971.

Kerouac, Jack. *On the Road*. New York: Viking Press, 1959.

Kesey, Ken. *One Flew Over the Cuckoo's Nest*. Ed. John Clark Pratt. New York: Viking Press, 1973.

Lanham, Edwin. *The Wind Blew from the West*. New York: Longmans, Green & Co., 1935.

Lewis, Sinclair. *Dodsworth*. New York: Harcourt, Brace, 1929.

Lurie, Alison. *The Nowhere City*. New York: Coward-McCann, 1965.

Melville, Herman. *Clarel: A Poem and Pilgrimage in the Holy Land*. Ed. Walter E. Bezanson. New York: Hendricks House, 1960.

————. *The Works of Herman Melville*. Standard Edition. 16 vols. London: Constable, 1922-23.

McMurtry, Larry. *All My Friends Are Going to Be Strangers*. New York: Simon & Schuster, 1972.

————. *Horseman, Pass By*. New York: Harper, 1961.

————. *The Last Picture Show*. New York: Dial Press, 1966.

————. *Leaving Cheyenne*. New York: Harper and Row, 1963.

————. *Moving On*. New York: Simon & Schuster, 1970.

————. *Somebody's Darling*. New York: Simon & Schuster, 1978.

————. *Terms of Endearment*. New York: Simon & Schuster, 1975.

O'Hara, John. *Butterfield 8*. New York: Harcourt, Brace, 1935.

Poe, Edgar Allan. *The Complete Tales and Poems of Edgar Allan Poe*. Intro. Hervey Allen. New York: The Modern Library, 1938.

Rolvaag, O. E. *Giants in the Earth*. New York: Harper and Row, 1927.

Roth, Philip. *The Great American Novel*. New York: Holt, Rinehart and Winston, 1973.

Simpson, Louis. *Selected Poems*. New York: Harcourt, Brace and World, 1965.

Steinbeck, John. *The Grapes of Wrath*. New York: Harper and Brothers, 1951.

Stevens, Wallace.*The Collected Poems of Wallace Stevens*. New York: Alfred A. Knopf, 1954.

Styron, William. *Set This House on Fire*. New York: Random House, 1960.

Thoreau, Henry David. *The Writings of Henry David Thoreau*. Houghton Mifflin, 1946.

Twain, Mark. *The Adventures of Huckleberry Finn*. Ed. Henry Nash Smith. Boston: Houghton Mifflin, 1958.

Updike, John. *Rabbit, Run*. New York: Alfred Knopf, 1960.

Welty, Eudora. *A Curtain of Green and Other Stories*. Garden City, N.Y.: Doubleday, Doran, & Co., 1941.

Wharton, Edith. *The House of Mirth*. London: Constable, 1966.

Whitman, Walt. *Complete Poetry and Selected Prose of Walt Whitman*. Ed. James E. Miller, Jr. Boston: Houghton Mifflin, 1969.

Wolfe, Thomas. *You Can't Go Home Again*. New York: Signet Books, 1966.

B. Secondary Works Consulted

Abrams, M. H. *Natural Supernaturalism*. New York: Norton, 1971.

Aldredge, John W. Review of Malcolm Cowley, *A Second Flowering*. *Commentary*, 56, no. 5 (November 1973), 37-41.

Allen, Walter. *The Urgent West: The American Dream and Modern Man*. New York: E. P. Dutton, 1969.

Anderson, John M. *The Individual and the New World*. State College, Pa.: Bald Eagle Press, 1955.

Arvin, Newton. *Herman Melville*. New York: William Sloane Associates, 1950.

Baroness, John A. "Ken Kesey: The Hero in Modern Dress." *Bulletin of the Rocky Mountain Modern Language Association*, 23 (1969), 27-33.

Baym, Nina. "The Erotic Motif in Melville's *Clarel*." *Texas Studies in Literature and Language*, 16 (1974), 315-28.

Bercovitch, Sacvan. *The Puritan Origins of the American Self*. New Haven: Yale University Press, 1975.

Bezanson Walter. "Introduction" to Herman Melville, *Clarel: A Poem* and *Pilgrimage in the Holy Land*. New York: Hendricks House, 1960.

Bier, Jesse. "The Bisection of Cooper: *Satanstoe* as Prime Example." *Texas Studies in Literature and Language*, 9 (1968), 511-21.

Blackmur, R. P. *Form and Value in Modern Poetry*. Garden City, N.Y.: Doubleday, 1952.

Bleikasten, Andre. *Faulkner's As I Lay Dying*. Translated by Roger Little. Rev. and enl. ed. Bloomington and London: Indiana University Press, 1973.

Bloom, Harold. *Wallace Stevens: The Poems of Our Climate*. Ithaca: Cornell University Press, 1977.

Bluefarb, Sam. *The Escape Motif in the American Novel: Mark Twain to Richard Wright*. Columbus: Ohio State University Press, 1972.

Bowen, Merlin. *The Long Encounter: Self and Experience in the Writings of Herman Melville*. Chicago: The University of Chicago Press, 1960.

Bowron, Bernard. "*The Grapes of Wrath*: A 'Wagons West' Romance." *Colorado Quarterly*, 3 (1954), 84-91.

Boyers, Robert. "Attitudes toward Sex in American 'High Culture'." *The Annals of the American Academy of Political and Social Sciences*, 376 (1968), 36-52.

Bridgman, Richard. "As Hester Prynne Lay Dying." *English Language Notes*, 2 (1965), 294-96.

Brooks, Cleanth. *William Faulkner: The Yoknapatawpha Country*. New Haven and London: Yale University Press, 1963.

Broughton, Panthea Reid. *William Faulkner: The Abstract and the Actual*. Baton Rouge: Louisiana State University Press, 1974.

Burke, Kenneth. *The Philosophy of Literary Form*. 3d ed., rev. Berkeley: University of California Press, 1973.

Butterfield, R. W. "*The American*." In *The Air of Reality: New Essays on Henry James*, edited by John Goode. London: Methuen and Co., 1972.

Campbell, Joseph. *Hero with a Thousand Faces*. 2d ed. Princeton, N.J.: Princeton University Press, 1968.

———. *Myths to Live By*. New York: Viking Press, 1972.

Cargill, Oscar. *The Novels of Henry James*. New York: Macmillan, 1961.

Carpenter, Frederic I. *American Literature and the Dream*. New York: Philosophical Library, 1955.

———. "John Steinbeck, American Dreamer." *Southwest Review*, 26 (1941), 454-67.

———. "The Philosophical Joads." *College English*, 2 (1941), 315-25.

Cawelti, John. *The Six-Gun Mystique*. Bowling Green, Ohio: Bowling Green University Press, 1971.

Chase, Richard. *The American Novel and Its Tradition.* New York: Doubleday, 1957.

———. *Herman Melville: A Critical Study.* New York: Macmillan, 1949.

Chew, Samuel. *The Pilgrimage of Life.* New Haven: Yale University Press, 1962.

Cowley, Malcolm. *A Second Flowering: Works and Days of the Lost Generation.* New York: Viking Press, 1973.

Daiker, Donald Arthur. "The Motif of the Quest in the Writings of Herman Melville." Doctoral dissertation, Indiana, 1976. Abstracted in *Dissertations Abstracts International,* 30: 4979A-80A.

Davidson, Edward H., and Simpson, Claude M. "Historical Commentary" to *The Centenary Edition of the Works of Nathaniel Hawthorne.* Columbus: Ohio State University Press, 1968.

Davis, Joseph Addison. "Rolling Home: The Open Road as Myth and Symbol in American Literature, 1890-1940." Doctoral dissertation, University of Michigan, 1974. *Dissertations Abstracts International,* 35 (1975): 4509A.

Day, Martin S. "Travel Literature and the Journey Theme." *Forum* (University of Houston), 12, no. 2 (1974), 37-47.

Day, Robert A. "Image and Idea in 'Voyages II'." *Criticism,* 7 (1965), 224-34.

Dembo, L. S. *Hart Crane's Sanskrit Charge: A Study of The Bridge.* Ithaca: Cornell University Press, 1960.

Douglas, Harold J., and Daniel, Robert. "Faulkner and the Puritanism of the South." *Tennessee Studies in Literature,* 2 (1957), 1-14.

Elgin, Donald Dean. "The Rogue Reappears: A Study of the Development of the Picaresque in Modern American Fiction." Doctoral dissertation, Vanderbilt University, 1973. *Dissertations Abstracts International,* 34: 4256A-57A.

Enck, John. *Wallace Stevens: Images and Judgments.* Carbondale: Southern Illinois University Press, 1964.

Feidelson, Charles, Jr. Introduction to *Moby-Dick.* Indianapolis: Bobbs-Merrill, 1964.

Fiedler, Leslie A. *Love and Death in the American Novel.* Rev. ed. New York: Stein and Day, 1966.

———. *The Return of the Vanishing American.* New York: Stein and Day, 1968.

Folsom, James K. *The American Western Novel.* New Haven: College and University Press, 1966.

Fontenrose, Joseph. *John Steinbeck, an Introduction and Interpretation.* New York: Barnes and Noble, 1963.

Forster, E. M. *Aspects of the Novel.* New York: Harcourt, Brace, and World, 1954.

Frye, Northrop. *Anatomy of Criticism.* Princeton, N.J.: Princeton University Press, 1957.

————. *Fables of Identity.* New York: Harcourt, Brace, and World, 1963.

Fuchs, Daniel. *The Comic Spirit of Wallace Stevens.* Durham, N.C.: Duke University Press, 1963.

Galloway, David D. "The Absurd Man as Picaro: The Novels of Saul Bellow." *Texas Studies in Literature and Language,* 6 (1964), 226-54.

Gibbs, A. C. *Middle English Romances.* Evanston: Northwestern University Press, 1966.

Gilman, Richard. "Ball Five." *Partisan Review,* 40 (1973), 467-71.

Gove, Philip Babcock. *The Imaginary Voyage in Prose Fiction.* London: The Holland Press, 1961.

Guereschi, Edward. " 'The Comedian as the Letter C': Wallace Stevens' Anti-Mythological Poem." *The Centennial Review of Arts and Science,* 8 (1964), 465-77.

Heimert, Alan. "Puritanism, the Wilderness, and the Frontier." *New England Quarterly,* 26 (1953), 361-82.

Hemenway, Robert. "Enigmas of Being in *As I Lay Dying.*" *Modern Fiction Studies,* 16 (1970), 133-46.

Hinz, Evelyn J. "Hart Crane's 'Voyages' Reconsidered." *Contemporary Literature,* 13 (1972), 315-33.

Holder, Alan. *Three Voyagers in Search of Europe.* Philadelphia: University of Pennsylvania Press, 1966.

Houghton, Donald E. " 'Westering' in 'Leader of the People'." *Western American Literature,* 4 (1969), 117-24.

Howe, Irving. "Philip Roth Reconsidered." In *The Critical Point: On Literature and Culture.* New York: Horizon Press, 1973.

James, Henry. *The Art of the Novel.* New York: Charles Scribner's Sons, 1946.

Jones, Howard Mumford. *O Strange New World.* New York: Viking Press, 1964.

Jubak, James. "The Influence of the Travel Narrative on Melville's *Mardi.*" *Genre,* 9 (1976), 121-33.

Karolides, Nicholas J. *The Pioneer in the American Novel, 1900-1950.* Norman: University of Oklahoma Press, 1967.

Kasson, Joy S. "*The Voyage of Life*: Thomas Cole and Romantic Disillusionment." *American Quarterly,* 27 (1975), 42-56.

Kenny, Vincent. *Herman Melville's Clarel: A Spiritual Autobiography.* Hamden, Conn.: Archon Books, 1973.

Kerr, Elizabeth M. "*As I Lay Dying* as Ironic Quest." *Wisconsin Studies in Contemporary Literature,* 3 (1962), 5-19.

Klein, Marcus. *After Alienation*. Cleveland: The World Publishing Company, 1964.

Knapp, Joseph G., S.J. "Melville's *Clarel*: Dynamic Synthesis." *American Transcendental Quarterly*, 7 (1970), 67-76.

Kramer, Maurice. "Six Voyages of a Derelict Seer." *Sewanee Review*, 73 (1965), 410-23.

Landess, Thomas. Review of Larry McMurtry, *Moving On*. *Southwestern American Literature*, 1 (1971), 38-39.

Lavender, David. "The Petrified West and the Writer." In *Western Writing*, edited by Gerald W. Haslam. Albuquerque: University of New Mexico Press, 1974.

Lawrence, D. H. *Studies in Classic American Literature*. New York: T. Seltzer, 1923.

Leonard, John. "Cheever to Roth to Malamud." *Atlantic Monthly*, 231, no. 6 (June 1973), 112-16.

Levant, Howard. *The Novels of John Steinbeck: A Critical Study*. University of Missouri Press, 1974.

Levin, Harry. *The Power of Blackness*. New York: Knopf, 1958.

Lewis, R.W.B. *The Poetry of Hart Crane: A Critical Study*. Princeton, N.J.: Princeton University Press, 1967.

Lieber, Todd M. *Endless Experiments: Essays on the Heroic Experience in American Romanticism*. Columbus: Ohio State University Press, 1973.

Lisca, Peter. *The Wide World of John Steinbeck*. New Brunswick, N.J.: Rutgers University Press, 1958.

Mancing, Howard. "The Picaresque Novel: A Protean Form." *College Literature*, 6 (1979), 182-204.

Markos, Donald W. "Life Against Death in *Henderson the Rain King*." *Modern Fiction Studies*, 17 (1971), 193-205.

Marks, Lester Jay. *Thematic Design in the Novels of John Steinbeck*. The Hague and Paris: Mouton, 1969.

Marre, K. E. "Narrative Comedy in Wallace Stevens' 'The Comedian as the Letter C'." *University of Dayton Review*, 12, no. 3 (Summer 1976), 133-50.

Melton, John R. "The Novel in the American West." In *Western Writing*, edited by Gerald W. Haslam. Albuquerque: University of New Mexico Press, 1974.

Melville, Herman. *Journal of a Visit to Europe and the Levant, October 11, 1856-May 6, 1857*. Edited by Howard C. Horsford. Princeton, N.J.: Princeton University Press, 1955.

Millgate, Michael. *The Achievement of William Faulkner*. New York: Barnes and Noble, 1965.

Monaghan, David. *"The Great American Novel* and *My Life as a Man*: An Assessment of Philip Roth's Achievement." *International Fiction Review*, 2 (1975), 113-20.

Morris, Wright. *The Territory Ahead*. New York: Harcourt, Brace, 1957.

Muscatine, Charles. "Locus of Action in Medieval Narrative." *Romance Philology*, 17 (1963), 115-22.

Nuhn, Ferner. *The Wind Blew from the East: A Study of the Orientation of American Culture*. New York and London: Harper and Brothers, 1942.

Parsons, Thornton H. "Doing the Best They Can." *Georgia Review*, 23 (1969), 292-304.

Paul, Sherman. *Hart's Bridge*. Urbana: University of Illinois Press, 1972.

Philbrick, Thomas. *James Fenimore Cooper and the Development of American Sea Fiction*. Cambridge, Mass.: Harvard University Press, 1961.

Pilkington, William T. Review of Larry McMurtry, *All My Friends Are Going to Be Strangers*. *Southwestern American Literature*, 2 (1972), 54-55.

Pinsker, Sanford. *The Comedy That "Hoits": An Essay on the Fiction of Philip Roth*. Columbia, Mo.: University of Missouri Press, 1975.

Poulin, A., Jr. "Crispin as Everyman as Adam: 'The Comedian as the Letter C'." *Concerning Poetry*, 5 (1972), 5-23.

Quinn, Patrick F. *The French Face of Edgar Poe*. Carbondale: Southern Illinois University Press, 1957.

Requa, Kenneth A. "The Pilgrim's Problems: Melville's *Clarel*." *Ball State University Forum*, 16, no. 2 (1975), 16-20.

Rodgers, Bernard F., Jr. *Philip Roth*. Boston: Twayne, 1978.

Ross, Stephen M. " 'Voice' in Narrative Texts: The Example of *As I Lay Dying*." *PMLA*, 94 (1979), 300-310.

Roth, Philip. *Reading Myself and Others*. New York: Farrar, Straus and Giroux, 1975.

Sanderlin, Robert Reed. *"As I Lay Dying*: Christian Symbols and Thematic Implications." *Southern Quarterly*, 7 (1969), 155-66.

Sanford, Charles L. *The Quest for Paradise: Europe and the American Moral Imagination*. Urbana: University of Illinois Press, 1961.

Scholes, Robert, and Kellogg, Robert. *The Nature of Narrative*. New York: Oxford University Press, 1966.

Sealts, Merton M., Jr. *Melville's Reading: A Check-List of Books Owned and Borrowed*. Madison: The University of Wisconsin Press, 1966.

Shulman, Robert. "The Style of Bellow's Comedy." *PMLA*, 83 (1968), 109-17.

Siegel, Ben. "The Myths of Summer: Philip Roth's *The Great American Novel*." *Contemporary Literature*, 17 (1976), 171-90.

Simons, Hi. " 'The Comedian as the Letter C': Its Sense and Its Significance." *The Southern Review*, 5 (1940), 453-68.

Simonson, Harold P. *The Closed Frontier: Studies in American Literary Tragedy*. New York: Holt, Rinehart, and Winston, 1970.

Simpson, Louis. *Selected Poems*. New York: Harcourt, Brace, and World, 1965.

Smith, Henry Nash. "Western Chroniclers and Literary Pioneers." In *Literary History of the United States*. 3d ed. rev. New York: Macmillan, 1963.

Sojka, Gregory S. "From Roth to Gaedel to Reiser: Factual Analogues for Fictional Characters." *Notes on Contemporary Literature*, 7 (1977), 3-4.

Spears, Monroe K. "Hart Crane." 1965. Reprinted in *Six American Poets*, edited by Allen Tate. Minneapolis: University of Minnesota Press, 1969.

Stegner, Wallace. "Western Record and Romance." In *Literary History of the United States*. 3d. ed. rev. New York: Macmillan, 1963.

Stern, Milton R. *The Fine Hammered Steel of Herman Melville*. Urbana: University of Illinois Press, 1957.

Stewart, George R. "The West as Seen from the East." In *Literary History of the United States*. 3d. ed. rev. New York: Macmillan, 1963.

Stout, Janis P. "Biblical Allusion in *Henderson the Rain King*." *South Central Bulletin*, 40 (1980), 165-67.

————. "The Possibility of Affirmation in *Heart of Darkness* and *Henderson the Rain King*." *Philological Quarterly*, 57 (1978), 115-31.

Strout, Cushing. "Henry James and the International Theme Today." *Studi Americani* (Rome), 13 (1967), 281-97.

Sugg, Richard P. *Hart Crane's The Bridge: A Description of Its Life*. Birmingham: University of Alabama Press, 1976.

Sukenick, Ronald. *Wallace Stevens: Musing the Obscure*. New York: New York University Press, 1967.

Swiggart, Peter. *The Art of Faulkner's Novels*. Austin: Univeristy of Texas Press, 1962.

Thompson, W. R. " 'The Paradise of Bachelors and the Tartarus of Maids': A Reinterpretation." *American Quarterly*, 9 (1957), 34-45.

Thorp, Willard. "Pilgrim's Return." *Literary History of the United States*. 3d ed. rev. New York: Macmillan, 1963.

————. "Redburn's Prosy Old Guidebook." *PMLA*, 53 (1938), 1146-56.

Trachtenberg, Alan. *Brooklyn Bridge: Fact and Symbol*. New York: Oxford University Press, 1965.

Unterecker, John. *Voyager: A Life of Hart Crane*. New York: Farrar, Straus and Giroux, 1969.

Vendler, Helen. *On Extended Wings: Wallace Stevens' Longer Poems*. Cambridge, Mass.: Harvard University Press, 1969.

Vincent, Howard. *The Trying Out of Moby-Dick*. Boston: Houghton Mifflin, 1949.

Vogler, Thomas. *Preludes to Vision: The Epic Venture in Blake, Wordsworth, Keats, and Hart Crane*. Berkeley: University of California Press, 1971.

Walker, Franklin D. *Irreverent Pilgrims: Melville, Browne, and Mark Twain in the Holy Land*. Seattle: University of Washington Press, 1974.

Weber, Brom, ed. *The Letters of Hart Crane*. New York: Hermitage House, 1952.

Wegelin, Christof. *The Image of Europe in Henry James*. Dallas: Southern Methodist University Press, 1958.

Williams, George H. *Wilderness and Paradise in Christian Thought*. New York: Harper and Brothers, 1962.

Wilson, Robert F., Jr. "An Indisputable Source for the Spirited Account of a Baseball Contest Between the Port Ruppert Mundys and the Asylum Lunatics in *The Great American Novel* by Mr. Philip Roth." *Notes on Contemporary Literature*, 5 (1975), 12-14.

Wright, Louis B. *Culture on the Moving Frontier*. 1955; rpt. ed. New York: Harper and Row, 1961.

Wright, Nathalia. *American Novelists in Italy. The Discoverers: Allston to James*. Philadelphia: University of Pennsylvania Press, 1965.

Zink, Karl E. "Flux and the Frozen Moment: The Imagery of Stasis in Faulkner's Prose." *PMLA*, 71 (1956), 285-301.

Zweig, Paul. *The Adventurer*. New York: Basic Books, 1974.

Index

tel," 44; "The Bride Comes to Yellow Sky," 44, 45-46

Day of the Locust, Nathaniel West, 111
"Death of a Travelling Salesman," Eudora Welty, 111
Deliverance, James Dickey, 95, 100
Descent, 133-34, 142-43, 146, 194, 223. *See also* Night journey
"Descent into the Maelstrom," Edgar Allan Poe, 92
Desert, 133-35, 142, 145-221, 225
Dickey, James, *Deliverance*, 95, 100
Didion, Joan, *Play It As It Lays*, 114-15
"Directive," Robert Frost, 66
Dodsworth, Sinclair Lewis, 81
Dolliver Romance, The, Nathaniel Hawthorne, 74
Dos Passos, John, *Manhattan Transfer*, 109
Dr. Grimshawe's Secret, Nathaniel Hawthorne, 74

Eakins, Thomas, 83 n.5
Easterly journey, 5, 66-67, 68, 112
Eden, 9, 13, 235. *See also* Bible, the
Edgar Huntly, Charles Brockden Brown, 89, 92
Education of Henry Adams, The, Henry Adams, 68-69, 69-70, 217-19
Eliot, Thomas Stearns, 82, 83 n.5
Ellison, Ralph, *Invisible Man*, 33
Emerson, Ralph Waldo, 83 n.5
"Encantadas, The," Herman Melville, 96

Entrapment, 12, 29, 32, 34, 35, 38, 39 n.7, 40 n.14, 100
Epic, 15, 45, 56, 88, 165, 178, 185
Escape, journey of, xi, 4, 5, 29, 30, 31-38, 53-54, 96, 99, 116, 124, 178, 230
Ethan Frome, Edith Wharton
Europe, American artists in, 5, 68, 72, 83 n.5, 85 n.24
Europe, journeys to, xi, 5, 67-82, 89, 217, 218
Exploration, journey of, xi, 4, 5, 30-31, 198
Explorers' accounts, 5, 22 n.1, 30-31

Far from Cibola, Paul Horgan, 34
Faulkner, William: *Absalom! Absalom!*, 58, 70-71; *As I Lay Dying*, 95, 101, 159-70, 173; "The Bear," 34-35, 95, 170; "Delta Autumn," 34; *Go Down, Moses*, 33-34, 170; *Light in August*, 170, 171, 173; *The Reivers*, 170, 173; *The Sound and the Fury*, 171; *The Unvanquished*, 170
Fitzgerald, F. Scott, 81; *The Great Gatsby*, 32, 34, 108; *Tender Is the Night*, 107-8, 109
"For the Marriage of Faustus and Helen," Hart Crane, 178, 180
Fragmentation of narrative pattern, xii, 32, 99-100, 103 n.23, 106, 118, 177, 247
French and Italian Notebooks, Nathaniel Hawthorne, 73
Frost, Robert, "Directive," 66
Fuller, Margaret, 83 n.5
Futility. *See* Wandering

Garland, Hamlin, *Main-Travelled Roads*, 66

About the Author

JANIS P. STOUT is Coordinator of Graduate Programs and Lecturer in English at Rice University in Houston, Texas. She is the author of *Sodoms in Eden: The City in American Fiction before 1860* (Greenwood Press, 1976) and articles that have appeared in *Nineteenth Century Fiction, Texas Studies in Literature and Language, Research Studies, Western American Literature, Concerning Poetry,* and *Philological Quarterly.*